Praise for Positive Influence: The First and Last Mile of Leadership

"*Positive Influence* recognizes human connection as a universal and enduring need. In an evolving world facing crises of disconnection where loneliness, division, and polarization have become commonplace, Tsun-yan Hsieh and Huijin Kong offer a substantive, go-to guide to build a personal craft for nurturing human connection."

Laxman Narasimhan
CEO, Starbucks Coffee Company

"Influence is a critical ingredient for the ultimate impact of any innovation. *Positive Influence* is a must-read for all professionals thirsty to have more traction for their ideas and technical contributions. Highly recommended."

Victor Dzau
President, United States National Academy of Medicine and James B. Duke Professor of Medicine, Duke University, USA

"A superb guide on how to positively influence for those with the courage to fight for what matters. Tsun-yan and Huijin's new book is an informative, insightful and practical primer on how to assess and improve your ability to positively influence organizations small and large – an essential skill for leaders in every occupation."

J. Craig Nixon
Brigadier General (US Army, Retired),
Former Commander of the 75th Ranger Regiment

"Our communities — and arguably the world itself — have never had more need of the power of positive energy, thinking and action. Tsun-yan and Huijin's book *Positive Influence* decodes brilliantly how leaders can drive positive influence and outcomes as a starting point to making business and the world a better place."

Jamie Wheal
Author of the global bestseller *Stealing Fire*

"The trajectory of all successful leaders hinges on their ability to influence a few stakeholders to do the right, often difficult things to benefit many. Tsun-yan is a master of the craft of such influencing because of his vast experience and his guru-like wisdom. Above all, he influences from his deeply spiritual character. This book trumps all works I know in this genre, taking it beyond techniques and principles to guide us in shaping our personal approach to influencing."

Sunil Mittal
Founder and Chairman, Bharti Enterprises and Bharti Airtel

"Tsun-yan and Huijin highlight the essential combination between focusing on facts and KPIs to drive performance and at the same time the need for an emotional connection between leaders and their organization in order to be truly influential. This is a highly sophisticated approach to a very complex problem all leaders have to solve at one stage of their career. This book gives examples from long-standing experience on how positive influence can be achieved. A worthwhile read for everyone."

Roland Krueger
Global CEO of the Dyson Group

"This book should be of interest to people beyond the world of business. It is about leadership and the qualities of heart and mind which a good leader should possess."

Tommy Koh
Ambassador-At-Large, Singapore and
Professor, National University of Singapore

"Tsun-yan is the deepest and most complete thinker on the subject of leadership and personal mastery that I know. This book brings together all his wisdom in one place and is a treasure trove for anyone looking to master the art and science of leadership. It combines theory and practice, and not only explains but coaches and directs the learner. If young people today can absorb and practice even part of it in their professional lives, they will stand apart in their organizations and win deep respect as leaders. For students to CEOs, this book is a masterclass in leadership, from the master himself."

Pramath Raj Sinha
Founding Dean, Indian School of Business, India

"*Positive Influence* will help you encourage, uplift, and lead other people to a better future from any position in life. Let these practical tools and proven techniques guide you to discover your best qualities and motivate you to do good, do well, and love getting it done."

Ron Kauffman
New York Times **bestselling author of** *Uplifting Service*

"As leaders, we often focus on the 'what' and neglect the 'who'. Getting the 'right answer' is not sufficient, we need to influence the 'right people' to do the 'right thing'. Tsun-yan and Huijin have devoted their professional careers to helping people to be better leaders; their extensive global, hands-on experiences would help no matter where you are in the world."

Jessica Tan
Co-CEO, Ping-An (China) and
Chairman, Ping-An Technology

"Tsun-yan is a consulting legend, and I have learned even more from reading this book than from watching him in action. As a coach, mentor, advisor, or leader within your organization, you need to exert positive influence. Here is a practical guide to mastering this rare skill, which requires both cool rationality and a genuine connection with emotions. Hsieh and Kong bring their method to life with a rich library of case studies, presenting real-life leadership dilemmas that are rarely discussed but that any businessperson will recognize. An invaluable tool for those of us who teach influencing skills, and a great read for anyone who aspires to make a positive difference."

Olivier Sibony
Professor, HEC Paris, France and
New York Times **bestselling author of** *Noise*

"Prof. Hsieh is a world-renowned advisor to many business leaders. This book stock-takes his thinking on inspiring and positive leadership. Both practicing and aspiring business leaders would be inspired by the book."

Bernard Yeung
Stephen Riady Distinguished Professor and
Former Dean, NUS Business School, Singapore

"Tsun-yan and Huijin's new book is a powerful guide for anyone seeking to influence others in a positive way. Through compelling real-life stories and practical advice, they show how empathy and understanding can be powerful tools for achieving meaningful change."

Michael Katchen
Founder and CEO, Wealth Simple

"If you care about growing your business sustainably and making a real difference in the circular economy, *Positive Influence* is a book you must read to learn about getting outcomes that benefit everyone in a more sustainable future."

Susan Chong
Founder and Chairman, GreenPac

"*Positive Influence* is a living testament to the power of action inquiry and adult development, how we can all transform ourselves to face life with greater courage, compassion and equanimity."

Bill Torbert
Professor Emeritus, Carroll School of Management,
Boston College, USA

positive INFLUENCE

THE FIRST AND LAST MILE OF LEADERSHIP

Other Titles by Tsun-yan Hsieh

Heart, Smarts, Guts, and Luck

Other Titles by Huijin Kong

Indelible Youth

NEW YORK TIMES BESTSELLING AUTHOR OF
HEART, SMARTS, GUTS AND LUCK

positive INFLUENCE

THE FIRST AND LAST MILE OF LEADERSHIP

TSUN-YAN HSIEH + HUIJIN KONG

LinHart Group

NEW JERSEY · LONDON · SINGAPORE · BEIJING · SHANGHAI · HONG KONG · TAIPEI · CHENNAI · TOKYO

Published by

World Scientific Publishing Co. Inc.

27 Warren Street, Suite 401-402, Hackensack, NJ 07601, USA

Head office: 5 Toh Tuck Link, Singapore 596224

UK office: 57 Shelton Street, Covent Garden, London WC2H 9HE

Library of Congress Cataloging-in-Publication Data
Names: Hsieh, Tsun-Yan, author. | Kong, Huijin, author.
Title: Positive influence : the first and last mile of leadership /
    Tsun-yan Hsieh, National University of Singapore, Singapore & LinHart Group, Singapore,
    Huijin Kong, LinHart Group, Singapore.
Description: New Jersey : World Scientific, [2023] | Includes bibliographical references and index.
Identifiers: LCCN 2022059903 | ISBN 9781944660567 (hardcover) |
    ISBN 9781944660574 (ebook) | ISBN 9781944660581 (ebook other)
Subjects: LCSH: Leadership. | Influence (Psychology)
Classification: LCC HD57.7 .H745 2023 | DDC 658.4/092--dc23/eng/20221215
LC record available at https://lccn.loc.gov/2022059903

British Library Cataloguing-in-Publication Data
A catalogue record for this book is available from the British Library.

For any available supplementary material, please visit
https://www.worldscientific.com/worldscibooks/10.1142/Y0025#t=suppl
and www.positiveinfluence.life

Desk Editor: Shaun Tan Yi Jie

Typeset by Stallion Press
Email: enquiries@stallionpress.com

Printed in Singapore

Prologue

You don't have to be a "person of influence" to be influential.

— Scott Adams

We are either the influenced or influencers in different situations.

— Jenny Xu, LinHart's LIFE2 China alumni

Influence is ubiquitous, in life and at work.

You can't avoid it even if you wanted to. You have 30 seconds or so to influence the maître d' for a better table than the one he is taking you to. You can choose not to. But the opportunity for a different outcome is clearly there.

You are influencing, well or not, in your everyday life— *e.g.,* getting your friends to play tennis when they are just content hanging out.

What about the high-stakes situations in which your ability to influence could make all the difference to what you care most about in your career — or in your life? Your boss has the budget to promote only one person — either you or your colleague. You know you two have performed neck-to-neck, but your introverted nature made you reticent to push for the promotion; your colleague is a better promoter in claiming credit for himself.

The stakes are even higher when, after 25 years in your organization, the Board will pick the next CEO between you and one or two others who are your colleagues now but will become fierce competitors.

Some of you may find yourself advocating a cause, hoping to influence people around you to act in concert for the collective good, trying to persuade everyone in your workplace to forgo disposable cups perhaps that you believe are unfriendly to the environment. Logic alone doesn't seem to work as people are slow to change their habits and do not like being inconvenienced. How do you create such a movement for the greater good?

Influence has never mattered more, with the world as it is and where it is going. With deep divisiveness within a country, let alone between countries, while the sustainability of our planet is called into question, more among us feel the need to do more in producing better outcomes than just win-win. Benefitting bilaterally in a 'win-win' approach is no longer good enough in complex situations in which multiple stakeholders may have legitimate but conflicting claims.

Whatever challenges you are confronting in work or in life, you are influencing in every situation that involves getting people to do things that will benefit others and the greater collective, not just you.

This book is about positive influence or "+influence"— conscious and constructive—for people directly or indirectly affected by your influence and for yourself. We are not advocating manipulation or coercion, but rather +influence, an attempt to produce "+outcomes" that are constructive and beneficial for all. All other (negative) influences are motivated by selfish gain at the expense of others.

In my nearly 50-year career, I can tell you that it is the most powerful yet most underrated skill I wished I had learnt decades earlier.

It's not a simple technique or tool. You've got to get into the critical details to see how your influence may affect others. And importantly, your heart has to be in the right place to produce the right outcomes. You may not always achieve a balanced outcome, but it's your intent that counts. And people can sense it.

Countless times in my younger days, I rubbed my colleagues the wrong way. No doubt irritated and even annoyed at me, they still said to others, "But he didn't mean it; his heart was in the right place."

I took that to mean I've got to be aware of my effect on people and act to change how they experience me. I did and still do. I worked on myself in this regard for over 30 years—observing, learning from just about anyone, everywhere, and kept practicing.[1]

I keep a Mont Blanc notebook with each page an entry on how I have helped a person make a significant step towards his/her full potential. It would not become an entry till I have received unsolicited gratitude from that person, often years later. In each entry, I would note what I have done that made that difference and how that made me feel. In influencing others towards their personal best potential, I also influence myself to keep becoming a better mentor and a better person.

Some of you may think, "I've accomplished enough to get to where I am, so why do I need to be better at something I don't even think much about?" Well, you could do a lot more or better in a lot less time and with less stress. There are always life goals we defer because we are so entangled and consumed in the hard work of shepherding people to get things done.

You know that to be true. You really have no choice but to become better and better at +influence if you want to accomplish more in your time on Earth.

So, +influence is not just about work, it is about life, the life you choose to live in relationships with others. We could use more empathy for others and better ways out of conflicts or impasse in relationships. Through my own and Huijin's experiences, we hope to inspire and equip you to evolve your influence into a personal craft, unique to you, that will strengthen your character that you'll need to draw upon in tough situations that invariably will chance upon you in life.

So how can you be at your best in +influence? This book dissects and decodes our experience and craft for your benefit.

First, we have drawn on our experience in helping founders, owners and CEOs ('FOC') across 33 industries and 30 countries—one at a time and with their top teams, year after year, typically for three to five years, and a handful for a decade or more. It is not too much to say that the LinHart Group,[2] our commercial platform, is an engine for building +influence.

Second, we selected course materials[3] from our graduate degree and executive programs, which adapted the same principles to people whether Master degree students or highly seasoned CEOs.

Third, we checked for validation in research done by others, very few in business, but have found nourishing truths from other fields like anthropology, neuroscience, psychology, primatology and natural history.

Our impact on the work and life of thousands of people we touched gives us conviction that the principles codified in this book are universal — applicable to all career stages and seniorities, and, as you will see, across most enterprise and cultural contexts. And it works especially well for high-stakes work and life situations.

Three mindsets can help you maximize the value of this book.

Lean in. You won't master +influence just by reading this book. Improvement comes with practice. We chose case studies from our experiences to cover the most encountered influence situations, curated for early executives and a set specifically for FOCs. They intend to bring alive the principles, raise your self-awareness, and inspire you to try different influence pathways. Think of delving into these stories like reveling in a historical drama: the circumstances and characters may be different, but the principles remain instructive.

Apply to your own situation. "Use it or lose it" as Ian Davis,[4] a wise leader, told me. Your learning from this book will fade if you don't use it in your life and work it *daily*. Not content for this to be just a textbook, we encourage you to use it as a guide for continuous improvement by yourself, or with a learning partner. We hope you will develop your own craft at +influencing, drawing on and shaping with each attempt your character as a person. Our dedicated website[5] enables you to access the application kit, start your +influence journey, and join the community.

Inquire into your own influencing bottlenecks. To help you easily get what you need from this book, we begin with an overview of the book structure, summary of each chapter, and some suggested "itineraries" through select chapters for different readers. See which "type" or combination of types resonates with you to navigate your own way to get the most out of it.

Let this journey through life and work, using our single lens of +influence, begin.

Tsun-yan Hsieh
Localita Querceto
Casole d'Elsa, Italy
September 2022

Key Terms and Definitions

A definition helps crystallize the specific meaning that distinguishes it from other interpretations; it differentiates it from other proximate words; and, specifically for this book, it is instrumental in driving the application techniques espoused to build +influence.

1. +Influence
2. Leadership
3. Moment
4. Conative
5. Qualities
6. Self-leadership
7. Judgment
8. Pressure points
9. Context
10. Presence
11. Inner being
12. Mastery
13. Outcome
14. Inquiry
15. Mental model
16. Pace
17. Power

18. Habit of mind
19. Conduct
20. Character
21. Craft
22. Pride
23. Fear
24. Hope
25. Status
26. Whole person
27. Unconditional positive regard

+Influence

An attempt to mobilize oneself and others to positively impact an interaction, a task, a relationship, a group of people or a community, without the use of raw power (*e.g.*, coercion) or authority, to produce good outcomes beneficial to all stakeholders.

Leadership

The social influence that causes people to go beyond normal efforts in doing things better and faster while creating a new reality.

Moment

A time window in which a reasonable influence may still produce the desired outcome.

Conative

A proclivity (*i.e.*, a bias, a tendency) to process emotional and rational stimuli in a particular way that results in actions in a preferred but often intuitive direction.

Qualities

A specific or a set of attributes, native to the person, shaped by life experiences, and accentuated by repeated application in practice that can be intuitively harnessed, together with knowledge and skills, in influencing others (*e.g.*, judgment of the counterparty's personality in selecting the most likely influence pathway).

Self-leadership

- The deliberate practice of influencing your thoughts, feelings, and behaviors — typically in the moment — toward your +influence objectives.
- A learned discipline to access your inner being and motivations to deploy for that influence.
- The deliberate practice sustained over time of getting in touch with your inner being and aligning it with thoughts, feelings, and behaviors toward espoused values and/or qualities.
- Habit of mind over time.

Judgment

The capacity to make consistently good decisions in complex or uncertain situations — with limited information and within a time window in which a reasonable influence may still yield the desired or required outcomes.

Pressure points

People and/or task issues and prevailing conditions in the context that exert the most influence on a person to act in a particular manner, in a certain direction and in a certain time.

Context

Salient forces at work in the situation that span four realms — the company in the marketplace, the organizational dynamics (*e.g.*, organizational culture, prevailing moods, and tensions), the key stakeholders involved (or interested parties in the situation), and the key leaders involved — and how the different elements materially affect each other (*e.g.*, constraining regulations that limit the scope of competition; the impact of the central leader's personal motives on the pace of the transformation).

Presence

Is not….

- A powerful personality
- Charisma
- Posture

Is….

- Being there
- Paying attention
- Having multiple senses engaged
- Whole person (rational, emotional, physical and spiritual) engaged

Inner being

Multiple, distinct inner qualities (*e.g.*, courage) and energies that exist in a person and can be mustered subconsciously, cohering into a flow of biases in service of +influencing. These qualities and energies become, with time and practice, more consistently available on call to +influence.

Mastery

Able to consistently bring constructive thoughts, feelings, and aspects of your being needed for +influence and minimize unconstructive aspects.

Outcome

The comprehensive set of consequences of an influence attempt, direct and indirect, now and later.

Inquiry

The central unanswered question upon which an insight is contingent, focusing on information searching or gathering and problem solving in discovering the most salient contextual issues at work and insights that guide effective +influence.

Mental model

A mental construct with which people interpret a set of things or process a set of variables — how the pieces add up to a gestalt and relate. It is shaped by past experiences, values, and personality. While it takes conscious effort to piece it together initially, unchallenged and refreshed, it tends to submerge and become instinctual mental processes.

Pace

How fast and how frequent the intervals are between influence attempts to produce desired outcomes.

Power

The ability or capacity to act in a manner to produce voluntary or involuntary behaviors in the recipients. This includes, but is not limited to, authority embedded in a position, but the actual power in that case can be more or less than the authority, depending on the position holder's mastery of influence.

Habit of mind

A learned disposition toward thinking and behaving in a particular way when confronted with a problem to which there is no immediate answer. It is more of a mental approach than any one specific algorithm, and a more generalized bias than a heuristic or a rule of thumb.

Conduct

A behavioral pattern of a person, persistent over time and consistent across a wide range of interactive situations, guided by a set of self-selected principles and corresponding norms.

Character

The habitual flow of moral biases, unique to a person.

Craft

Emerges when a suite of conduct covering work and life (and usually the overlap between them) is practiced as an expression of one's character in +influence.

Pride

"Self-esteem, confidence and satisfaction" derived from being associated with noble purpose, excellence and meaningful accomplishments.

Fear

Inner sensation that drives us to move away from what we don't want.

Hope

Desire for a better future that motivates people to a voluntary choice to go for achievement.

Status

An universal need for standing, where we stand in the pecking order of a social group or organization.

Whole person

Not just rational, but also emotional, physical and spiritual being.

Unconditional positive regard

Basic acceptance and support of that person just as (s)he is and where (s)he is; enabled by a suspension of the urge to judge others based on what (s)he says or does.

Contents

1

Overview of Chapters & Suggested Itineraries

This overview explains how the book is structured, including what the sections and chapters cover so you can see the arc of the journey that will be taken and how the chapters connect and flow. Suggested 'itineraries' are laid out, which some readers may wish to explore to better determine where to deep dive into during practice sessions. For others, these itineraries might stimulate their own creative routing through the book.

Section I. Fundamentals of Influence

2. +Influence in the Context of Interactions

This chapter examines how people influence each other and how to approach any situation that requires influence. It's much broader than selling, persuading, or converting. We define +influence to include pathways that benefit ourselves and others simultaneously. This brings into focus the intent behind the attempt that differentiates positive influences from all other influences, including coercion and manipulation.

3. <u>What Makes a Good +Influence</u>

A good +influence starts with the outcomes — not just what you want but also from the perspectives of others. It also takes, with deliberate practice, skilled execution that accounts for the context, stakeholders, and your being. As soon as influence begins, all parties involved start to react, giving off new data that can be incorporated by a mindful, attentive practitioner. That's why what works for you might not work as well for others. And what works for you at this moment may not work as well in a different moment or setting.

4. <u>Just How Good Are You at +Influence?</u>

In this chapter, you score yourself on a test of your effectiveness at +influence for high-stakes situations. From experience and research, we array influence situations at work that are commonly encountered by CEOs and, for contrast, by younger professionals. Younger professionals may encounter influence situations that arise many times: How do you say no without offending? How do you ask for a raise? How do you give your boss constructive feedback? Later, case studies will be provided for you to practice most of these common situations. For CEOs, a list is shared of real influence challenges you are likely to run into, with examples, to show how to better manage the stakeholders in spite of complexities.

5. <u>Why All of Us Can Be Better at +Influencing</u>

For most people, influencing is all about persuading and communicating. Subconsciously, we have certain beliefs about how we do it and we don't consciously think a lot about it. Influencing in everyday life involves engaging people with diverse outlooks, agendas and expectations. This will take more than communication. Trying to persuade others often have the opposite effect, as people can sense you aren't open to other views. Like it or not, effective or not, we are all "influencing." If the stakes are low — say, we botched the chance to change seats with another passenger on a plane — it won't be the end of the world. However, in higher-stakes conversations, we may not get another chance. Like playing a musical instrument, our inner being also impacts our interpretation and approach. Being conscious of our inner being helps us to respond with our whole self. This allows us to be true to ourselves while getting to +outcomes more effectively. But our inner being may just turn up in a way we cannot fully expect. It just impinges — more or less, good or bad — on the outcomes desired. So, we might as well get better at it by combining our influence skills with inner qualities that can be expressed in the moment.

6. +Influencing Against All Odds

Six diverse real short stories help to richly illustrate what good +influence looks like, as practiced by very different influencers. This chapter aims to show how it all comes together, thus inspiring you to lean into difficult influencing situations to benefit yourself and others.

Section II. Transform Your +Influencing Effectiveness

7. The Basics of +Influence

Principles, techniques and habits taught in Chapters 7–9 will help when practiced deliberately, similar to learning to play a musical instrument well. From our client work, seven basic principles that transcend all +influence situations have been condensed:

- Be <u>deliberate</u> (take a more planful approach).
- Understand the <u>context</u> (for the <u>pressure</u> points requiring <u>judgments</u>).
- Set +<u>influence objectives</u> (from others' and your perspectives).
- Draw <u>insights</u> and surface <u>inquiry</u> (*i.e.*, key unanswered questions on which insights pivot).
- <u>Seize the moments</u> within which influence might (still) be productive.
- <u>Pace</u> through the influence for good outcomes.
- Engage your <u>being</u> (often the best source of effective influence).

This chapter deals with the first three principles because they guide you in preparing and planning for the +influence. Just the first three principles will help you better prepare and avoid 'winging it'.

We have curated a good selection of cases for practice with an interlocutor, a facilitator, or a small group.

8. +Influencing in the Moment

The remaining four principles in this chapter deal with guiding principles for executing +influence during the attempt itself. Insights and inquiry are also applicable to the planning phase, but because there is often little information available to the +influencer while planning, the most valuable insights and inquiry typically come during the interaction itself.

9. Habits to Raise Proficiency in +Influencing

Presence — whether your mind, heart, body, and spirit are all showing up and attentive — is the next opportunity. It's more than a set of postures to improve your body language. It is one of five habits that enables anyone, together with the consistent practice of principles in Chapters 7 and 8, to become more proficient at +influence. The other habits include genuinely caring about others, stretching yourself, getting feedback, and reflecting.

10. Aligning Our Being to +Influence

By observing thousands of live interactions in LinHart's work, we discovered four rather startling factors regarding our being that will upshift our mastery of +influence: whether we can unleash the personal qualities that will help +influencing, whether we can align our emotions with what we think and our +objectives, whether our state of being in the moment is calm and collected, and the all-important but hidden conative — our more instinctive stance that predisposes us to act in a certain way, distinct from what our (cognitive) thoughts and (affective) emotions prompt us to do. Strong +influencers align their thoughts and emotions with these four elements of being to power their +influence attempts.

11. +Influencing Through the Written Media

Since remote work and staying in touch have become more prevalent, we believe the written media — email, messaging services and more — can be a powerful supplement to in-person influence. When do we use the written forms judiciously to help us in our +influence? How do we do it well? This chapter shares some practical tips (and mistakes to avoid), from a +influencing perspective.

Section III. Becoming Your Better Self Through +Influence

12. From +Influence to Development

Our being, not just technique, comes into play in any influence attempt. Developing yourself will help your +influence skills, and vice versa. Being comfortable in your own skin is foundational to good +influence because you will be centered and congruent and more of the "real you" will get expressed. At the same time, your readiness to get out of the comfort zone serves both the influence and development. Having a role model helps, and so does having a diet of opportunities to stretch and apply yourself. The more you ask for and receive help, try again after a setback, and face tension and conflict, the faster you will overcome challenges to become a better influencer and a better person.

13. How Others Can Help You Develop

Asking for help when it's needed occurs less than it should, for reasons that will be explored. Research says it conveys strength — not weakness — to ask for help. How to open ourselves to have others help us? We have observed that the best learners have learning groups or partners as well as mentors. They practice High Challenge High Support to accelerate their own and peers' influence skills — and personal development. By exploring and practicing radically different approaches, with high-quality feedback and suggestions, everyone can see their blind spots and possibility of other styles. Mentors take that a step further, by providing opportunities and role models that would otherwise not be accessible. Testimonials from alumni of LinHart courses, programs, and community events are abundant in showing the accelerated benefits within a year and the transformative release of personal qualities when sustained over a few years.

14.   From +Influence to Leadership

Leadership in any enterprise is a social influence that causes members to go beyond the normal, doing things faster, better, and creating new things. We have learned across industries and countries that influence is the first and the last mile to desired outcomes. When an executive gets a new job or promotion, what is the first thing that should happen? In research, many subsequent failures can be traced back to mismatched expectations between the executive and the stakeholders providing that mandate. Few are aware that the problems begin the moment they sign on the proverbial dotted line. They assume that what they think is the mandate also matches the stakeholders' perception. And stakeholders' expectations can be diverse and divergent. So, the first mile is to align, through influence, the stakeholders regarding common expectations. Ultimately, it's the last mile — of making enough of the right things happen in time — that produces the required results. Many executives assume that the hierarchy will carry out the orders they enunciate, not recognizing that many rings of consequences — intended and unintended — dynamically emanate from the initial influence. Ultimately, each of us put in charge of something, big or small, cannot expect to lead others if we are not good at leading ourselves. And leading the self is all about raising awareness of the inner self, harnessing the hidden qualities in service of good outcomes for yourself and others.

15. <u>Shop Floors, Boardrooms and the Great Culture Divide</u>

Most people think that shop floors and boardrooms are vastly different contexts, and that to effectively influence in both is daunting. The same is taken to be true in crossing cultures. We have found that when stakes are high, certain common threads help bridge those divides: when we connect personally to stakeholders as human beings, behind the veneer of their work roles, and beyond their outward persona. Curiosity to know the person and unconditional positive regard are a powerful combination to +influence with humanity. Harnessing primal emotions such as Pride and Hope turn them into compelling forces to cross cultural divides, much more than Fear and Status. Finally, find your own unique blend to pursue +outcomes with passion and value-add shines the light on potential paths forward. This will allow you to cross those big divides, time and again, when the stakes are high.

16. <u>Conduct, Craft and Character</u>

This final chapter shows how a personal blend of self-chosen principles, with corresponding norms and behaviors, could enable each person to develop his/her unique +influence craft that will improve with use and work in more contexts. Conduct is the consistent pattern of behaviors and practices which, when coupled with the moral decisions that each person routinely faces, shape each person's character. This character will increase the courage, confidence, and speed with which the being and its inner qualities can be deployed consistently in challenging situations. That is why no two effective +influencers will approach the same situation exactly the same way, and why apprenticeship with caring masters will accelerate progress rather than just training. +Influence is thus not just a bag of tools or techniques but a craft that helps to bring the best out of people, moving them towards shared +outcomes.

A table with a <u>brief description of all the cases</u>, *e.g.*, on the industry, geography involved in each case, etc., is available in "Mapping of Cases". It draws from the authors' professional experiences from shop floors to boardrooms/CEOs, 30+ industries and countries as discussed in the Prologue.

Suggested Itineraries

We recommend everyone start with the Prologue to get a sense of what the book is about — and not about. Then it would be very helpful to scan essentially a Summary of the book presented in this Chapter 1 — the Overview of Chapters — to see at a high level how the chapters and sections build on one another. As you read this, pick out topics and words that catch your attention as interesting and/or pertinent to your situation, and go to the relevant chapters. The itineraries described below depends less on your seniority in your workplace, but more on your starting point of belief. The cases are color-coded by seniority: for young professionals they are colored in light grey (YPL), senior executives in dark grey (EXE), and founders/owners/CEOs in black (FOC).

If you are wondering about the importance of influence and whether anyone can improve their ability to influence themselves and others, read Section I thoroughly. As you read, try to keep an open mind and question your own existing assumptions and beliefs. Where do they come from, and how do you know they are true? Can you recall vividly influence situations in which your assumptions may have betrayed your effectiveness? The rest of the book may be more useful to you when you have a mindset to want to see more, learn and grow and ready to explore.[6]

If you are already convinced that influence is vital to navigating life and business, then you may get the most starting with Chapter 3 — What makes a Good +Influence — then go to Section II, Chapters 7–9 (to learn the principles). View the summary of case studies listed in Chapter 4 and pick out cases you can practice throughout the book. The cases are listed for easy reference and access, along with a table describing each case's most pertinent characteristics, *e.g.*, industry, seniority of people involved, etc., in "Mapping of Cases". As you gain traction, fill in your learning with Chapters 2 and 5 for broader context of influence, and Chapters 11 (written media) and 15 (influencing across shop floors, board rooms, and cultural divides). Use Chapter 16 (conduct, craft and character) for inspiration and to motivate your development as a +influencer, leader and +craftsman.

If you have been trying to improve your influencing but feel some part of your being is a bottleneck (*i.e.*, holding you back from being more effective), then Chapters 9 and 10 (on proficiency in +influence and aligning your being) and Chapter 12 (from +influence to development) could be a catalyst for your improvement. Have a quick read of Chapter 16 (conduct, craft and character) to give you a sense of how your craft in +influence could come together and Chapter 6 (+influence against all odds) for inspiration on what good could look like in highly challenging situations. Do this even before you go to the other chapters on principles (7 & 8).

For the senior executives and highfliers, you are advised to take the self-assessment at the beginning of Chapter 4 to see how good you really are and how ready you are to take all comers in high-stakes and high-challenge situations in which you are already immersed. Then fast forward to Chapter 14 to see how well you have handled the First and Last mile of your leadership mandates. You may be up against the next make-or-break assignment or big promotion. So you'll need the timely principles to manage your stakeholders' (high) expectations. You will need Chapter 15 if the opportunity requires you to +influence on the shop floor, in the boardroom or cut across them and other cultural divides.

If you need some inspiration to keep trying despite an unsupportive environment or stakeholder, Chapter 6 (on influencing against all odds) and Chapter 15 (influencing across shop floor, boardroom, and cultural divide) may light your fire again, and then you can peruse earlier parts of this Overview Chapter to see which parts of the book might uplift your influence effectiveness the most.

There is nothing like success to encourage you to keep going. For all reader types, Chapter 13 (on how others can help you develop) might give you some ideas on how you can benefit from similar-minded and similar-hearted people to keep journeying. Do reach out for help from some of these resources; otherwise your improvement may stall or you don't reach your best potential in +influence when you find yourself in high-stakes situations (*e.g.*, competing for a make-or-break contract) requiring more efficacy in +influence than you can pull off in the moment.

Finally, the book, however read, is a touchstone and guide to accompany you in your journey to become a better person and a better leader, whenever and wherever you might find challenging opportunities in which +influence is central to doing well and doing good for yourself and others. We hope it leads you to the ultimate payoff, which is a unique +craft that is personal to you and that strengthens your conduct and character, even as you draw on them readily to yield +outcomes.

Section I

Fundamentals of Influence

Overview

Section I Fundamentals of Influence is about why and how anyone — young professionals to CEOs — should care about improving their +influence skills in the context of interactions. This section makes the case for positive influence ("+influence"), examines what good +influence looks like, and invites you to self-assess how good you are at it for high-stakes situations. For CEOs and aspiring leaders, there is a collection of real-life stories of +influence against all odds to inspire you. By the end of Section I, we hope you are ignited and mobilized to improve your +influence! This section includes one mega case with six episodes to help you get hands-on in practicing +influence. The episodes take learners through the vantage points of different seniorities or roles using a myriad of real-life examples to bring to life the nature, challenges, and opportunities of +influence across business, life, and war.

2

+Influence in the Context of Interactions

We know from our lives that there are many things that can and do influence our behaviors. Many of us are awed by the presence of greatness, be it beauty, wealth, scholarship, or authority. Settings — a holy place, a beautiful sunset, or even a cramped airplane cabin — also affect how we behave.

This book primarily addresses influence that occurs in interactions between people. Where pertinent, case examples may highlight the non-interactive factors involved as additional considerations of the context in which influence takes place. These factors, such as stature and reputation of a person, can indirectly but powerfully affect an interaction.

Unique Nature of Interactions

What in the nature of interactions makes influence, especially in high-stakes situations, complex and challenging?

1. **Context.** Every interaction takes place in context — of the influencer's and influencee's (influenced person) needs and wants, the environment that affects each (often differently), what it takes to get the relevant task done, and

an array of situational factors, such as the time available, preexisting perceptions, biases, and assumptions.

2. **Opacity.** Many factors in the context are opaque (*i.e.*, not visible) to the influencer. This includes things that might be discoverable, but you may not have the time or means to discover them before the influence attempt (*e.g.*, confidential performance targets not typically known to outsiders). There are also things not even conscious to the influencer, influencee, or both (*e.g.*, hopes and fears).

3. **Dynamism.** As soon as the interactions begin, new data emerges, including non-verbals such as body language, and rational and emotional reactions begin to affect how each party thinks, feels, and acts. Preexisting impressions may be deepened or disrupted and new information injected.

Later chapters will look at a systematic way to examine the context (Chapter 6); how to discover pertinent but opaque data before, during, and after the interactions (Chapter 6); and how you can learn to pick up on signals and new developments and adapt, in real time, your influence approach to the targeted outcomes (Chapters 7 and 9).

+Influence Defined

Case 2.1.A New service launch

You are Bill, a high-potential young professional on a very important project for a facilities services company that is trying to evolve its business model. In particular, your team has launched a new service that is struggling in the marketplace. The company has historically provided companies with cleaning services via multi-year contracts. Now, your team has introduced a direct-to-consumer cleaning service

(Continued)

(Continued)

---

for families without stay-in helpers. You have had significant concerns regarding the attractiveness of the new service since the beginning of the project eight months ago, but you don't know the right way to convey your concerns. You are not sure if your project leader, Vik, is open to your concerns, because he seems to share primarily good news with the project sponsor, Sue-Ann, and minimize the bad news from the project. Sue-Ann also seems distracted due to some personal issues in her family, even though this project could significantly impact her career. The rest of your team have a range of attitudes: some are frustrated that the project isn't going so well, while others are just going through the motions until they get off the project. You are still excited about the project and have some ideas that could significantly increase the attractiveness of the service to customers. You think the price point is too high, and instead, an annual subscription with a 20% unit price reduction might work.

Young professionals (and senior leaders) are in these situations all the time: the project or situation is suboptimal, and the designated leaders don't seem to be on the right path or won't make the tough call. Who has influence over the outcome of the project? Conventional thinking would say the designated leaders (*i.e.*, the project leader and the project sponsor). The reality isn't so straightforward. All the team members, including this thoughtful young professional, Bill, can affect the trajectory and outcome of the project and the personal satisfaction and growth of the team members and project leaders through their mindset and actions. Not acting is also a choice.

+Influence is an attempt to mobilize oneself and others to positively impact an interaction, a task, a relationship, a group of people, or a community without the use of raw power (such as coercion) or authority, to produce good outcomes beneficial to all stakeholders.

In Case 2.1.A "New service launch," even if the ultimate leaders of this company (*e.g.*, the CEO) were watching the project closely, there is not much they could do using hard power and authority. They can change out the project leader and project sponsor and mandate the goals and timeline for the project, but the CEO can't command this young professional to share all his concerns and ideas or suddenly motivate the rest of the team members. Following the COVID-19 pandemic, the Great Resignation[8] phenomenon shows that people don't work for money and promotions alone. There are many personal, family, and interpersonal reasons that enhance or reduce enthusiasm and performance. A highly observant leader can find and use these levers of influence. This book helps you do this better, faster, with a broader range of people, especially in high-stakes, challenging situations.

Case 2.1.A New service launch (*continued*)

2.1.A.1 You are Bill. The pressures are mounting inside you as the deadline nears for a press release about this new service for the media. What should you do?

2.1.A.2 You are Jane, the CEO of the company above. You sense things are not coming along well as early results have been mixed, and the team doesn't seem to know why. Reasons provided by project leader Vik sound like excuses. Who could you influence to change the trajectory of the new service introduction? How might each person need to think, feel, and do differently?

+Influence Versus Persuasion, Communication, and Manipulation

How does +influence differ from persuasion, communication, and manipulation? There are essential differences — in orientation, intent, direction, and nature.

Unilateral versus mutual or collective <u>orientation</u>. The orientation of communication and persuasion is primarily unilateral, where the initiator (persuader or communicator) wants to convince the other parties of a typically fixed point of view or position,[9] hence the use of words like "buy-in" as in "you subscribe to my view and position." Lawyers making a case in front of a judge or jury are a prime example of this, where they work in service of a fixed outcome (*i.e.*, winning the case on behalf of their client).

On the other hand, +influence's orientation is mutual, even collective, where influencers are looking to positively move themselves, other people in the same situation, the project, the company, their family, and even society at large.

Many people would be open to accept "win-win"outcomes, except that "win-win" is often not good enough. First, "win-win" could end up being "what do I give up minimally so you feel you are getting enough of what you want to go along with my position." Second, the further from "I" you go, *i.e.*, "(s)he", "we" quickly slide into "they" where "they" could get non-specific. Collective entities like community and society at large are often given lip service. Third, when there are multitudes of stakeholders and entities involved, there is typically no fixed single outcome that will carry all stakeholders. Trade-offs and sacrifices are inevitable if human existence is to be sustainable. The positive outcomes that can work have to be discovered among all the different stakeholders. In other words, +outcomes must be treated as a third entity, apart from 'your' and 'my' interests. One has to work hard to discover the overlaps between the three entities. You cannot simply rely on persuading others to agree with your point of view by communicating more clearly or compellingly. You must identify the needs and pressure points of all stakeholders and address the pertinent ones that would move everyone. It will involve openness to learning new ways to step up and beyond what we normally are willing to do in service of the greater good even when self-interest is short-changed. We see a lot of examples of this tension in today's world — *e.g.*, saving endangered species by curtailing human encroachment, reducing carbon footprint in pursuing growth paths that are less financially attractive but gentler on the environment, *etc.* This is still a rare and under-appreciated skill (even in the age of ESG).

For example, in Case 2.1.A "New service launch," the key people have some personal needs in addition to wanting the project to do well: the project leader, Vik, wants to look good in front of his bosses, whereas the project sponsor, Sue-Ann, wants minimal problems from work so she can focus on family issues. Any successful raising of concerns by the young professional, Bill, must account for the task (project) and the stakeholders' personal needs.

Intent: Self-interest versus mutual or collective interest. This is the most important distinction between influence and manipulation. Manipulation is when one party influences other parties for the sole benefit of the influencing party, and it is often harmful to the parties being influenced.[10] Examples of manipulation include political propaganda, blackmail, and sowing discord among people. In business, manipulation often occurs too, such as spreading negative rumors about a competitor. Like +influence, manipulation uses some of the same sources of power, but the intent is fundamentally different.

One <u>direction</u> versus interactive. In interactions, all parties can +influence each other and the task at the same time (*i.e.*, an in-person meeting) or asynchronously (*i.e.*, across time), as opposed to mass media (*e.g.*, open letters, annual reports, Twitter, TikTok), where the initiator broadcasts to many people, but each of the recipients has a limited ability to influence back.[11] The interactive nature of dialogue is powerful: individual pressure points can be discovered, empathy can be expressed, assumptions and beliefs can change, and mutual inspiration can occur.

<u>Nature</u>: Indirect or contextual versus direct. The case examples in this book focus on direct influence, a particular genre of interactive influence, where one party makes a direct attempt to influence the thoughts, feelings, and actions of another party, without going through an intermediary party. The latter is what we call indirect influence.[12] Sources of contextual influence related to an individual will not be touched on, such as reputation, stature that results from many years of personal actions and people's perceptions and responses to those actions, and general bias or sentiment. Some of the more common contextual influences we have worked with include dealing with a climate of discontent or fear as well as a cultural bias to be inclusive, or "leave no one behind." Indirect and contextual influence is particularly important for more senior leaders, especially those in public domains with a lot of external stakeholders; therefore, this will be covered separately in our client work, blogs, or in another book.

Influence can be used for good and for evil, for selfish reasons or for the collective good. Influencers, even without conscious choice, know their intent. +Influence is a constructive type of power, essential in all human endeavors — be it business, family, social, or political situations — when raw power, as in authority, is not sufficient in getting people to face up to reality and change their behavior. As the world struggles with its interdependence and diversity, the rise of +influence is inevitable and long overdue.

Putting Oneself at Risk for Worthy Outcomes

Coming back to Case 2.1.A "New service launch" at the beginning of this chapter, Bill's influence depends on his relationships with the project leader and sponsor, and his own being — not just how persuasive Bill's logical arguments are. Is he just their underling, or is there enough of a personal relationship where he can share with them that their behaviors are detrimental to both the project's success and their own success? After all, the poor results of the launch can only stay hidden for so long, and it is better for them to course-correct when they still have a chance than to have to explain the non-success later. What is the risk and reward of Bill stepping up to influence team members to course-correct the project?

Bill's being — his personal qualities and beliefs — affect what he does and how those actions impact others. Will they see his comments as being for their good or for his own agenda? How does Bill see the risk and reward of having these courageous conversations? What is the power relationship between Bill, project leader Vik, and project sponsor Sue-Ann? What is Bill's conative? **Conative refers to a proclivity (*i.e.*, a bias, a tendency) to process emotional and rational stimuli in a particular way that results in actions in a preferred but often intuitive direction.** While the cognitive part of our mind argues for one rational action and the affective urges a different, more emotionally satisfying one, the conative takes in both and gets us to act. Will Bill be driven to achieve, to stand in harmony with others, or to serve a higher purpose? +Influence is as much about what a person does as who he or she stands for.

There's a Chinese saying that to get the tiger's cubs, you need to go into the tiger's den (不入虎穴，焉得虎子). If Bill wants to positively impact the project by improving the launch with his own ideas, he will have to put himself at risk in some fashion. With diligent practice, using the principles of this book and the excavation of his being, Bill will reduce the risk greatly and increase his influence to make the kind of impact he ultimately can have.

Case 2.1.B New service launch

Our young professional, Bill, summons up his courage to have a one-to-one chat with his project leader, Vik. Vik is at first taken aback that a junior person would pass judgment on the project. Vik had spent most of his career in India, where hierarchy is strongly respected. However, he recognizes that times have changed. Moreover, the strong case Bill has made is so compelling that he can't ignore the need to do something. Bill was also sincere and earnest, assuaging concerns that he might backstab Vik. Lastly, the solution Bill proposed was also intriguing. How can Vik talk to the project sponsor, Sue-Ann, who has cancelled their last three one-on-one meetings due to family emergencies?

Bill has taken a decisive step to change the outcome for the project and for the key stakeholders. This influence attempt to create things that are not there at all, or get things done faster, better, and more consistently makes Bill a leader.

Making +Outcomes Happen

Defining the right positive outcomes worthy of putting yourself on the line for is just the beginning of the work of a conscious influencer. The skilled design and execution of an influence attempt considers the context, stakeholders, and your own being during planning while also remaining open-minded during the influence attempt. This book guides you through the mastering of preparation to execution, if you practice using your own situations and the cases in this book. Additional professional help can be found on the book's website.[13]

As said earlier, all parties involved begin to react as soon as the influence begins. The new data given off consciously or unconsciously by different parties can be incorporated by a mindful, skilled practitioner living in the next moment. Because your influence will naturally draw on your own unique blend of personal qualities, preferences for an influence approach, and skill level, the same (case) situation will draw forth different behaviors from different people. What works for you might not work as well for others. Circumstances change as well, so what works for you at this moment may not work as well in a different moment or setting. For example, waiting a day or two could change the ripeness of Bill's approach.

Case 2.1.A.3 New service launch

How might Bill's influence attempt need to be different depending on project leader Vik's profile?
- Profile 1: Vik is a veteran of the company with little to prove; he was recently appointed to take over for another project leader.
- Profile 2: Vik is known to be a highly indecisive leader who shies away from bad news.
- Profile 3: Vik is a highflier who has had a long history of success and is in line for a promotion, so he is anxious to show quick results.

Bill would need to tailor his influence strategy to the subjective profile of Vik, his project leader. Each of the three profiles of Vik would have a different path toward the desired outcome of acknowledging that the launch needs a change in tactic.

Whatever the profile of Vik, the influence strategy also must be grounded in the being of Bill. A confronting person cannot suddenly be highly sympathetic, just as a highly relational person might need to work up to the tough message. Just like the adage that all roads lead to Rome, each influencer should find the unique influence path that bridges the existing thoughts, feelings, and actions to what is required by the differentiated +outcomes. Excellent influencers have this unique insight into this path and bridge, via a combination of data collection and analysis, intuition, and inspiration. Chapter 7–8's principles help you to find these paths and bridges.

Once in the conversation itself, there can also be many dynamics to be contended with; for example, Vik's mood will impact his willingness and ability to listen and absorb, or he might get a call during the meeting or be interrupted by his child while working from home. The mood can only be sensed and dealt with in the moment. Expert influencers pick this up in the first 30 seconds and adapt their outcome and strategy in real time.

With so many different aspects of +influence, you might feel daunted: where do I start? There are so many ways to improve your influence, and you can start anywhere. Each aspect is a way to improve your influencing. Once you improve one aspect, you will have more insight and more consciousness about other aspects. There is a virtuous cycle that is particularly powerful when you work on your doing and being simultaneously.

What Makes
a Good +Influence

Few will have the greatness to bend history itself, but each of us can work to change a small portion of events. **It is from numberless diverse acts of courage and belief that human history is shaped.** *Each time a man stands up for an ideal, or acts to improve the lot of others, or strikes out against injustice, he sends forth a tiny ripple of hope, and crossing each other from a million different centers of energy and daring those ripples build a current which can sweep down the mightiest walls of oppression and resistance.*

— Robert F. Kennedy

We can choose what kinds of outcomes to aim for, no matter how challenging the circumstances. Whether we exercise that choice doesn't depend on authority or power but rather on our values, courage, and attitudes.

As a young project manager assigned to cut costs for an insurance company in Canada in the early 1980s, Tsun-yan looked fear in the face.

+Influence Personal Story: Going Beyond Cost Cutting

He was asked to speak at the company town hall meeting to explain the cost-cutting program. The sponsoring senior executive had said little before passing the baton to him. The project leader hadn't bothered to show up. Tsun-yan got on stage. He looked at the audience, and the fear and anxiety of the people were palpable. Tsun-yan is a feeler according to the MBTI,[14] so he felt all the emotions in the room acutely. People feared for their jobs; social relationships would be disrupted; muscles important to basic services for customers might be damaged while some fat remained.

In that moment, he knew he couldn't just deliver his prepared presentation about the cost-cutting process. He took a deep breath as he felt his heart and spirit move within him. Without consulting anyone, he asked the people to go on a journey with him, to cut costs and to find growth opportunities that would deploy the people made redundant from the cost-cutting exercise. "Simultaneously tear down and build up," he said. He gave people hope, which he delivered with the help the audience willingly gave. To his working team members, he issued a choice: stay on the project but do two projects — one would cut costs and the other would raise revenues — or get off the project. All chose to stay on, even though it meant double the work.

The moral of the story is that you can't just focus on productivity; more people will be with you if you actually care about their growth and satisfaction.

Throughout Tsun-yan's career, he never did another cost-cutting study, choosing instead to help people grow and transform themselves to better cope with pressures from stakeholders. Sticking to this choice was costly. He turned a group CEO job down because it would have involved a lot of cost-cutting upfront. While the title and prospect of being a CEO tantalized him, his soul searching told him that he should continue devoting himself to helping people grow and evolve toward their best potential — not to cut people down with job elimination, no matter how lucrative financially.

People will forget what you said, people will forget what you did. But people will never forget how you made them feel.
— *Maya Angelou*[15]

Core +Outcomes: Productivity, Satisfaction, and Growth

A good influence starts with the outcomes — not just what you want, but also from the perspectives of others affected and the system (*e.g.*, company, family, industry) as a whole. This takes, with deliberate practice, skilled execution that considers the context, stakeholders, and your own being.

Three core outcomes undergird +influence: productivity, satisfaction, and growth (Table 1). One without the other two

Table 1.   Examples of positive productivity, satisfaction, and growth.

Productivity	Satisfaction	Growth
• Higher profits (higher revenues or lower cost) • Less effort/waste while maintaining output • Less capital while maintaining profit • Greater resilience (bounce back from negative shocks) • Team output greater than sum of the individuals	Individuals feel • Respected • Competent • Can see impact of work • Connected to others • Getting traction to achieve goals • Working with people who "accept me"	Business • Extend product to new customer segment • Grow revenue through more outlets • Strong leadership bench to grow business with • Accelerate learning of high-potential staff • Attract people who are effective in multiple contexts Personal • Diversity of leadership styles • High aspiration • Push yourself outside of comfort zone • Able to operate in multiple contexts

would not be motivating to all the key stakeholders and/or not be sustainable.

- **Productivity**: more performance for the same effort/ inputs, or less effort for the same performance.
- **Satisfaction**: do people like working here? Are they respected, do they have joy, do they have a threshold sense of self-worth?
- **Growth**: business growth, personal development, improvement in a system's capacity to deal with certain needs (*e.g.*, health care system to care for mental health issues).[16]

Rarely can a situation be resolved well purely through productivity, as demonstrated by so many cases in which leaders have gone wrong in the singular pursuit of profit and winning (*e.g.*, a gold medal).[17] Despite the unfettered capitalism of the last hundred years, businesses don't exist just to make profits for owners.[18] Businesses provide valuable services to customers, impact the way society evolves, and provide the environment for employees to grow and develop themselves. Businesses' potential for positive and negative impact is enormous, but it depends on whether leaders, young and old, can channel people's energies toward worthy, positive outcomes, no matter how challenging and risky the situation.

Despite how challenging a crisis or failure might start off being, there is always a direction that increases shared productivity, satisfaction, and growth. The word "shared" is important because when everyone has a stake and can benefit meaningfully from their perspective, they will invest more of their energies into the shared endeavor, braving thunder and storms.

Working in service of shared productivity, satisfaction and growth is not easy, but doable because human beings have evolved newer parts of the brain (namely the frontal cortex) to "*make you do the harder thing when it's the right thing to do*", as Robert M. Sapolsky, author of the book *Behave*,[28] aptly put it. While the older parts of our brain are more automatic and instinctive, a well-developed frontal cortex gives us the ability to delay gratification, motivate ourselves to benefit self and others, and not give in to first instincts. The frontal cortex gets stronger with use, *i.e.*, willful effort to apply ourselves in a certain direction.[19] So with a lot of practice, aiming for shared productivity, satisfaction and growth will become automatic at some point.

─────────────── ✝ ───────────────

+Influence Personal Story: Taking the Road Less Traveled

The work for productivity, satisfaction, and growth starts with individual choice, to not take the easy road, but have the courage to take the path less traveled. Marie Cheong (a participant of LinHart's first LIFE2 program)'s recent career choice (as told in her own words) illustrates this character-forging process, how she sacrificed a higher salary and approval of others, to keep uncovering herself.

In July 2019, I was 18 months into an early-stage startup that I had taken a leap of faith and a financial hit to join. As the general manager and close personal friends of the founders, I had given my all, but it was clear our objectives and values were no longer aligned. It was time to look for a new role.

An alumna of Huijin and Tsun-yan's LIFE programs, I had spent five years putting in the work to re-discover, or uncover, who I was at my core. Like so many young professionals, I had internalized external markers of success — brand names, promotions, salary, and titles — as who I am. The pursuit had left me unmotivated and dissatisfied. Through my journey with LinHart, it became clear to me that for me to be fulfilled, I wanted to build something great for the world. The only downside: I had no idea what that was.

A few months into the job search, I had an attractive offer on the table. A large tech company was building out a new product and was looking for a customer success manager. It was an exciting, dynamic team. I would have the flexibility to work around my young family and the compensation was more than double what I was earning.

The offer felt good. A big brand wanted me, and they were willing to pay! The job would justify the risk I took joining the startup and was something I knew I could do well. I was tempted to fall back to past behaviors.

Using my LinHart training, I built a framework (based on the LIFE2 'sweet spot' and Ikigai framework) of what I could do well, what I enjoyed and what I felt the world needs. At the intersection of all three was my driving motivation: to build something great for the world. When I evaluated the opportunity through this framework, I realized the job on offer would be paying me for what I was already good at and a little of what I enjoyed, but nothing on my list of impact on the world. This would not get me closer to my sweet spot of building something great for the world.

The day I turned down the job, I felt an incredible sense of freedom. This gave me the courage to be vulnerable and speak more about what I wanted from life, sharing ideas from my framework, even when I thought people wouldn't understand. I was surprised by the overwhelmingly positive response and how this deepened my connection with friends and people in my network. It was through these conversations that I discovered what building something 'great' meant to me — building startups that fight climate change. I was 'all-in'.

Nine months later, I was in a new role building climate tech startups and learning as much as I could about what it would take to transition the world to a carbon-free future. I kept growing and got better at evolving and articulating my purpose. Momentum started to build and life got more and more exciting.

In October 2021, along with four other founding partners, I launched Southeast Asia's first climate tech venture builder VC fund. Our mission is to build a portfolio of startups that can reduce the global carbon budget by 10%. I go to work every day with an incredibly passionate and motivated team that shares this mission. I've chosen to dedicate the rest of my career to becoming better and better at building climate tech companies that can have the biggest possible impact on reducing carbon emissions. I found my sweet spot, and the journey is exhilarating.

Case 3.1.A.4 New service launch

In the new service launch project, what positive outcomes should the young professional, Bill, aim for — for the project or company and for key individuals (project leader Vik, project sponsor Sue-Ann)?

Answers to this exercise can be found in Chapter 5.

+Outcomes for the Group

When we consider good outcomes of productivity, satisfaction, and growth, we must often consider the groups that are affected by our +influence — not just one or two individuals. That's true for an enterprise involving collective efforts: in businesses, government, social enterprises, families, schools, and so on. In theory, it's simple, but in practice, we observe quite a lot of fall-off. Only productivity goals seem to get the attention of the leaders. Sure, value statements declare loudly that the company is respectful and inclusive, but actions speak louder than words. Reality falls way short of ethos. To generate more productivity, satisfaction, and growth for all group members,

1. Individual group members must avoid the siren's call of maximizing one outcome (*e.g.*, productivity), but have the courage to look for paths that raise productivity, satisfaction and growth.
2. Group cohesion must be actively built by promoting a mindset of working towards group, not just individual, success. This is not easy: it requires putting the person, "the subject", to be as important as productivity considerations. That is the fundamental mindset +influence requires.

Group Cohesion

We see individuals come together as a cohesive group during the course designed for NUS Business School MBAs. For more than a decade since the course was introduced, each cohort of around 200 has become more cohesive, and such a significant portion of students felt personally transformed that the school decided to rename it "Launch Your Transformation" to better reflect the personal impact of the program.[20]

———————————— *+* ————————————

+Influence Personal Story: Supporting Others to Grow

In a week, young MBAs learn to work on their own and others' development via mutual High Challenge High Support (HCHS). They reflect alone but learn in pairs, in small groups of five and in sections of 25, so they can scale their +influence objectives in small and larger groups. One of the faculty, Mike Jackson, a senior media executive and leadership coach, shares one such experience below.

> An MBA student vented his frustrations with his learning group of 5: "I have to drive all conversations! They aren't committed to learn. The day 5 team task would be a disaster." He only had one day left to figure this out. We discussed his learning group, their profile, their preferences, and how his style was different (from the rest of his group). He saw immediately the issue was himself, that he hadn't applied the course learnings to his group situation. A light bulb lit up in his mind. Applying high-quality feedback principles he learned earlier, he addressed the group first thing on day 5. He shared his frustrations but acknowledged his assertive approach hadn't and won't work for the team. He suggested more planning time to support the team and held back from driving the day 5 task solution. His group excelled in the day 5 task, and firm friendships started to emerge. The individual was so taken aback by his "light bulb" moment that he came back the next year as an assistant faculty.
>
> So, what is the key learning? It's recognizing that in any influencing situation, the starting point is the subject or subjects of influence (i.e., the people), where are they coming from, pressures, and how you need to adapt your style to influence them.

In the real world, a CEO's effort to build cohesion in the top team is a lot tougher. Most team members didn't choose one another to be on the team, they have very limited bandwidth on collective issues since they are mostly paid on their own business results, and collective results translate into too small a portion of their rewards and are often too abstract to motivate. That's even before considering the reality that they compete for scarce resources: good talents and capital. Because the stakes are high in terms of team performance, most CEOs intuitively aim to build high-performing teams. However, few know what it takes. The bar is very high. Tsun-yan's experience certainly concurs with the research of his mentor, Jon Katzenbach:[21] only a very small percentage of work groups should and can be a high-performing team. It takes hard work that must be rooted in the heart and spirit of every team member in creating a shared purpose, agreeing on norms for acceptable behaviors, aligning around a common standard of what is good enough/fast enough, developing protocols to resolve conflict, and holding people accountable to achieve goals and uphold norms.[22] Groups need to be clear and aligned on how becoming a high-performing team could pay off — in productivity, satisfaction, or growth — for the effort to be worthwhile.

The most elusive but most powerful ingredient of a high-performing group is a leadership climate or culture that encourages people to stretch themselves, go beyond their comfort zone, and change or evolve as demanded by the environment and as inspired by themselves and others. A conducive leadership culture will lift people's sense of what is expected. Just imagine when personal development is the norm (not the exception), when people give each other high-quality feedback regularly, when everyone has specific development goals they are working on, and when people challenge and support each other actively on task issues and personal development. We actively encourage this in LinHart's programs and courses and among its client leaders and have been awed by the power of it.

Caring for the "Subject" Promotes Collective Outcomes

Winning is fun, but those moments that you can touch someone's life in a very positive way are better.

— Tim Howard

Mike's emphasis on the "subject" is spot-on and underappreciated by the vast majority (90%+) of professionals and senior leaders alike. The "subject" is the person or people doing the task, dealing with challenges — professional and personal — and contending with the pressures; the task and challenges are the "object."

Tsun-yan has a great parable to illustrate "subject orientation,"[23] which undergirds everything we and LinHart do; we help people become more "subject-oriented."

John picks an apple.

Most people focus on the apples and apple picking (objects) part of the sentence. How big is the market for apples (market sizing)? What are the market positions of the producers (market share)? What tools are needed to pick the apple (processes, technology)? At what rate can the apples be picked (productivity)? And so on. The world is well trained to execute the analysis.

Very few people ask: How good is John at picking the apples? How many apple pickers do we need for a year's production and to grow the business? How do we recruit and train enough apple pickers? How motivated is John, and how best do we continue to motivate him? Can he make a decent living wage from picking apples? How might he want to upgrade himself? Can he grow to manage an apple orchard? How do we make John feel respected as a person and worker?

Most businesspeople focus on the apple picking, the object. The focus on John — the subject — is still highly unusual now and certainly when Tsun-yan started his career in 1980. It is likely to apply even more to the government and social sectors, where emotional issues often trump logic, and individual needs and feelings can amalgamate into a swirl of social sentiment.

+Influence Personal Story: Developing Personal Formula for +Influence

Tsun-yan developed his extraordinary focus on the person or leader (in addition to content) as a means for survival. He was great at content and analysis but couldn't develop new clients and projects by being great at content alone. Marvin Bower, the founder of McKinsey and Tsun-yan's hero, sat next to Tsun-yan during the new associate training in the United States and pooh-poohed Tsun-yan's aspiration to be a counselor to CEOs. "What do you have in common with most American CEOs? Do you watch the same sports they do? Did you go to the same schools, clubs? How will you build a relationship with them?" As an introverted Singaporean Chinese, the first ethnically Chinese person to join McKinsey, he didn't have cultural affinity, a school's network, or natural charisma to rely on. He had to develop his own formula.

Dejected by Marvin's comments, Tsun-yan was determined to prove Marvin wrong. The "Whip" and "Fastest Analyst in the East" (two of Tsun-yan's early nicknames) moved beyond the ability to chase down any data and out-analyze anyone. Throughout his subsequent adventures across four decades — developing strategies, doing deals, expanding internationally, and growing global champions — Tsun-yan's secret sauce was in addressing the subject.

> *I always focused on helping the person behind the role become successful, in ways that are meaningful to the business and to the person. I have an airport test: if I ran into a client a decade after the work was done, would he or she be really glad to see me?*

Tsun-yan inspired himself to focus on the person: Why do they think the way they think, do the things they do? What do they care about, and how can they align more closely doing well with doing good? How do I get them to dream bigger, be better (not perfect) leaders, and act more impactfully?

Good outcomes start with not only productivity but also growth and satisfaction of the individuals. Don't stop there. As leaders, you should set +outcome objectives for the group of people — teams, groups, and larger connected networks. By focusing on the subjects and subjective aspects, you can more easily include the growth and satisfaction of these larger collectives in targeting +outcomes for doing well and doing good.

4

Just How Good
Are You at +Influence?

Young professionals and senior executives alike approach high-stakes situations much like day-to-day influence attempts: they wing it. They may get the content ready, typically in a presentation, an outline, or even a script for the opening. They have some gut feel for the audience or the counterparty — their likes and dislikes and, therefore, what to lead with and what to avoid (*e.g.*, "He hates PowerPoint!"). Especially for top executives, past success may reinforce the belief that they "have a sixth sense that's on the money and works most of the time," not realizing that their success might not be replicable as circumstances change.

So, just how good are you at +influence? In a totally new, unfamiliar environment (*e.g.,* different cultures, foreign countries, moving to a different company), is your grasp of the influence fundamentals good enough to adapt to the different context, task demands, and relational dynamics?

You are invited to complete the simple questionnaire below to sense how well equipped you are for high-stakes influence that you want to get right. All statements should get a "yes" or "no" response only — no "maybe" or "it all depends." "Yes" means at least "most of the time" or "all the time."

Assessment: How Good is My +Influence Ability?

1. You classify the desired outcomes based on your understanding of the situation into must-haves, should-haves, and nice-to-haves.

2. You create a different, less charged setting in which you could meet the other person so you can have a direct, personal read of the person you're about to meet in the "arena" later.

3. You frame the outcomes not just in terms of how they would benefit yourself or your organization but how they would benefit others.

4. You continue to gather data at the venue, including first impressions (<5 minutes) of the people before serious conversations get under way; you pay attention to the settings, the body language of the counterparty, the tone and sincerity of their initial behaviors, and the strength of personal connection.

5. You work up at least two different pathways to achieve the desired outcomes and, depending on the flood of new information from #4, you decide which path to take or improvise a new one if the information is fundamentally calling for a different approach.

6. You take a few minutes on arrival to meditate on how you'd like your whole person to show up, (*e.g.*, by looking out the window in the reception area or some private space if necessary to center yourself) and meditate or ground your being on those thoughts.

7. As the meeting gets under way, a part of you gets "on the balcony" to see, sense, and perceive the dynamics — gauging the next moment you could pivot the meeting more toward achieving the desired outcomes — and adapt your behavior accordingly.

8. Notwithstanding the flood of information — content and emotions — on the interaction dynamics, you observe key people's behaviors but refrain from judging with finality the key person's character, motivation, and attitudes.

9. You form judgments based on earlier evidence, updated with immediate in-meeting behaviors, and you ask yourself, "Even if this were true, what else can *also* be true?"

10. Even if the going is tough, you ask yourself what you could uniquely do to add positive energy to the room, since an extraordinary amount of positivity is required to spread goodwill and outcomes to all stakeholders.

If your total number of yeses is 0–2, you are probably winging your influence attempts too much or all the time. This book will hopefully help you see that there is a lot of upside for you to influence more consciously (see Chapter 7). You have already experienced a lot of hit or miss in your influence attempts. You rationalize your misses. But you need to be persuaded that one can improve beyond native instincts.

With a total of 2–4 yeses, you are likely aware that certain influences don't go your way, and you're not sure why. But you know it's important to be better at it and are open to improvement if possible.

4–6 yeses: You are probably aware of the upside of improving your +influence ability but have not yet mastered your own way to make it work more often than not.

7–9 yeses indicate you are already conscious of what you could bring to bear from your inner being and meld it with the immediate goings-on to be present and +influence yourself and others effectively.

If you scored a 10, you should be writing the book with us and teaching others at one of our programs.

A bit facetious, perhaps, but the above test is a quick gauge of a person's influence effectiveness and potential areas for self-improvement. If you remain skeptical about whether you could be better at influencing, the questions were based on real-life challenges and opportunities people like you are already facing out there — whether a CEO or young professional in the first few years out of school. The remainder of this book goes into these challenges and opportunities in detail.

The Most Common Influence Challenges CEOs Face

From our work in counseling founders, owners, and CEOs (FOCs) and investors dealing with them, a list has been created of the ones encountered multiple times. For brevity, each will be grounded with a disguised, highly abbreviated example drawn from real-life experiences and will include some cases you can read and practice to better appreciate the nature of the challenge and how you might tackle it by applying +influence principles. The case code indicates the chapter where a case example can be found; for example, case 7.4 means case 4 in Chapter 7. The cases in the later chapters may not be the exact example before, but another situation that illustrates the essential nature of the challenge.

1. **Managing stakeholders' expectations to align (divergent) interests.**
    a. **Management versus union.** Automation of a car assembly meant a dramatic shift in skill required. A lot more robotic and electrical engineers and technicians, and a lot less of the largely mechanically trained workers are needed. Executives often focus too much on making the investment in technology

and changing the operational processes, and not enough on engaging with the workers who need to adopt new mindsets and skills and thus deal with the fear of losing relevance. (Case 15.23)

b. **Shareholders' interest versus regulator**. After securing the broadcast rights to Premier League football with a bid >$200 million, a telco is instructed by the regulator to allow cross-carriage to its arch rival telco so "more residents could watch the matches without having the inconvenience to switch their cable subscription." It is a tough balancing act: how to set the price in a way that residents can afford it (hence not complain), and yet not give too much ground to the competitor, and still make some money.

c. **Majority shareholders versus minority shareholders**. A controlling shareholder continued to ignore minority shareholders' clamor for better governance, expressed as rising dissenting votes at the company's Annual General Meeting on every resolution put forward. The super-voting shares held by the controlling shareholders ensured the resolutions were passed. The non-independent chairman insisted on chairing the nominating committee and appointed 'independent directors' who are friendly to the controlling shareholder. (Case 10.11)

d. **Activist shareholders (or Greenmailer) versus all shareholders**. A U.S. hedge fund bought 5% of an iconic Asian company's share and challenged management to divest some profitable businesses that the fund partners deemed to have no synergy with the core business. Management disagreed, but performance of core businesses reached an all-time low. The CEO must personally deal with the activist shareholder, potentially make compromises while trying to restore the confidence of the larger shareholder base in management.

e.   **Aligning the top team on strategic agenda** (with resultant shifts in allocation of scarce resources). An outsized global acquisition of a private equity-owned business has taken up much of the attention of the CEO and CFO and distracted the rest of the top team, just when the core business has suffered some substantial, unforeseen setbacks, including a lawsuit from a dominant customer alleging serious contract breaches. While everyone is coping with keeping all the balls in the air, the CEO must find precious time to align everyone on the future vision of the business and on who does what. (Cases 14.18 and 14.19)

2.   **Balancing leadership priorities across horizons**: short versus long term. The CEO of a capital-intensive, high-growth business must convince the principal investors that a big investment in technology to refresh its marketplace/transaction platform is imperative. The pandemic has hit the business hard with revenue shrinkage and an alarming cash burn that necessitated cash rationing to all units. Engineers believe this is an existential decision whereas others in sales believe that the expenditure can be postponed while sales staff must be retained to arrest further revenue decline. Morale is low as employees wonder how the investors comprising the board will swing the decision on the technology investment.

3.   **Setting performance expectations**. Commodity prices have plunged by >50%, and the company is running out of cash in three months. The chief of sales is retiring in

nine months and is more avid to shop for a sailboat for leisure than coming up with a viable sales turnaround. The CEO, Ron, is noodling on how to inspire someone to put in extraordinary effort (versus cruising) when he is on the cusp of retiring. The story can be found in Chapter 6.

4. **Managing performance shortfalls**. A commercial bank is underperforming budgets by a wide margin with half of the 24 industry verticals earning less than cost of capital. Of the vertical heads, 17 were veterans and used to be peers to the newly appointed COO, who is a highly experienced banker with great technical skills. But he likes to tell more than he listens.

5. **Influencing the stock analyst/market perception of performance trajectory**. Notwithstanding consecutive profitable growth, the stock price has languished, with returns to shareholders well below par. The CEO is sure that legacy businesses destroy value, but past tries to divest have not worked. There could be other reasons, with 18 lines of businesses. The CEO needs some help to gain insight into what is really going in each of the 18 lines of business and to be able to effectively communicate this and what he plans to do to the market.

6. **Making the tough decision to move, separate, or terminate underperformers and managing fallouts/debris**. A long-tenured VP of engineering has clearly underperformed and is tired and wants a way out with dignity. The CEO was hired 20 years ago by him. Everyone is tiptoeing around the VP out of respect for his past "glory." This has gone on for two years. For tough conversations like these, the CEO needs to first influence himself and then influence the VP to confront the underperformance and figure out a way forward. (Case 9.7)

7. **Attracting top talent** — young or senior — to join your team. The chair of the new talent development taskforce is a frontrunner for CEO succession. Big efforts in ESG (Environmental, Social, and Governance) have not changed the company image as a big "polluter" in the war for talent, especially in fast-growing Asia where young talents have a lot of better options. There is also a dearth of Asian women in the middle to upper ranks, hollowed out by attrition to greener pastures in the last decade. While corporates may spend a lot of money on employee branding and sponsoring conferences, a top leader's personal credibility on a theme like "gender/diversity" has a disproportionate impact. (Cases 11.14 and 14.19)

   A. A wealthy family owner is having trouble replacing the retiring CEO. The pipeline is poor inside and paltry outside after two searches. Two shortlisted candidates are both financially independent from the recent change in ownership. The owner's attitude and being become all-important: these candidates don't need another CEO job but are instead looking for purpose, camaraderie, and a great adventure. (Case 9.8)

8. **Building extraordinary energy behind change initiatives** (on top of business-as-usual). A venerable airline has fallen on hard times. After a private-public recapitalization, a new CEO was hired. There are many low-hanging fruits, but the old culture of inertia and insouciance lingers. The demand for talent to drive the large portfolio of initiatives far outstrips the paltry supply of committed, capable change champions. A CEO must win the minds and hearts of the people, in addition to executing the key early wins. (Case 15.23)

9. **Dealing with a crisis.** A hospital CEO presides over a massive data leak following a cyberattack with alleged loss of electronic medical records, in addition to basic personal information. This happened when there was an ongoing investigation into the death of a preschooler whose mother has made a Facebook post alleging a cover-up and mishandling. The central challenge is how can the CEO project humility and competence while he or she may not immediately know much about the cause and impact of the data leak?

There are many other challenging situations facing CEOs (and relevant CXOs). Suffice to say, these are the genres we have encountered more than others that illustrate well some common themes where influence is concerned:

- Multiple stakeholders with non-aligned interests.
- Complex, ambiguous circumstances unfolding dynamically.
- Unique context rendering general purpose solutions less useful.
- Enormous internal and external pressure points, including ticking time bomb effects demanding timely judgment.

The owners are encountering most, if not all, problems for the first time and are, at best, partially ready to deal with all the issues.

Common Influence Situations Encountered by Younger Professionals/Executives

Younger professionals and executives (roughly speaking, 0–12 years out of graduate school) face a myriad of more basic influence challenges when their native self-awareness is still developing. Here are the ones Tsun-yan compiled for the pilot course[24] at the NUS Business School, subsequently enriched by Huijin who is LinHart Principal responsible for our leadership programs for universities and corporates.

- Managing expectations (cases 7.3 and 14.20)
- Saying no (to a request) (case 10.9)
- Dealing with irate/angry customers or external partners (cases 8.4 and 8.6)
- Making a pitch (case 8.6)
- Giving or taking (negative) feedback (cases 9.7, 10.9, 12.15)
- Giving constructive feedback to a superior (case 2.1.B)
- Working with an uncooperative peer (case 7.2)
- Instructing others on tasks (cases 7.2 and 8.5)
- Addressing underperformance of project or individuals (cases 2.1.A, 5.1.C–E, 11.1.F–G)
- Motivating/encouraging a colleague or team members (cases 8.5 and 11.13)
- Connecting well while being your true self (case 5.1.E)
- Doing well in a job/new role/interview
- Accepting a new assignment or promotion
- Turning down a new assignment or promotion
- Asking for more or different opportunities than assigned
- Asking for more pay, benefits, or time off (case 10.10)
- Dealing with self-promoter peers
- Quitting well
- Giving voice to change versus conforming with norms (case 12.16)
- Balancing work and life demands (case 5.1.E)
- Charting career choices with divergent personal stakeholders (*e.g.*, parents, siblings, friends).

The above list is obviously not comprehensive but represents a wide array of challenges that younger people often face. Some people may do well in some genres and not so well in others. As shown in Chapter 5, everyone can improve regardless of the starting point. Common factors making them challenging are as follows:

- Self-talk impeding more data acquisition and a thoughtful approach.
- Unresolved inner tensions that cause either a "to do or not to do" or "do now or do later" type of dilemma. Nothing happens and the moment passes.
- Demanding authority figure stakeholders (*e.g.*, boss, parents) that persist in engaging in a difficult style (*e.g.*, condescending, lecturing, judging).
- Failure to engage the other person as an equal, most often with authority figures.
- Lacking self-confidence, fearful that the other person will pounce on any sign of weakness or anxiety.
- Fear of difficult emotions (*e.g.*, disappointing or angering others).

The chapters ahead will return to pick up some of the above common challenges and how you can best overcome them through reflection, and hands-on practice with someone.

5

Why All of Us Can Be Better at +Influencing

Even the best influencers had to overcome many hurdles to influence effectively. Or perhaps because they didn't let hurdles stop them in their tracks, they uncovered the ability to influence.

Initially, Tsun-yan struggled at Harvard Business School (HBS), which is famous for its case study method. Less well known is that 50% of grades are based on verbal comments made. Three months into the fall semester, he still had not spoken up in his classes. He risked failing his classes, "hit the screen" in HBS colloquial language.

One day, he got the dreaded cold call, "Mr. Hsieh, would you start the discussion for us?" He could no longer avoid speaking up. The professor looked at him expectantly, waiting. He was trying to help Tsun-yan, by forcing him to speak up.

Tsun-yan knew this logically but found it nerve-racking. In 1980, the 28-year-old had little confidence in his communication ability. He had been an extreme introvert all his life, and that was largely okay in Singapore where he had worked as a mechanical engineer. But not at HBS, where BS, also known as bullshit, is jokingly referred to as an art form.

It also didn't help that Tsun-yan hadn't finished reading the case, since it was a struggle to finish preparing 3 × 25 pages of cases a day. So he had to quickly flip through the unread portion of the case.

For what felt like an interminable three minutes, there was silence in the classroom. All 89 fellow students looked upon Tsun-yan intently. Then, something clicked in him. He took a deep breath and found his voice. His opening analysis was so comprehensive that the class clapped, though the professor was a bit miffed that so few angles remained to be debated.

That experience was one of many across his four decade-long career where Tsun-yan ventured outside of his comfort zone and dug deeper into his being to influence more people, more effectively. Such experiences taught him that people can go far beyond their upbringing, personality, and discomfort to influence better, making positive connections with people who are very different. These experiences humbled and inspired him to keep improving his influencing.

How We Short-Change Our Influence Attempts

For many of us, influencing is not something we *consciously* think about much, so we make a lot of avoidable mistakes. In fact, by leveraging some deeper preparation methods used only by a minority of people, our influencing effectiveness could increase significantly. We have been brought up to think of it as communicating or persuading (refer to Chapter 2). We are quick to conjure up certain beliefs about how we do it and where we would not be comfortable to go. Influencing in our everyday lives is a lot broader and is two-way: it includes engaging with people with a wide variety of outlooks and agendas as well as managing expectations of diverse stakeholders. We have seen earlier that when the stakes are low, say, we botched the chance to change seats

Table 2.   Influence attempt preparation methods for high-stakes situations.

Question: For the high-stakes conversations that affect the trajectory of my relationship with people and/or task performance, I prepare in the following way.

	Used often or always (% of respondents)
• Think through how the other person(s) might react, and how to deal with each possibility	65%
• Reflect after the episode to see what worked vs. not worked and what to do differently	59%
• Analyze the situation and prepare an influence plan (with objectives and alternative strategies)	58%
• Identify my self-talk and reframe it to be more constructive	43%
• Meditate to align how I think, feel and do to what is needed for good outcomes	40%
• Reflect on how I can be triggered, and coach myself on how to avoid being triggered	38%
• Roleplay with the help of others	25%

Source: LinHart research involving 189 American professionals and leaders.

with another passenger on a plane, it won't be a disaster. However, in high-stakes conversations, our doubts, self-talk, low awareness, ill-preparedness, and instinct-led execution short-change our attempt. With proper analysis and preparation, as you will see, we can significantly reduce these drawbacks. Also, it's not just the techniques we learn and practice; we can become aware of how our inner being unconsciously limits — or broadens — our instantaneous choice of approach and therefore impact on others.

Case 5.1.C New service launch

As the project leader of the new service launch, it has not been easy for you, Vik, the day-to-day project leader. The early result indicators are not good. The online reviews are particularly problematic, with 45% of sign-ups budgeted to be coming through online channels. You are a bit lost as to how to address the issues with the online channel. Your personal expertise is B2B sales, where you get to talk to a client, but digital sign-ups is quite new to you. You do have younger chaps who seem to be more digitally savvy, but some aren't so motivated, and most don't know how to express their thoughts. One management associate, Bill, always seem to want to say something but doesn't. The pandemic years must have really dented the development of communication abilities. Sue-Ann, the project sponsor, has been distracted by family issues, but you really need her to lean in more for everyone's sake. In the last project's steering committee with the CEO, Jane, who was frowning at Sue-Ann's distracted behavior, including taking a phone call in the middle of the meeting. You don't know Sue-Ann well, so you hesitate to ask her what is going on. You wonder, how do you minimize the damage from a non-success in this project? You are near the end of your career, so non-success won't impact you much personally. It can impact Sue-Ann's and Bill's careers a lot though, given the visibility of the project. Moreover, you actually think the new service is a good idea, but the execution has been very problematic.

Common Drags on Influence Attempts

1. Doubts

When there are a lot of problems and the solution isn't evident, and others don't seem so motivated to address them, a sense of futility can set in. It is very easy to have what one CEO (Seah Chin Siong of Singapore Institute of Management) calls goal erosion, "*Do what is easy, go through the motions but not do the hard things the ultimate mission requires.*" It is true that no one person alone has the power to impact the person and/or situation, but every person can make attempts to impact the situation positively. Acknowledging the current reality, including issues, is a powerful first step.

Vik could start by acknowledging the issues the project is having and seeing what the juniors' ideas are. That might encourage Bill to open up. A similar conversation with Sue-Ann could also be had to see what is going on with her.

People also tend to give up too early. Endeavors encounter many challenges: technical, social, and political. The more ambitious the project, the greater the obstacles. Many people let these challenges and obstacles stop them in their tracks, rather than see them as inevitable steps to work through. This can be the case when it comes to personal, interpersonal, or organizational issues, which are less straightforward to address. For example, by asking Sue-Ann why she has been distracted, Vik could be wary about getting too personal — "whether it is his place to ask, might she be offended." While well-intended, this and other concerns are limiting beliefs that stop necessary conversations and influence attempts from occurring. Like it or not, how we are as individuals affects our productivity and conversations, and *vice versa.*

2. Self-talk

"Maybe Sue-Ann has some issues specific to her being a young mother that she wouldn't feel comfortable talking to me about since I am a 60-year-old man." One can easily imagine this self-talk in Vik's mind.

The intent of our self-talk is positive but not necessarily oriented toward achieving +outcomes. A lot of self-talk keeps us safe and considerate of others' feelings based on what we have experienced in the past, but doesn't consider what will raise productivity, satisfaction, and growth for ourselves, others, and the project or company. These different instincts need to be interpreted, reconciled, and directed by the command center of our brain to determine the best way forward. If the command center is missing in action, we will react strongly or won't know what to do. Vik's concern of "Is it my place to ask?" about Sue-Ann's distraction shows that he defines their relationship narrowly, as direct report and boss, where work is compartmentalized from life. Instead, if he stepped out of the box, he might see a struggling colleague who needs help, and the caring thing to do is to ask what is going on.

3. Low awareness or unawareness

Case 5.1.D New service launch

Sue-Ann has been feeling terrible lately, like she is letting everyone down. Her three-year old daughter was diagnosed with childhood diabetes a month ago, and it has been difficult to learn how to manage that condition. The blood glucose level of her daughter has to be monitored constantly, and if it goes above a certain threshold, then her daughter needs an insulin injection right away. While she has her domestic

(Continued)

(Continued)

helper to assist at home, the helper is new, and Sue-Ann is not sure that she can be fully trusted yet. Sue-Ann's mother promised to come and help but can only come by the middle of next month. The new service launch is having problems, and Sue-Ann has a lot riding on that, given it is her first cross-company project. A lot of eyes are on her. It frustrates Sue-Ann a lot that she struggles to get a full grip on what the problem is and what the solution therefore could be. It doesn't help that the project leader (Vik) may not be on top of things and that the team is a mixed bag.

Often, people are not doing what they should be, not because they don't want to but because of pressures with which they are struggling. As mentioned in Chapter 2, these pressures are typically opaque (not known to others), since most people have been trained to compartmentalize life and work and to view sharing challenges a weakness. Therefore, it is quite normal for Vik to be unaware of Sue-Ann's pressures.

Sue-Ann is experiencing two distinct types of pressure: her desire to make the project a success to further her own career, and her needing to be on call to deal with her daughter's health condition. So, any conversation Vik wants to have with Sue-Ann about her distraction would go better if he were to start by exploring the pressures she is facing. Most people in Vik's position would try to solve or go around the distraction, and that could put Sue-Ann on the defensive and result in a tactical conversation at best.

Any conversation to understand the distraction is courageous for Vik since he is stepping beyond the current boundaries of their relationship. There are several influence paths he could consider, depending on his own style, preferences, and being. Moreover, talking to someone who knows Sue-Ann well, who might know what pressures Sue-Ann is facing, would enable Vik to choose his path more insightfully.

- Path 1: Share a time when he struggled with family issues.
- Path 2: Express concern for Sue-Ann, ask how she is coping with different demands.
- Path 3: Express his willingness to step up in leading the project more to offload her.
- Path 4: Point out to her the precariousness of the project and the need to get on top of it within a few weeks.
- Path 5: Excite her about a potential solution to the launch problems and position it as a solution to her problems.

4. Ill-preparedness

Most people worry and agonize over issues and challenging conversations but don't necessarily put in the time to prepare for the conversation. Rehearsing the presentation is a far cry from proper preparation; gathering data on the people involved and rehearsing the interaction can more than double the effectiveness of a challenging influence attempt.

Basic preparation of an influencing attempt consists of 1) analyzing the context and pressures that the project or company, stakeholders, and you face; 2) identifying what would improve productivity, satisfaction, and growth for all the stakeholders and entities; and 3) distilling how each stakeholder needs to think, feel, and act differently to work toward the target of improved productivity, satisfaction, and growth. Chapter 6 lays out this whole process in detail. The conversation with each of the key stakeholders can then be practiced to anticipate each stakeholder's reactions and concerns and to prepare your heart and mind for each of the influence attempts. The higher the stakes, the more systematic analysis and preparation will help. For medium-stakes situations, even 10 minutes in the taxi before a meeting can yield significant benefits.

Case 3.1.A.4 New service launch answer

What positive outcomes could Bill (and Vik) aim for, for the project or company and for key individuals (project leader Vik, project sponsor Sue-Ann)?

- For the company: Turn the new service launch around, by effectively addressing the early problems, and deliver the intended business benefits.
- For Sue-Ann: Turn a setback into a career-making episode by showing courage in acknowledging her personal challenges and calling out the project's early problems; get help in the form of empathy and support from the project team and CEO on how she can support her daughter while also leading the project.
- For Vik: Build personal relationships with key stakeholders and channel that to fix the project, by drawing on the ideas of Bill and other younger team members; show empathy to Sue-Ann but also challenge her to refocus on the new service launch issues.
- For Bill: Find his voice and share his ideas for turning the new service launch around; get Vik and Sue-Ann's support to try these ideas out.

With these outcomes defined and the pressure points of each stakeholder excavated, Vik can start to design his influence strategy to move each person.

5. Instinct-led execution

Instincts, "an innate, typically fixed pattern of behavior in response to certain stimuli,"[25] are powerful but can also be wrong-headed. They enable us to respond instantaneously to danger and opportunity, and they work well when the situation is similar to past situations where the instincts were developed. Going with our instincts is problematic when the situation or stakeholders differ from those past situations. For example, one culture might find confronting a conflict acceptable (*e.g.*, American culture), but another culture (*e.g.*, many Asian cultures such as Japan) might be offended by a direct confrontation. In today's disruptive world, situations are more different than similar; people generally overestimate the similarity between situations and overuse their instincts (including heuristics).[26]

Our instincts come from various sources, creating in each of us a unique combination of instincts, a "habit of mind"; therefore, it is important to reflect on where your instincts come from, in what narrow situations they are useful, and the limitations of those historical instincts.

Top sources for our instincts include our personality inclination,[27] shaping people and situations that had a big positive or negative impact on us (*e.g.*, parents, authority figures, teachers, trauma, triumphs), environments where we spend a long time (that shape our sense of right and wrong, good or bad), and our worldview.

Instincts can overwhelm us when our amygdala (brain region) is triggered, unless it is moderated by the prefrontal cortex (PFC, brain region) in a timely fashion. The amygdala is triggered when we are anxious or afraid, from a real or perceived threat or source of stress. It leads to the 4 Fs – flight, fight, fawn, and flee, which can temporarily prevent bad things from happening, but not particularly useful for +influence. The PFC override is the key to avoid amygdala "hijack", giving one the ability to take a pause, and figure out a better response. This is essentially what Steven Covey called "Response-ability", the ability to choose your response, part of his famous 7 Habits of Highly Effective People (1989). *"The PFC chooses between conflicting options—Coke or Pepsi; blurting out what you really think or restraining yourself; pulling the trigger or not. And often the conflict being resolved is between a decision heavily driven by cognition and one driven by emotions."*[28] It is not, however, that emotion/instinct is always wrong, but rather taking the time to get on the balcony, think about what is really going on, sense more deeply what is going on, and consider different ways to address the situation is more effective. The best solutions inevitably leverage logic and thought to +influence self and others.

Vis-à-vis Sue-Ann, Vik's experience from dealing with older male colleagues could be very limiting. In Vik's upbringing, older or senior colleagues typically have spouses and relatives to take care of personal matters, whereas Sue-Ann herself must deal with her daughter's ongoing health situation. Women may also have different norms on discussing personal challenges, with each other and with men, though it is important Vik doesn't use generalizations to pigeonhole Sue-Ann and himself.

Vik is better off to suspend his instincts, treat her like the unique individual she is, and explore her pressure points and how those pressures could be resolved. Whether Vik cares about Sue-Ann personally, versus just trying to get the project back on track, will make or break this influence attempt.

How We Improve Influencing with Our Being

Love leads me one way, my understanding another.

— Ovid

Why is harnessing our being critical to good influencing? Like it or not, our being will find a way to express itself, and when it does, it is often not the same as what we say, nor what our rational mind may necessarily want, with resultant impact on outcomes, good or bad. So if we want to achieve the positive outcomes we care about, we need to consciously deploy our whole being to support our words and argument. In critical moments, our ability or inability to bring all of ourselves — mind, heart, and soul — will be keenly felt by others and will determine the influence attempt.

Our whole being is an amorphous concept that is hard to pin down. But it is also very real. Two-thirds of the impact of communication and influence come from all the non-verbal aspects (*e.g.*, body language, expression, and energy), which reflect our being, "the nature or essence of a person." This explanation makes it sounds like our being is one coherent thing. The reality is more complex. Our inner being consists of multiple inner qualities and energies that exist independently, sometimes cohered if our conative is clear and if we have worked through our inner tensions. More often than not, for the average professional and leader, younger and senior, different parts of their being are left alone in unconscious, dynamic chaos. We may get lucky sometimes, when we are unconsciously supercharged by the right aspects of our being, but other times we're befuddled with our influence attempt short-changed. Chapter 10 discusses how you can consciously and consistently align your being with your influence attempt.

Conscious influencers recognize that their being is their most powerful influencing weapon and consciously wield it.

Tsun-yan is an expert in handling tough, difficult people, including ones that aren't liked by others. What is his secret? His unconditional positive regard for people.

In the late 1990s, there was a female executive at a client company's (an EVP of a bank) that everyone avoided like the plague. She was controlling and difficult.

One day, Tsun-yan had to get her to sign off on a set of recommendations that was going to a project steering committee she sat on. Five minutes before he went to her office, he meditated on one good thing about her. He genuinely appreciated her creativity, and he meditated on all her creative ideas that had benefitted the bank.

He then went to her office. When she saw him, she asked, "What did you do to yourself?" She meant the positive attitude he exuded toward her, absent in others' interactions with her. She must have been thirsting for a different kind of connection with others but became locked in a cell due to all the perceived hostilities from others.

Tsun-yan would practice and deepen this unconditional positive regard[29] for others for the rest of his life. The power of this deep regard was popularized by psychologist Carl Rogers in the book *On Becoming a Person*,[30] where he described the lessons learned from working with prisoners, including those on death row. By focusing on a real, positive part of a person, that aspect and other positive qualities have a higher chance of coming out, helping to find a constructive way forward in even the most difficult and highest-stake situations.

Our being isn't a fixed thing on tap. By calling on it and using it, we gain access to singular aspects of the being (*e.g.*, courage) and make sense of and bring together different aspects of our being despite seeming tensions (*e.g.*, caring and courage). With this conscious deployment and mastery of our inner being, we come into our inner power, to channel toward our own success and worthy people and causes — one of the truly magical and profound aspects of our human existence.

Case 5.1.B New service launch

Note: this continues from Case 2.1.B.

5.1.B.1 Given Sue-Ann's struggles, what aspects of his own being does Vik need to call on to maximize the chances of a constructive conversation that helps both Sue-Ann and the project?

5.1.B.2 The same question as above, except now you are Jane, the CEO of the company.

The Joy of Influencing Effectively

From his first accidental success at influencing senior clients as a baby consultant to many adversarial situations in which he managed to get +outcomes in spite of unreceptive stakeholders, Tsun-yan has always found his influencing skills and being to be his trusty companion in navigating life and business challenges. He finds it joyful to develop different influencing tactics and dig deeper into his being, practicing congruently on everyone, from housekeeping staff to CEOs. For him, it is a genuine way of showing that he cares, a great way to express his calling, which is to help others reach their best potential.

Huijin's joy of influencing comes from being able to make her ideals into reality. More of an intellectual and reformer,[31] she is driven by her sense of mission: to help people uncover their true and whole self and channel that toward better decisions and +influence. The more she can effectively influence people to find parts of themselves that bring +influence, the happier she is. She loves the moment when people realize there is something they can do, that they can remove their own inner barriers like fear and unhelpful assumptions no matter what the external situation is. Honing her influence skills allows her to avoid her fear from coming true: ending up as a frustrated idealist who can't impact in the real world.

Reflection: What deep fears or aspirations motivate you to improve your influence skills?

Is it to better navigate your career, get recognition for the work you have done, or make more money? Or is it to help people more, get people to care about a cause, or cope with life's pressures better (from being in the driver's seat)?

Take a moment to reflect on this, write it down, and share it with someone else. The strength of this rationale and accountability for progress will fuel your journey to increase your +influence effectiveness.

Case 5.1.E New service launch

Sue-Ann was relieved to have had an open chat with Vik. It was about the project's challenges. It was also about life, and how to ask for help when you need it. She learned that Vik had had a teenage son who died of acute leukemia five years ago. It was a sudden diagnosis, and his son died within four

(Continued)

(Continued)

months. Vik was very busy with a project during most of the four months, thinking surely the cancer could be controlled and there was time still to spend with his son. By the time he woke up to the reality that his son was physically still alive but largely unconscious and sleeping all the time, it was too late. When Vik shared this, Sue-Ann teared up and shared her challenge of controlling her daughter's blood glucose levels. This shared experience broke the veneer of polite colleagueship that had defined their collaboration so far and opened up the field for a real conversation about Sue-Ann's distraction and how she could reengage with the project while still having the ability to attend to her daughter if there was an emergency. They discussed how to share this issue with the broader team and CEO, including a plan to support Sue-Ann. Though still concerned how this will change the way people look at her, Sue-Ann is largely relieved that she doesn't have to hide this anymore. She can feel herself breathing more easily, with more energy to think about the project.

Vik brought out the empathy and caring parts of his being, via the gut-wrenching sharing of his personal experiences. He knew he would need to use his heart to get through Sue-Ann's distractedness and any defense mechanisms (*e.g.*, she needs to project a strong front since she is more senior than Vik). Making a heart-to-heart connection enabled the two leaders to connect more as peers, tackling the problems together from the same side of the table.

While not a hard and fast rule, we find often the most challenging task issues first need a relational connection that is genuinely human to build a foundation of trust to confront the issues. As human beings, we are warmth-seeking creatures who possess the capacity to relate to others with our inner selves. This, beyond improved techniques, is what always increases our +influence.

+Influence Personal Story: From Reserved to Leader

While a lucky few are naturals at influencing, most people must work at it to become dramatically better. Shaw Voon Hau is the story of that work — how the conscious decision to change one's environment and behaviors changes oneself.

> *I had always felt that I was not good with words and was even told to improve my fluency in speaking. I saw it as a defining weakness, compared to other high-potential leaders who have charisma. Through LIFE2[32] and mentorship from Huijin and others, I found the courage to not see it as my weakness and to not stop me from sharing my views and showing my leadership.*

Shaw Voon was an MBA student of Tsun-yan and Huijin at NUS Business School. She learned about the importance of self-leadership and building trustworthy relationships, and diligently practiced speaking up more and being more influential. Her initial hard work paid off. She was picked to be part of a high-potential leaders' program in her company, an industrial multinational company.

Soon, though, she felt another bottleneck in her career. Her career advancement was slowing down. Shaw Voon found it hard to position herself for a bigger regional role due to her shyness, under-developed verbal leadership, and challenges balancing work and family as a mother of a young child. As much as she was "showing up more," she knew it was inconsistent in quantity and quality.

Shaw Voon wanted more. She felt deep in herself that there were better things she could do and more she could achieve personally and professionally. But the possibilities and steps to move forward were far from clear. She needed more help to accelerate herself. That was when Shaw Voon lunged at the opportunity to attend LinHart's LIFE2 program.

Shaw Voon first worked on her personal vision. Before LIFE2, like most people, she was busy with all her day-to-day responsibilities, and lacked a longer-term vision with which she could steer her life in the direction she most wanted. Though the vision wasn't crystal clear during the LIFE2 program, the implications were: although her work in sales was meaningful, she wanted a bigger regional role; furthermore, she wanted to help families with special needs. The latter she acted on immediately, volunteering to lead a CSR (corporate social responsibility) initiative.

Her identity started to evolve, and her confidence increased, resulting in bigger changes. At the time, Shaw Voon was very attached to her comfort zone. She struggled to see how she could move as she lacked the confidence to tackle a new, foreign environment. After getting feedback and input on the many other plausible paths that she could take and mapping out her strengths and gaps, Shaw Voon realized that moving to another industry and/or company was not such an insurmountable challenge. "*I needed a place of quietness to step away from my busy routine. To bring clarity to things that I wasn't able see before.*"

With an inner vision that anchored her and courage to try other paths, Shaw Voon was ready for the open seas. After LIFE2, she moved to an adjacent industry with a new organization. This step involved great risk and uncertainty, but she aced it, quickly filling in her learning gaps and building new relationships and networks. The +influence skills and habits she had learned from Tsun-yan, Huijin and faculty like Robert Tan, Nalin Advani and Mathia Nalappan paid off handsomely.

> *I had to gain traction fast and count on new relationships for support. I did this by communicating that I was new and willing to learn. I had to take a chance with everyone. For people to trust me and show me the ropes, I had to first open up and reach out. When I went for my first on-boarding training session, I showed my passion to drive ideas differently and left a great impression on seniors. It does not matter if you're 100% spot on, or new. It is most important to show the essential qualities of being a fast learner and driving results.*

All of Shaw Voon's hard work paid off in 2019, four years after her LIFE2 program, when she was promoted to the executive ranks as business VP, leading a business in Thailand. She moved out of her comfort zone again and, shortly after, braved the pandemic — a double challenge that pushed her to her limits — but she stayed resilient because she had an inner vision and a set of +influence habits and skills that equipped her to navigate in rough seas.

6

+Influencing Against All Odds

Most of us want to make a positive impact on our families, work, and societal issues, but we are daunted by seemingly insurmountable barriers and difficulties. "What can I do that actually sticks?" "Can I pull it off?" Sometimes, these challenges just exist in our mind, while other times the risks are very real and could cost us a great deal. We come upon these moments all the time and need inspiration in these moments of choice. This chapter hopes to provide such inspiration, through stories of +influence against all odds, by well-known people of influence and regular but influential people alike.

As you read through this chapter, you may be inspired but also feel, "That person is special. I can't do that." Hold that thought and ask yourself if that really is true. What if there is courage and conviction in you and a choice to inspire yourself instead of disbelieving your own potentiality?

Zelensky — from Comedian to Rallyist of a Continent

Since this book was written in 2022, the first example is Volodymyr Zelensky, the president of Ukraine, who has rallied not only his own country but also the whole continent of Europe.

How did a comedian who was losing popular support before the invasion inspire himself and so many people to fight, when conventional wisdom predicted Ukraine would be overrun in a few days? As of October 2022, eight months after the invasion started, Ukraine had taken back some of the territory it initially lost, forcing Russia to begin a highly unpopular partial mobilization of conscripting young men. Europeans have expressed their solidarity in living with energy prices that doubled or rose even to 10 times the usual cost, the direct result of Russian gas being cut off.

Zelensky's influence came from what he did, thought, and felt and his ability to convey this clearly, concisely, and compellingly via speeches to decision makers worldwide and through social media videos, both of which touched the hearts and minds of millions. He is truly the 21st-century Winston Churchill, the British prime minister who inspired fearlessness among the British between 1940 and 1941, when it seemed all but certain that Britain would fall, along with France and the rest of Europe, to Nazi Germany. Churchill refused to surrender and negotiate for peace, instead fighting on despite nightly bombing raids that extracted a terrible cost. Against all odds, he had Britons revolt against the brutal bombings and produce enough aircrafts to mount counterattacks. His speeches were some of the all-time most inspiring any leader has made.[33] Despite the risk of death, he would go on top of buildings during the nightly bombing raids by the *Luftwaffe* (the German Air Force), because he understood that as a leader, he must brave the same burdens as his people.

Words alone cannot exert positive influence when the odds are so strong against a particular positive outcome;

personal actions to embrace the real risk and danger must be taken. *"The fight is here; I need ammunition, not a ride,"* Zelensky told the U.S., according to the U.S. embassy and what was widely reported in the press at the time.[34] Zelensky stayed in Ukraine, instead of fleeing, in stark contrast to the former Afghan president, Ashraf Ghani, who fled as the Taliban entered the Afghan capital of Kabul just a few months earlier. When the stakes are high and the odds are against something, you must put yourself at the same risk in which you are asking others to put themselves.

Zelensky's words, thoughts, and feelings were also extraordinarily powerful in influencing decision makers and public opinion to support Ukraine. An example of this is the European Parliament speech on March 1, 2021,[35] when the translator teared up as he did the simultaneous translation. It is an incredible example of giving voice to the existential challenge that the Ukrainians face and challenging the audience to care and act:

> *Now, we are dealing with reality. We're dealing with killed people... I believe that we today we're giving lives for the rights, for freedom, for the desire to be equal as much as you are. We are giving away our best people, the strongest ones, the most value-based ones.*

> *So I would like to hear that from you to us. We could hear that Ukrainian choice for Europe from you. I have some time off here because we have breaks between the missile strikes and bombardments. And this morning was a very tragic one for us. Two cruise missiles hit Kharkiv, the city which is located to the borders of the Russian Federation.*

> *There were always many Russians there, and they're always friendly. There were warm relations there. More than 20 universities are there. It's the city that has the largest*

number of universities in our country... The people who gathered all the time and was gathering there all the time for celebration...in the largest square in our country, the Freedom Square.

And this is the largest square in Europe. And that's true. This is called the Freedom Square. Can you imagine this morning two cruise missiles hit this freedom square. Dozens of dead ones. This is the price of freedom. We're fighting just for our land and for our freedom.

He killed 16 people just yesterday. Our people are very much motivated. Very much so. We are fighting for our rights. For our freedoms. For life. For our life. And now, we're fighting for survival. And this is the highest of our motivation. But we are fighting also to be equal members of Europe I believe that today we are showing everybody that's exactly what we are.

The European Union is going to be stronger with us. That's for sure. Without you, Ukraine is going to be lonely, lonesome. We have proven our strength. We have proven that at a minimum, we are exactly the same as you are. So do prove that you are with us. Do prove that you will not let us go. Do prove that you indeed are Europeans.

And then life will win over death and light will win over darkness. Glory be to Ukraine.

Shortly after President Zelensky's speech, the president of the European Parliament, Roberta Metsola, said: "*The message from Europe is clear. We will stand up, we will not look away when those fighting in the street for our values stand down Putin's war machine.*"

Analyze: How did Zelensky want the European Parliament to think, feel, and act?

Don't Take No for an Answer

Having the odds against you is not limited to presidents and CEOs; it happens to all of us every day. Huijin encountered such a situation when she first interacted with Tsun-yan, in 2008, 14 years ago.

She was at a conference for the McKinsey Center for Asian Leadership,[36] which she had just joined to begin her career in leadership and organization development, away from the strategy consulting work in which she had invested for the previous six years. It was a high-risk move: there was a window on being promoted to associate partner, and changing practices during such a window might delay — and even jeopardize — the promotion. Though afraid, that was a cost Huijin was willing to pay, for she had realized that her calling was in helping people uncover the leaders in themselves and in influencing positively. She also knew that having a calling was just the start; she needed to learn and apprentice with a seasoned practitioner. The conference convinced her that the person was Tsun-yan. He, alone, had the values, skills, being, and impact she aspired to uncover in herself.

She quickly approached him, but his response was pretty much no, because he was retiring from McKinsey after 28 years. She wouldn't take no for an answer, going back to him again and again, sharing with him that she was in stormy seas with barely a wooden plank, that having a teacher and a kindred spirit to work with and learn from might be the difference between failure and success. She put into words images she saw in her mind's eye.

Tsun-yan was impressed by her persistence and decided to give her a challenge. "If you can get yourself to India where most of my leadership projects are happening in the next two years (that Tsun-yan would still work on part-time), then you can watch how I do things and see what you can pick up yourself."

Huijin took this lifeline, and a moment of inspiration struck her. She had come to know Dominic Barton when he was then Chairman for Asia for McKinsey. She also knew that Dominic was a mentee of Tsun-yan and appreciated his unique skills and being. She approached him and said, "Dominic, there is a unique opportunity that I need you to support. Tsun-yan is retiring but just beginning to pass his craft to help clients accelerate the development of hundreds of leaders. There is so much more that the firm could learn from him. Send me to India so I can learn from that, and then share that with the rest of the firm for those who want to learn it." To Huijin's surprise and delight, Dominic said yes. Tsun-yan was quite surprised that Huijin managed to pull it off and intrigued by what would happen and flow from there. The rest is history.

Finding the Key

Tsun-yan had a long-time friend (and client), Ron Oberlander, who taught him much about business and life. Their working relationship lasted about 15 years, evolving into a deep, loving friendship in its later years. In many ways, Tsun-yan is the consummate advisor and person he is because of Ron. Ron was probably Tsun-yan's greatest mentor, not only in business but also in life — how to parent, relax, and be more centered.

Ron would test and tease Tsun-yan that while what he recommended may be true, other explanations and pathways could also be plausible. This saying Tsun-yan would remember and use forever going forward. This applied to business issues, and people issues even more. Tsun-yan would go to Ron with many logical observations about people, only to find that Ron had a very different, more humane take on it. One memorable example was when Tsun-yan shared his frustrations about one of Ron's leadership team members, even going as far as suggesting that Ron may be better off without this person. Ron stopped Tsun-yan dead in his tracks: "You don't understand. He is the only person on the team that gives me any warmth." From this and many other dialogues with Ron, Tsun-yan learned to appreciate that the heart has different needs than just the logical business mind.

Ron had an uncanny ability to figure out the "key" to move an individual. There was a veteran of the company approaching retirement who needed to be fired up. As the EVP leading sales, whether he was fired up or not made a huge difference to the company's performance and survival. The company was struggling, like most of the pulp and paper industry in Canada. A few more percentages in top-line performance would make a huge difference to the bottom line and to cash flow.

Ron asked this executive what he planned to do after retiring, which was coming up in a year. The executive responded excitedly, "Sailing," but that he could afford only a small sailboat and not the dream boat he wanted. Ron said: "What if I bought you that dream sailboat from my own money, and you give your all in the next two years to fuel the transformation?" The executive was surprised and intrigued. HR said no way, and the board's compensation committee thought Ron should just let him go then and appoint a younger executive who was two years away from being ready. Ron knew that his sales chief was unstoppable when fully fired up. After all, Ron was mentored by him when he first joined the company. He knew what his mentor was capable of. So he went ahead anyway. The sales chief did apply himself fully and got his dream boat from Ron personally.

Ron's other success against all odds has inspired Tsun-yan to influence despite unfavorable odds in his career. Ron rose from an EVP of a small division to become the CEO of the whole company. He survived a cash crunch and avoided bankruptcy by making tough decisions, like selling the crown jewels: he sold his company and then became the chairman of the combined company, doing essentially a reverse takeover. Throughout all this, his focus on influencing people positively and going beyond conventional wisdom were critical to his success. Tsun-yan pointed out that the acquiror had paid a paltry premium for his company, "Surely you could have negotiated a better deal for yourself and your people in leadership roles." Ron demurred, citing his confidence in reading his and the acquiror's executives: "I'm no schmuck! Our people are better leaders. And the cream will always rise to the top. Just you wait and see." Just like he had said, in two years, his people had taken over all the top jobs, including the CEO role. By being the non-executive chairman, he appeared to have retired from the real action but had positioned himself for far greater influence. Another lesson for Tsun-yan.

One constant undergirded Ron's impact as a leader throughout the 13 years that Tsun-yan knew him. Ron's being made every interaction an experience of his full humanity, not just his intellect, not just an element of his being such as the enormous courage in the face of adversity, but his total being. More on this later in Chapter 16 when we share more about Ron's character at work.

Cleaning up the Carpet Stain

Whether you're a young professional or senior leader, one of the most unfair things in life is when you are misunderstood, misjudged, or condemned to corporate purgatory. This can happen anywhere, especially if the power is concentrated among a few people (*e.g.*, one owner or a powerful chairman), be it a CEO succession candidate with a mixed reputation, an executive damaged by a compliance investigation, or a former high potential who was too rash in pursuing a project 12 years ago. Tsun-yan calls the prejudices "carpet stains" because, like red wine on white carpet, it's almost impossible to make it lily white again.

Not content with just asking coaching questions, Tsun-yan has made it his mission to clean up the carpet stains for wronged candidates so that selection decisions can be fairer and objective.

For Ranjiv (disguised name), a brilliant CEO succession candidate in an Indian conglomerate, his carpet stains had to do with the chairman's misconceived perception that Ranjiv was arrogant. His bias was supported by anecdotes which he shared with other influential board members. Thus socialized, it became broadly circulated in top management and the board, hence the analogy of a deep carpet stain that hadn't been cleaned and had sunk deep into the fibers of the carpet. There is usually some grain of truth to the perception, like the time the entire management team had shown up for the retirement party of a senior colleague and Ranjiv "dared" to be absent. When the chairman heard about this absence, it became another example of arrogant behavior and took on a life of its own. Board members and incumbents talked about the episode with indignity, magnifying the issue and making it far worse than the original "offense" and making it impossible for Ranjiv to correct the impression. This in turn demotivated him to take any further corrective action. Tsun-yan decided to drill down on this anecdote and found unshakeable evidence that Ranjiv did care, by showing up at the retiring colleague's home the day before and giving him a personal well-wishing gift. Ranjiv couldn't attend the ceremonial farewell party because he had an important contract to close that required travel. "Why bother if people already made up their mind about me and won't pay attention to the truth?" This was Ranjiv's reply when confronted with the travesty.

Unless these carpet stains are deep cleaned, silent injustice will persist, and many companies make CEO selections based on these false carpet stains being perceived to be true and their opposites to be fake and fictional halos. This phenomenon is fed by both unconscious human bias and mental shortcuts as well as intentional perpetuation by certain stakeholders with personal agendas.

Tsun-yan has always had a special place in his heart for people who, like him, are misunderstood and misjudged. He vowed to shed light on and unveil the truth of complex situations. The board, including the chairman, graciously accepted Tsun-yan's deposition and cleared Ranjiv to become the next CEO. He is still serving brilliantly as the CEO as of this writing.

Tsun-yan labors to unearth all the facts and perceptions contributing to the carpet stain, to separate fact from fiction, and to get everyone to take responsibility for helping the executive to address the real (as opposed to false) issues. "I always tell client sponsors, sight unseen, that at least 50% of the change will have to come from them, the sponsors. It is not just the executive that has to change." Without acceptance of this condition, Tsun-yan will turn down the assignment. With this fierce stand for light and truth, he has helped many executives overcome their carpet stains, get fairly recognized for how they actually lead, and get into the right roles. The company is better off with a more realistic assessment of executives, and the people themselves feel more fairly treated.

High Trust in the Boardroom

(The section below is based on several real-life cases in the last three years. No identifying information is provided to protect the confidentiality of the companies and individuals involved).

You might wonder if there is such a thing: Do people in the boardroom and the C-suite actually trust each other? Your skepticism is well-founded. There is limited trust in the boardroom and C-suite; the odds are stacked against it, but high trust is possible depending on the being of the person.

It is his deep commitment to surfacing the truth, no matter how complex and difficult, that leads some of these executives to trust Tsun-yan in helping them decide whether to leave their companies.

Most executives who decide to leave their companies won't tell anyone related to the company until they tender. By then, typically, their disaffection with the company has become so deep, and/or they have talked themselves into going to a new place so much, that there is little their existing company can do to convince them to reconsider. Though this disaffection has been building up for some time, stakeholders are usually not aware or don't take it seriously. Because of Tsun-yan's trust-based relationship with these executives, built over years, some executives do come to him to help them decide whether to stay or go. Then, Tsun-yan has a chance to help them consider both options vigorously, in full transparency with the company. "Stay for the right reasons, or go for other right reasons." In the process of looking at the option of staying, Tsun-yan often helps executives realize their assumptions about their future at the current company could be wrong, and/or helps the sponsors recognize that they need to change certain perceptions of the disenchanted leader, show more appreciation, or give a bigger mandate so the leader can grow.

This sounds so logical, but these conversations rarely happen at the senior-most levels because the stakes are too high, and the trust level required just isn't there between the executive, the CEO, and the board.

Why do these executives who are considering leaving the company trust Tsun-yan so much? They believe he will act with their and the company's individual and shared interests in mind. These interests are not mutually exclusive. He is devoted to making the executive successful and satisfied in the company. Considering alternatives at a certain juncture is arguably in the interest of the company because the executive will be settled in his or her loyalty to the company instead of wondering whether the grass is greener on the other side. Tsun-yan believes that supporting executives to address their deeper career concerns is truly beneficial for the company. He brings these concerns into the light to be dealt with, rather than allowing them to be driven underground until it is too late. In this, he becomes an invaluable aid to the wise CEO and board who value their talent and understand that talent has choices.

Advocating the Quiet Leader

Nizam was a quiet oil executive who had been twice passed over for a promotion because he was taciturn, and nobody knew what he really thought. Known for his technical skills in upstream exploration, he had become too old for a purely technical role and too introverted for a more senior leadership role, where he'd be required to secure acreages in foreign oil fields. Not classified as a high potential, his career floundered.

Being an introvert himself, Tsun-yan empathizes deeply with the quiet leader,[37] so he sought Nizam out and spent time finding out what his passion at that stage of his life was. Behind the scenes, it turned out that Nizam was encouraging many young petroleum engineers to stay and make a career with the company. Although his career was floundering, he still believed that other talents better than him should stay to help grow the oil company into a global champion. Needing to have a technical expert support a case for an investment, Tsun-yan called upon Nizam to make two presentations in the allotted time for one: one for the technical expert case and the other a plea for the company to develop better career paths for younger engineers. Nizam rehearsed vigorously to make his points succinct and concise so that the two presentations could fit into the time for one. When the time came, Nizam soared like an eagle in his impassioned plea, stunning the CEO whom Tsun-yan knew had a habit of dropping in informally to hear lower executives argue their business cases. Nizam was asked to work with HR to come up with a career proposition for these young talents and was promoted in the next round of advancement exercises.

The foregoing six stories tell a similar tale: One can influence against all odds and bring truths to light to prevail. +Influence can make a big difference in whether you are a person of influence or, more likely for most of us, if you can learn to be influential.

Section II

Transform Your +Influencing Effectiveness

Overview

Section II Transform Your +Influencing Effectiveness lays out the main principles, practices, and techniques of +influence to improve your proficiency in commonly encountered influence situations. They are based on LinHart's CEO counseling experiences across industries and cultures, and teaching materials the authors codified in LinHart's courses for MBA-level and other university and open-enrollment programs. Through the 12 cases, covering all seniorities, you can gain a deeper grasp and digestion of the principles, enhance insights about your own instincts and skills, and inform your learning edge for deliberate practice. To further equip you for greater efficacy in +influence, this section guides you through the habits to adopt, the ways to draw on your inner qualities more readily, and the use of written media to complement in-person +influence.

7

The Basics of +Influence

While there are many books on good practices for influence, they tend to deal with persuading others, especially in sales situations. Below are eight basic principles that transcend all +influence situations:

1. Be <u>deliberate</u>.
2. Understand the <u>context</u> for <u>pressure</u> points with <u>judgment</u>.
3. Set <u>task and relationship</u> influence objectives.
4. Draw <u>insights</u> and <u>inquiry</u>.
5. Time the <u>moments</u>.
6. <u>Pace</u> through the influence.
7. Seize the <u>moments</u>.
8. Engage your <u>being</u>.

This chapter will focus on the first three principles, which are mostly about getting yourself ready for the +influence episode. Like an army preparing for a coming war, you must know the context — yours and other people's — to appreciate the pressures on you and on them. For example, you have ammunition to last only three days and will run out of rations in two days. The other side has a month's worth of each. Judgments must be made to come up with your strategy for the war, with special attention on the first battle. Troop deployment, including supporting arms like artillery and demolition, must be envisioned based on experience and the latest intel. Above all, "Take Hill 105 by 07:00 hours with minimal losses and hold ground" is a clear and concise objective for the upcoming battle that would place your side at an advantage for the rest of the war.

The remaining five principles will be addressed in the next chapter. In many ways, they are the vital essence of winning a hand-to-hand combat. Yes, you'd better believe it because no strategy or resources could save you if you don't engage the other side well and adjust tactics in the melee.[38] The mechanical execution of even a well-laid plan will ill-prepare you for the dynamic, fluid flow of the interactions.

A selection of cases has been curated for practice with an interlocutor, facilitator, or small group. The section below, "Be Deliberate," and the sections in Chapter 9, "Be Present" and "Give and Receive Feedback," will equip you to observe, provide feedback, and debrief each other's attempt at +influence to improve yourself or in small group learning format.

Principle 1. Be Deliberate

Deliberate means done consciously and intentionally. A deliberate influencer has a +influence outcome in mind and goes through the cycles of plan–do–adjust (PDA)[39] with a strong focus on target outcomes — not rushing and certainly not winging it. We get lucky sometimes, but being intentional will result in greater +influence, all else being equal. In high-stakes situations, there is no opportunity for a do-over, so conscious planning is a must.

The most effective influencers can go through multiple rapid cycles of PDA in the first few *minutes* of an important meeting. The process allows the influencer to apply the basic principles laid out in this chapter toward the target outcomes, activate the relevant parts of his or her being, and execute well.

Plan refers to the conscious effort to understand the context, identify the pressure points, and make timely judgments — both about what business or people actions to take and how to +influence the stakeholders to move toward the right direction. Good planning includes data acquisition and consideration of who the key (influencee) people are, how they may respond, and alternative strategies to achieve the same or different (but still good) outcomes. A broad understanding of the audience and a judgment of their needs, pressures, fears, and hopes are foundational to good planning.

Do refers to carrying out the +influence attempt, noticing the spontaneous reactions and feedback from the other party (said and unsaid), and deepening your understanding of the audience and contextual forces and pressures at work. What people say is a small part of the feedback. Their non-verbal response and actions speak far louder than words.

Adjust refers to both real-time adjustments, as well as repeated tries (not common in high-stakes situations), which take into account the effectiveness of your initial +influence strategy and new information about the context and pressure points you have gathered through the previous "do's."

The integrated application of the eight principles in PDA cycles has been codified in the Deliberate +Influencing Process. You can use this process on your own or together with others, by being highly observant of how others react or respond, asking people for feedback, and trying to be objective. Be aware, though, that your own bias and relationships with people could lead to them not telling you everything, or your unconsciously rejecting certain aspects. Therefore, it is recommended that you involve others in improving your influencing effectiveness.

Deliberate +Influencing Process

a. From the perspective of the influencer: What are your task and relationship objectives, and why these objectives as opposed to other possible objectives?

b. Test that the task and relationship objectives promote shared and higher levels of productivity, satisfaction, and growth.

    i. If not, brainstorm what task and relationship objectives would promote shared and higher levels of productivity, satisfaction, and growth.

c. Roleplay the interaction. The influencer can play him or herself. The selection of the person to play the influencee requires a bit more thinking. Picking someone who resembles the influencee's personality, mannerism, mindset will increase the chances of the actual interaction dynamics coming out in the roleplay, *e.g.*, the influencer might get triggered emotionally.

d. Check with the +influencer, and if possible the influencee, on what the impact of the influence attempt was and why.

    i. Ask what led to the impact: Was it what the influencer said or did, body language, voice level, his or her being, assumptions the +influencer made, what the influencer saw or didn't see?

    ii. What were some pivotal moments where the impact was achieved, or a better impact could have been had?

    iii. For moments the +influencer missed, what was going on in his or her mind and heart that led him or her to not see or seize the moment? What assumptions, beliefs, and feelings does the person have toward the other person or situation?

e. Point out gaps between:
   i. The intended and actual outcome.
   ii. The difference between the +influencer's assumptions about the influencee and what the influencee actually thought and/or how he or she behaved.
   iii. How aligned is the being of the +influencer relative to what the task or relationship objectives require, and how the +influencer tried to get the influencee to think, feel, and do.
f. Brainstorm different ways to get to the intended (or even better) outcome.
g. Roleplay again (cycle repeats).

When you consistently apply this process, you develop a habit of understanding the context and audience, defining desired outcomes, reading further data and reactions, and checking whether the +outcomes were achieved. This will raise your awareness and consciousness of what is going on within yourself, others, and the situation.

Some individuals, especially those who have been content experts or are used to being in charge, might struggle with this process for several reasons. They see themselves as having the "answer" or knowing the answer more than other people. They like telling other people what to do. They have poor or average listening skills.

If the above applies to you in a significant way, you will need to consciously adopt the process, fight your instincts to judge, and try to be truly open to where others are coming from or what they are driven by.

Throughout Section II, there are disguised real-life cases that you can roleplay with others. This will help you to cement your usage of the Deliberate +Influencing Process and to digest the basic principles of better influence. Instructor's notes and additional role cards for the cases are available for purchase separately from the book's website.

Principle 2. Context, Pressure Points, and Judgment

Each influence situation is unique because the context for each situation is unique. What worked before in a similar situation may not work as well or at all the next time. There is no shortcut; heuristics are no replacement for deliberateness.

Context refers to important forces at work in the situation and spans four realms — the company in the marketplace, the organizational dynamics (*e.g.*, organizational structure and culture), the key stakeholder involved (or is interested in the situation), and the key leader(s) involved — and how the different elements are related to each other (*e.g.*, constraining regulation limits the scope of competition, the impact of the central leader's personal motivation, and the time horizon for a transformational initiative). The question of which aspect of the context affects the central issues requiring influence the most is the starting point for planning an +influence attempt.

While some contextual information is opaque and hard to find out before the interaction, a lot can be found through diligent research, analytical thinking, and talking to people who might know the stakeholders. Guided by the central issues, you can scan the Internet for information and use initial takeaways to gain deeper insights. Do watch out for developments, since late-breaking news could change the dynamics of the context. Pay attention to opaque areas and weak signals — "Just because you can't see it doesn't mean it's not there." Weak signals can lull us to gloss over them because they are not significant yet or we have more urgent things to attend to.[40]

Below are some common questions you can ask to understand these four contexts of the situation you want to influence. This list of questions are illustrative, not comprehensive. You can use them to generate additional questions.

Company in the marketplace

- What is the company's competitive position in the market (*e.g.*, attacker, incumbent)?
- In which stage of development is the enterprise (*e.g.*, start-up, growing, mature)?
- What is the scope of business? What are the boundaries of their business (*e.g.*, multiple lines of business, monoline (one business), online only)?
- What is their financial flexibility[41] (*e.g.*, high liquid assets, credit line dependent)?

Organizational dynamics

- How might the company's overarching goal be characterized (*e.g.*, profit, social service)?
- What are its core capabilities (*e.g.*, IP, low-cost producer)?
- How strong is its performance culture (*e.g.*, focused on delivering value, internally focused)?
- What are its *de facto* core values[42] (*e.g.*, winning, service)?
- What bias may be evident in its organizational structure (*e.g.*, geographic fiefdom, functional silos)?
- How adequate is its leadership capacity relative to demand (*e.g.*, demand < supply)?

Stakeholder dynamics

- What are their regulatory constraints (*e.g.*, they can't get into adjacent areas)?

- How adequate is their <u>access to further capital</u> (*e.g.*, constrained or capital markets darling)?
- How good are their <u>relationships with the press or public</u> (*e.g.*, collaborative, adversarial)?
- What is their <u>ownership structure</u> (*e.g.*, family controlled, diverse share ownership, state controlled)?

Key leaders

- What <u>mandate</u> does the leadership team have (*e.g.*, broad, limited, short-term results only)?
- What is the horizon of the leadership team (*i.e.*, how long will key members be around)?
- What characterizes their leadership team dynamics (*e.g.*, collaborative, dysfunctional)?
- What are the needs and motivation of key leaders (*e.g.*, CEO seeks a legacy)?

Pressure points arising from the context are important to factor into any +influence attempt. Contextual factors could create negative pressure points (*e.g.*, a deal is falling apart in the last six months of a successful CEO's tenure, endangering his or her legacy) or offer relief for pressure (*e.g.*, a supportive major shareholder could inject much-needed cash). Some of these pressure points are obvious (*e.g.*, business, financial), while others (*e.g.*, personal, family) can be opaque from a distance but only confirmed through engagement with the person and relevant networks. People who can leverage positive pressure to relieve a negative pressure point are more influential.

Head and heart are both needed to gain insights into the context and pressures and to deploy the insights to good judgment. Good contextual and pressure point analysis will shed light on the specific issues where business and leadership judgments should be made, but that isn't enough.

The ability to be calm and collected is central to making good judgments in high-pressure situations. Pressure, especially emotional pressure, makes people reactive and anxious. At the same time, heightened emotions need to be acknowledged[43] and relevant underlying concerns must be factored into the decision-making process. A person who is present with feelings and retains a rational thinking capability has a significant advantage over a superb rational thinker who is neither aware of nor able to deal with strong emotional undercurrents.

Case 7.2 Assigning a task to an uncooperative peer

You (Antonietta) are about to approach Hilario, a 55-year-old veteran of your client company. Hilario has been assigned to your project team to find ways to improve the quality of business reviews while reducing the time and effort spent by 50%. For this project, your team — from a well-regarded consulting firm — will be working with three to four client team members, among which Hilario is one. You recently graduated from Wharton, and this is your second consulting project.

You anticipate this conversation to potentially be difficult. Hilario has a reputation for being cynical and aggressive. On the bright side, he knows the company inside and out and is known to be a bit of a walking encyclopedia. He didn't show up for the project kick-off, so your client leader VP of strategy (Francesco) asked you to meet with Hilario separately and get him to participate in the project.

Complaints about the business reviews have always been there, but the new CEO is determined

(Continued)

(*Continued*)

to do something about it. Business reviews are meetings in which the CEO of the company reviews the performance and health of each of the eight business units (BUs), and they occur every quarter. There is one review for each BU, which is typically a day long and requires around 300 pages of slides to be produced, although the management team views only 25% of the discussion as high value. Despite widespread dissatisfaction, things didn't change before, because the last CEO started these business reviews and loved to go into minute detail.

As a veteran who has worked in finance, marketing, and IT, Hilario might have a unique working-level perspective on the few central issues these business reviews should be about, where the data to inform these discussions sit, and how the reports to enable value-added discussions can be automated. The lack of automation and difficulty in accessing data is killing people involved in the preparations and frustrating the discussions in the business reviews, since the CEO often asks about customer or market data, and it would take days or weeks to get the data.

You are wondering what might get someone like Hilario excited about working on this project and how he became so cynical and different from his younger hotshot, impatient self. Maybe it has something to do with how slowly things moved under the last CEO. You knock on his door.

Analyze: What key aspects of the context should Antonietta consider in designing how to approach Hilario? What pressures does Hilario face? What pressures does Antonietta face?

The common meaning[44] of **judgment** covers:

- An opinion or decision that is based on thought.
- The process of landing on an opinion or a decision.
- The ability to make good decisions about what is right or should be done.

In our +influence work, we found it useful to narrow in on judgement as the capacity to make consistently good decisions in complex or uncertain situations — with limited information and within a time window upon which a reasonable influence may still yield the desired or required outcomes.

When +influencing a high-pressure situation, you need to develop *business or technical judgment* about what to do (or not do) and the *leadership judgment* of what *+influence objectives* and *+influence strategies* to adopt for critical interactions to build momentum toward the overall desired positive outcome.

Business/technical judgment requires inquiry into what would lead to more shared productivity, satisfaction, and growth or what would minimize their erosion. The ultimate test of whether business or technical judgment is good is whether it works: does the product work, is it safe, is it cost effective, do customers buy the product, did we get to the market fast enough?

Leadership judgment requires insight into how different stakeholders think and feel; what they would like to do about the situation; and what would move them toward what is required for the positive target outcomes. For example, for those who seem to care only about their own KPIs, how can they be motivated to meet their own KPIs and help other functions? People's thinking, feeling, and action patterns are shaped by their personality and predispositions, past experiences, beliefs, values, the prevailing culture, and their stage of life and development. Influential people have a deep understanding of what has shaped their stakeholders and what helps people be their best.

Good business or technical and leadership judgments are:

- Analytically sharp (*e.g.*, What is/are the one to two numbers/assumptions critical to the decision?)
- Relationally sound (*e.g.*, What relationship dynamics must be addressed lest the task objectives are derailed? Who are the key stakeholders that need to be engaged?)
- Contextually pertinent (*e.g.*, What situational/stakeholder considerations impinge most on the situation and potential solutions?)

Relieving negative pressure and/or adding positive pressure on the situation and on stakeholders is core to most challenging situations. People look for relief to business and personal problems; a minority is driven by a strong sense of mission and vision.

There is a high premium on judgment (versus just analysis, facts, or conjecture). Nobody has enough time, but senior people have perhaps 15, 30, or 60 minutes to consider and then decide on a complex issue. So, put yourself in their shoes. If you were them, what would you want your team to tell you?

Case 7.3 Resetting investment expectations in a start-up

You are the co-founder and CEO of a digital health company facing tough choices and scared investors. You were flying high 10 months ago, when you

(Continued)

(Continued)

closed the Series D round, valuing your company at USD 5 billion, and were looking forward to IPO'ing the company in a few years. However, the market sentiment has turned dramatically against technology companies. Nasdaq is down 35% overall, and down 50% or more for the tech companies with a large cash burn rate. Late-stage venture capital has dried up, so you can't get any more funding. You have USD 500 million in the bank but need to spread it out across three to five years, since it is uncertain how long the dry spell will last. Your CTO (and cofounder)had given you a very ambitious re-platforming that would cost USD 100 million, but you know the company would struggle to afford that right now. While it would raise the fundamental competitiveness of the platform and raise revenues over the next few years, there are a few board members who would oppose any significant investment. You think a smaller investment, of around USD 50 million, would better balance the need to conserve cash while continuing to strengthen the fundamentals so the company is well positioned for the recovery. You see the CTO hurrying toward you; he likely wants to talk to you about the big platform investment.

Analyze: What should your +influence objectives be? How might you +influence the CTO to think, feel, and act toward +outcomes?

Principle 3. Set Task and Relationship Objectives for +Influence

Directionally correct business and leadership judgment helps the influencer identify who to influence and set +influence objectives for specific individuals.

You set influence objectives by answering the basic question of *"What do I want the influencee to think, feel, and do, to get the task done while improving my relationship with him or her?"*

- Thinking refers to the rational or logical argument for taking or not taking a course of action.
- Feeling refers to how people feel about themselves (*e.g.*, proud to be an initiative leader), about each other (*e.g.*, excited to be working together), and about the organization (*e.g.*, a sense of belonging).
- Doing refers to specific actions that individuals take or do not take. Too often, a meeting or exchange has no productive outcome because people are not clear about who needs to do what by when.

The +influencer needs to map out the path between the other person's *current* thoughts, feelings, and predisposition and how (s)he needs to think, feel, and do for the task and relationship objective to be realized. This mapping in turn requires a person to understand the other person's thoughts and feelings about the *central issues that need to be resolved.* The initial understanding is typically somewhere between a stab in the dark and a good guess, depending on how well the influencer knows himself or herself, as well as the other person, and "sees" what is going on in the context. The more data the person collects, the better the guess will be. Task and relationship objectives and thinking/feeling/doing paths should be constantly adjusted to better address both parties and the context's pressures while staying true to the overarching goal of shared and greater productivity, satisfaction, and growth.

To understand the other person's thoughts and feelings about the central issues that need to be resolved, one needs to mentalize, the ability unique to all humans to infer mental states of another person and to recognize that these mental states can affect behavior. For a typical person, the maximum number of separate mind states involved in such mentalizing is five, in what the author of the book *Friends* called the "5 orders of intentionality": "I <u>sense</u> that you <u>are</u> angry about how the bosses are <u>failing to recognize</u> how we <u>devoted</u> our last 2 years' days and nights to a project they <u>prioritized</u>."[45] This complicates influence attempts since higher orders of 'intentionality' are cognitively much more demanding (than, say, recalling a fact).[46] The cerebellum is especially important when managing several mind states simultaneously (including one's own), such as keeping the different mind states distinct in mentalizing the intent and emotions of particular players and across them in an influence situation involving multiple stakeholders with distinct agendas. Functional imaging/MRI studies have consistently implicated a network of brain regions including this in such tasks.

Central to correctly mentalize how other(s) think and feel about an issue, one must be able to suspend one's own perceptions and judgments about the other person, and the issue. Supposedly, as a child grows up, (s)he gains the ability to suspend his/her own thoughts and feelings, and *"understands more broadly that other people have different thoughts, beliefs, and knowledge than they, the landmark of achieving Theory of Mind."*[47] In reality, on an average day, adult professionals and leaders vary hugely in consistently and constantly having insights into how others think and feel, hence complicating any effort to say what is intended in a way that takes into account how others might think and feel to produce the right (*i.e.*, intended) effect and outcomes.

Skilled +influencers can get both tasks done and improve relationships in difficult situations, whereas younger people lack either the "will" to go after both types of impact or the skill. This requires addressing the head (thoughts), heart (feelings), and volition[48] (action).

The task and relationship both matter in most business, social, and even family situations. The relationship can impact the way people perform the task, especially if there is repeated interaction. Even in situations where individuals may never see each other again, a sufficiently negative impact on the relationship could result in a negative task impact and reputation. Most high-stakes situations require +influencing both the task and relationship dimensions simultaneously. For example, you need to develop a personal relationship with a key executive of your joint venture partner to better understand his or her pressure points and key concerns. At the same time, you also need to understand the task well enough to craft a solution. Otherwise, your counterpart might not want to talk to you, or find you to be a weak partner in addressing the real issues. While you don't have to be all-singing, all-dancing and solve the issues on your own, you do need to have sufficient task and relationship awareness and the ability to be an influential dialogue partner.

The impact of feelings on thought and action is particularly important to look out for because it is often not obvious and under-attended to. Strong feelings can disable thinking and action and catalyze extreme action, while logical leaps can contribute to strong but misplaced feelings. In these cases, feelings often need to be addressed before thoughts and action can be constructively discussed. Acknowledging and working through negative feelings is uncomfortable but necessary; it is a skill that can be developed along with emotional intelligence. The most emotional, intelligent +influencers can witness others' strong feelings, get to the underlying issues (relationship- and task-wise), and channel people's energies toward productive actions.

The most influential people get tasks done through others by building positive relationships and focusing people's energies and talents on what needs to be done. In a positive relationship, people are inclined to think positively of each other and are more willing to do things for each other (including work tasks). The more positive the relationship, the easier it will be to surface and deal with difficult issues. In intense conflicts, without a positive relationship and the basic trust that is implied, conflict resolution is very difficult. A positive relationship depends on caring about the other person and whether you have unconditional positive regard for the person, which is expanded on in Chapter 9.

+Influence Personal Story: Connecting with the Person

Few people, including Tsun-yan, are naturally strong in both task and relationship. Most people, especially younger people, have a bias toward focusing too much on a task or too much on a relationship. This bias typically stems from personality, shaping experiences, and the norms of the surrounding environment (especially role models such as parents). The depth of the bias varies from person to person. In extreme cases, someone could be close to 100% focused on a task but ignore the rewards and damage to the relationships, or alternatively, spend so much time on connecting with people that what needs to be done is fuzzy and lacking in energy.

Early in his career, Tsun-yan was known to be the "fastest analyst in the East," creating spreadsheets and financial models faster than most of his peers, driving clients hard to develop the data he needed to populate his spreadsheet. You get the picture: relationship was not at the top of his mind and therefore not his strength. One defining experience in 1982, his second year with McKinsey, changed this.

He was sent in to talk to a senior client executive, Jan Movil, who was about to throw the McKinsey team out of the small company town that was the client HQ in Norway. The team's relationship with the executive had deteriorated so much that the partner thought he didn't have anything to lose by sending in a 14-month associate like Tsun-yan. After all, the Scandinavian practice reputedly had a three-year backlog, and the partner thought he might as well create a learning opportunity on the way out to give a young associate a taste of entering the lion's den.

Tsun-yan was tense, as any young professional would be in the same situation. He walked into Jan's voluminous office, immediately proceeded to flip through the well-rehearsed lab visual (*i.e.*, a paper copy of what is today's PowerPoint presentation). Jan became quite impatient two pages in. "You are (ethnic) Chinese. You must be great in math." Taken aback, Tsun-yan explained that he was from Singapore and only decent in math. This started a conversation through which Tsun-yan found out that Jan's wife was Malaysian Chinese and "damn good in math." Notwithstanding such a tenuous connection, both Jan and Tsun-yan began to relax.

Three hours went by before Tsun-yan emerged without getting past page 2 of the two-inch thick document. The rest of the team had been anxiously waiting outside. Jan had decided to give McKinsey another chance, on the condition that Tsun-yan was on the hook for delivering something useful. The partner was delighted but also lost — how did Tsun-yan achieve such a feat?

Tsun-yan learned then and there that task is not everything; relationship is king when all else is headed south. Jan took a liking to him and took a chance. There was a big element of chance — the ethnic proximity between him and his wife, but Tsun-yan helped himself with his full humanity rather than insisting on going through the highly regimented content. He learned the principle of being subject oriented, *i.e.*, focused on the personal/human aspects that would undergird everything he did and inspired him to influence better. Though he was eager to walk Jan through the thick deck, he stopped himself in his tracks. The document was safety and a crutch, but Tsun-yan knew that only by taking risk, by putting himself in the uncomfortable zone of connecting with Jan as a human being, could he engender a different, better outcome.

Developing in yourself the underused aspect of a task or relationship is absolutely doable (refer to Chapter 9). It is like learning to write with your opposite hand: at first, you must force yourself to write with your weaker hand, despite the discomfort, slow speed, and bad handwriting. You must hold at bay the temptation to give up, and after persistent practice, your weaker hand becomes stronger, and using it feels more natural. This process of stretching yourself beyond your comfort zone is foundational to expanding your influence range.

Be deliberate — conscious and intentional — and grasping your and the influencee's context and pressures will enable you to make the best judgments, including the specific task and relationship objectives to achieve with key influencees that are appropriate for +outcomes.

Next, let's delve into the interactions: the meeting itself where +influence unfolds.

8

+Influencing in the Moment

What never fails to amaze us is how many influencers go into a high-stakes meeting with a presentation and proceed to blast away, totally blind to the wealth of information gushing forward even as the first slide goes on the screen. Roberto, one of Tsun-yan's most esteemed industry experts, was once invited to address a leading telco's management committee. Not even three slides in, he felt vaguely uncomfortable with the audience's silent reaction, which he countered with more vehemence and intensity in his content delivery. Tsun-yan, who convened the session, winced when he noticed the management committee members were mostly looking at their cell phones and not at all attentive to what he was saying or what was on the screen. What could Roberto or Tsun-yan do in that moment?

Once the interactions unfold, the flow of behaviors (including non-verbals like facial and body expressions), signals, and interaction dynamics (*i.e.*, pace, tone, openness/receptivity, intensity, and ebb and flow of positive or negative energies) are instantaneous, changing direction rapidly, seldom as intended or hoped for. Thus, they offer abundant opportunities in the form of moments, however short, to seize and turn the tide toward better +outcomes. That is the pinnacle of what makes this fun to learn, see more, and accomplish more.

Principle 4. Insight and Inquiry

Insight is about developing an understanding of the key contextual factors, the related pressure points, and the central issues requiring resolution, within the limited time of typical influence attempts. You don't want to be an executive who wasted 30 minutes of an hour-long interview with senior management on a discussion of little interest to them or that you could have found out from somebody else. Yet, we have all been in such wasted meetings, which happen every day in companies and organizations all over the world.

Two aspects of the dictionary definition for insight[49] are remarkably relevant for +influence:

1. An instance of apprehending the true nature of a thing.
2. Penetrating discernment; seeing into inner character or underlying truth.

Insight helps us understand:

- Relationships that shed light on or help solve a problem.
- Sources of emotional difficulty plaguing ourselves or others.
- The motivational forces behind our and their actions, thoughts, or behavior.

Insight into central issues that need to be resolved to move forward productively provides the necessary focus of people's energies. Insights on central issues can be placed into three categories: those relating to task issues (*e.g.*, How fast can this market grow?), relationship or people questions (*e.g.*, What will it take to motivate Bob?), and insights where business and people issues are intertwined (*e.g.*, How can we gain clinician support to migrate the electronic medical records to a new IT system?). As hard as it is to predict market growth, people issues flummox more, and the interaction between business and people issues is the hardest to "see" and influence.

If insight apprehends the true nature of things, then inquiry is the central unanswered question upon which the insight is contingent.[50] It is difficult to gain deep, valid insight into a situation without asking the right questions. In the heat of the battle, there is scant time to chase after all non-essential questions unlikely to drive your +influence pathway. For inquiry to be "seeking or requesting for truth, information, or knowledge,"[51] one must constantly suspend and question one's own assumptions and judgment. Inspired by his mentor and friend, Ron, Tsun-yan constantly asks: What still doesn't make sense? What could I be missing? What is this new data telling me about the dynamics of the situation? Believing that you are frequently right borders on hubris. Humility is needed to hold the unanswered question in our minds to sharpen our sensitivity to new data, especially during the influence.

"Seeing" is paying attention to what is going on and critically evaluating what you "see" from multiple perspectives (*e.g.*, different time horizons, goals, mental models, how different stakeholders might view and experience the situation) to discern the dynamics of the underlying situation and what it takes to move forward to achieve a positive outcome. Mentalizing how different people "see" and relate differently to the same objective phenomenon sheds light on how they might need to be influenced differently.

Our "eyes" can often be wrong. We easily get visual illusions wrong and don't see a lot of what is going on. In business situations, we have even more difficulty in seeing what is going on because our limited experience, bias, and beliefs lead us to filter out things that are not on our radars or are inconsistent with our mental models.

The best "seers" can hold and accept different and conflicting perspectives from which the current situation or people need to be understood, not just what they can easily "see." Different time horizons, goals, mental models, cultures, and stakeholders are common perspective differences that cause people to have vastly different interpretations of and attitudes about the same underlying reality. A mental model refers to a construct with which people interpret a set of things: how the pieces add up to a gestalt and how they relate. It is shaped by past experiences, values, and personality. Suspending our own perspective sounds simple but takes tremendous self-discipline to do consistently, especially when we feel threatened or feel we are right. It is when we are so certain that we have the greatest risk of not seeing something important.

One of Tsun-yan's favorite quotes of wisdom is, "There is always more to see and learn."[52] Seeing — the insight and inquiry it fuels — is one of the least visible limits to influence. To see deeply and wisely requires an openness of mind and humility of heart to fully embrace the situation and others as they are, while not compromising the quest for +outcomes. With high aspirations, emotional tension (*e.g.*, frustration at the lack of progress) is inevitable; it is easy to start judging others harshly and become cynical. Effective +influencers can convert that emotional tension to creative tension, inviting themselves and others to imagine different possibilities for moving forward with a positive regard for everyone.

The insights and inquiry section was placed here not because the only time to raise insights and inquiry is during the interactions in which +influence occurs. In truth, inquiry and insights should start at the beginning as part of the contextual analysis and carry all the way through and after the influence session. Post-session, one might ask: "What did we learn about what helped and what hindered the achievement of +outcomes?" "What insights could we glean from today that will inform future interactions with this person?" Our proficiency continues to improve when we submit ourselves humbly to enquire about the truths underlying our non-success as well as our success.

It's two days after IBM CEO Louis Gerstner's announcement recommitting IBM to mainframe (computers) at Chantilly in 1994.[53] You are an IBM sales leader who wants to get an old customer to buy mainframe computers again. Your customer, Mark, is the CIO (Chief Information Officer responsible for IT) of a large supermarket chain in the Midwest of the United States. You lost Mark's business a year ago because of IBM's prices being far above market and the inability to address Mark's frustrations with IBM. Now that mainframe prices have been reduced by 40% and IBM is coming out with a superior technology, you are eager to try to regain Mark's business.

Like many customers IBM lost, Mark was angry about IBM's arrogance. He pleaded with you to reduce prices. You wanted to, but under the old regime that was milking the mainframe business, there was nothing you could do. Mark was also upset that IBM let the rumor that "mainframe was dead" grow out of control. This myth made Mark (and other CIOs) who invested hundreds of millions of dollars in mainframes look silly and created a lot of unnecessary work for them to rationalize their expenditures ex post facto. Mark was fed up with IBM's bureaucracy, too.

You are excited about IBM's improved mainframe product and eager to share with Mark how, under Gerstner's leadership, IBM will serve customers better. Thankfully, Mark and you have remained on

(Continued)

(Continued)

---

good terms personally. Hopefully, he will give you and IBM a chance.

Analyze:

1. What are the central issues or concerns in your customer's (Mark) mind and heart?
2. What are your task and relationship vis-à-vis your customer, Mark?

Background information

1. Gerstner's keenness to revitalize IBM's mainframe computer business.
   - When Gerstner joined IBM in 1993, IBM was at serious risk of running out of cash.
   - Mainframes accounted for 90% of IBM's profits and thus were vital to short-term sustainability. Gerstner viewed mainframes as IBM's greatest asset, a reversal of the previous strategy of milking the business (milking: getting as much short-term profit as possible) and letting it die.
   - IBM mainframe prices were 30–40% higher than competitors due to the milking strategy.
   - Customers were begging for IBM to fix the problem with mainframes (e.g., high prices) rather than walk away.
2. IBM's troubles as illustrated by the conditions of EMEA[54] (one large geographic region).
   - Rapid decline in pre-tax profit margin: 18% in 1990, 6% in 1992.
   - Rapidly declining mainframe sales.
   - Lack of participation in client/server segment (e.g., PCs).

(Continued)

(Continued)

- Alarming decline in company image.
- Net cash change of −$800 million in 1993; couldn't pay corporation (HQ) any dividend for some time.
- All levels of organization: fear, uncertainty.
- Extraordinary preoccupation with internal processes as cause of problems > belief that tinkering with processes could provide solutions needed.
- Duplicate infrastructure in each country (23k of 90k employees belonged to staff functions).
- Enormously talented people, deeply committed and competent.
3. Gerstner's announcements to customers at Chantilly.
   - Acknowledged IBM's failures: failed to defend mainframe's role in a PC world (hence failed to defend CIO's previous choices), bureaucracy, difficulty in integration, high prices.
   - Lowered mainframe prices quickly.
   - Spoke from the heart and acknowledged that customers are angry, perturbed, and upset.
   - Put himself on the same side as customers: "The customer is now running IBM"; shared his own frustrations with IBM.
   - Set new expectations for customer/IBM relationship:
     - Define priorities based on customers and their performance expectations.
     - Develop open, distributed user-based solutions.
     - Recommit to quality.
     - Be easier to work with.
     - Establish a leadership position in industry (but not dominance).

Principle 5. Timing the Moments

Nothing focuses the mind more than a finite horizon.

— Kenichi Omae[55]

Assuming you have used insight and inquiry to determine an effective context and pressure analysis and arrived at a directionally correct judgment of what task and relationship objectives to aim for and what you need the other person to think, feel, and do, the next critical element is timing: When do you make the +influence attempt?

Contextual factors create a finite moment — a period within which task and relationship objectives can be achieved, where a reasonable influence can still have an impact. The starting inquiry is, "When does X need to do Y for Z to be achieved, and by when?" Are there any "hard" situational factors that affect the timing (*e.g.,* bidding deadline, mounting public or regulatory pressure)? What do stakeholders expect to be achieved and by when? Of particular importance is sensing the window of time that people will be open to being influenced on the central issues. Often, windows are short, and once they close, closing a sale or getting approval is next to impossible.

For complex situations, there could be multiple moments for influence. This could be embedded in the context (*e.g.,* if a decision process has multiple stages) or be created by influence (*e.g.,* someone is so compelling that multiple options, not just the default option, will be considered).

Moments can also be long. The Cold War between the U.S. and Russia lasted about 45 years.[56] Of course, there were junctures within this long moment for détente and pivot. Long or short, the key to moment is the ability to estimate the time available for +influencing and to be prepared to act when the window is open.

Skilled influencers will decide in which moments they are best equipped to have influence, or how different parts of the influence attempt take advantage of different moments. In general, influencing earlier will provide the greatest degrees of freedom. People's minds are less made up. They aren't tired yet of the issues and problems. There is some freshness and energy to consider possibilities. The later the influence attempt, the more vigorous and compelling it must be, much like the eagle that swoops in to get the fish that the sea lion has been chasing for a while.

Case 8.5 Convey news of a plant shutdown

You are the manufacturing leader of a global car company. You are about to tell the head of the Italian plant, Giovanni, that the global leadership team has made a final decision to shut down the Italian plant in two years.

This is a hard conversation for you and Giovanni. You ran the Italian plant before Giovanni and mentored him throughout his career. Giovanni worked at the Italian plant for more than 20 years, and so has most workers at the plant. Giovanni and the workers have been anxious over the last 12 months, as they and then the global management team did reviews to determine whether there was any way to keep the plant open. You fought hard for the Italian plant by looking at every possible option, even that of workers taking a 30% pay cut, but the numbers did not work out. At the end, you agreed with the rest of your colleagues that the Italian plant had to be shut down and the manufacturing moved to lower-cost locations.

(Continued)

(Continued)

You need to keep Giovanni motivated through the next two years to ensure the shutdown goes smoothly. There are difficult negotiations with the unions ahead, and Giovanni still needs to keep the plant running efficiently until six months before the shutdown.

You are sad it has come to this. You are keen to support Giovanni through this difficult time. Will he let you?

Analyze:

- What are Giovanni's pressure points?
- What are all the different horizons beyond this meeting whereby you can influence Giovanni to constructively approach this plant shutdown and support him through the difficult time?
- What might be your task and relationship objectives for each of these moments?

Principle 6. Pace

Finding the right pace — how fast, how frequent, intervals between influence attempts — requires influencers to align their internal sense of timing to what the situation calls for to have good +outcomes. What pace of moving the conversation along is most likely to get alignment around the issues and generate the resolution?

Roman emperor Augustus made famous the phrase, "Make haste slowly," or *festina lente* in Latin.[57] A fast pace is not necessarily the fastest way to achieve desired objectives. A slower pace gives influencees more time to reach their own realization of the outcomes for everyone and the opportunity to build relationships and increase ownership of the +outcomes. On the other hand, moving too slow risks running out of time to get good closure. Novice influencers tend to rush when out of time, thereby risking reaching agreement and, worse still, agreement in words only but without the commitment to follow through. The influencer may be better off summarizing the discussion and coming back another day to land the closure.[58]

A faster pace works well when all parties have a similarly high sense of urgency and there is sufficient trust between the parties. If there are difficult relationship issues that impede an open discussion of the issues, the influencer will be better off acknowledging and working through enough of the issues first. In a conflictual situation, a fast pace and the resulting higher intensity level require relational equity above a certain threshold or an ability to build sufficient rapport quickly; otherwise, conflict may erupt in the process and derail the tasks and relationship.

At any given point in time, an influencer must decide whether to make an influence attempt now or later. The central question is, "To what degree are key stakeholders willing to engage constructively on the central issues now versus later?" Skilled influencers sense that willingness changes continuously and will make the influence attempt when the counterparty is ready to engage. Sometimes, when the window is closing but willingness is low, you must still influence. In that instance, you should think through how to manage the risk of an initial unfavorable reaction (*e.g.*, shock, resistance) and work to get the person to be open.

Of course, now versus later also applies to selecting and sequencing the issues to influence. In some circumstances, we have taught practitioners with low relationship equity but urgent business needs to acknowledge the relationship issues upfront, show sincerity by requesting a separate meeting devoted to discussing these issues, and ask for dispensation to suspend such issues for now and move on to the business matters.

When pacing to achieve +outcomes, influencers must be aware of their native bias. Relative to the pressure points and the context and considering now-versus-later calls, mature influencers choose the influence objectives carefully, focus on the issues to address or avoid in an attempt, and sequence and plan the attempt. Then, in real time during the influence, they adjust the pace depending on the people's reactions and other dynamics emerging and what is required by the context and the people engaged.

Principle 7. Seizing the Moments as They Arise

Even the best-laid influence objectives and plans won't lead to outcomes if we fail to act in the moment. The sin of omission is very common.

Effective influencers seize far more moments than ineffective ones to produce differentiated positive outcomes.

If you were asked to name the important meetings you have coming up, it probably wouldn't be a problem: things like the annual shareholders' meeting, the final pitch for a major contract, the one-on-one performance review with your boss, and so on. But if you were asked to point to the two or three moments in each of these meetings that will disproportionately drive the outcomes, many of you would be flummoxed. We don't have a problem identifying critical moments from our past, yet predicting and preparing for those moments in the future is much more difficult — but no less essential than those past moments prove.

These critical moments are not quite the same as "moments of truth,"[59] but in real time, they're usually a moment of uncertainty and unclarity from which the trajectory to the desired outcomes will be made or broken.

So, how do we make the most of the defining moments coming at us in the near future?

First, let's identify them. Consider the duration of that influence agenda. Ask which ingredients are key to success.

Take the annual shareholders' meeting. There are often as many agendas as there are stakeholders. What is one thing you could pursue there that would also benefit the other stakeholders? A typical annual meeting could drag on for hours. At which juncture of the proceedings might it be most opportune to advance your agenda? Which outcomes in the other agendas might favor your cause? Who can you line up beforehand to lend support at the critical moment? By paying attention to the things that are crucial to your objectives, you can act purposefully to marshal the ingredients for success, or at least watch for the moment when they emerge together.

The advice above will increase clarity, but uncertainty is another matter — it could help you achieve breakthrough results in your upcoming important meetings. To be sure, uncertainties drive all of us crazy. They paralyze most of us because we become less sure of our plans; we feel exposed and vulnerable as we lose control and fear for the worst. This is the same whether we are talking about a situation broadly or a meeting specifically. Uncertain moments become frozen moments.

To get unstuck, someone needs to jump in and move us forward. The right intervention done well could lead to genuine appreciation of your leadership by everyone. So, how can you prepare for this?

It starts with knowing that uncertainty occurs at least once in most important meetings. Ahead of every important meeting, you should think about what those moments might be. Visualize the conditions under which you would jump in and what you might say or do. There is no need to be too precise here — it's more about mental alertness and awareness of what opportunities look like when they emerge and conditioning yourself to pounce when they do.

Time is a tyrant. It consumes unmade choices as it runs out. Inaction is a choice. When uncertainty reigns, the far greater danger is to stop and wait until uncertainty resolves. It may not. And those who choose to act are the ones who will +influence the outcomes. There is no guarantee, of course, that the uncertainty won't overwhelm the actions, along with, in some cases, the actors. We have seen enough cases in which the movement *per se* did not suffice but is nonetheless valuable as it upsets the equilibrium and causes reactions from others that create new opportunities. Often, that's all you can hope for — and all you need.

When we spend time preparing senior executives for critical meetings, less than 15% of the time is spent on the process design, content, and flow of agendas, and 85% is spent on what the leadership moments might be (*e.g.*, when there is a pregnant pause, when someone just called out a conflict, when someone openly dissents) and how they can prepare themselves for those breakthrough moments when they occur. The guidelines are simple: embrace the uncertainty, make a conscious choice to act on it through conscious influence planning and, most importantly, stand by your principles when you make your choice.

Case 8.6 Closing a deal with a stressed customer

You are a sales representative for a boutique data analytics software company. Your customers are Internet gaming businesses that use customizable software to track and analyze gameplay behavior to better monetize their users. Your firm's advantage over competitors is the ability to provide customized solutions that meet the clients' current needs and could be easily adapted to new needs. The co-founders of your firm are ex-Internet gaming veterans who have unusual insight into how game developers' analytics need to evolve over time. However, given that your firm is relatively young (only three years since its founding) and is still building its brand, salespeople, like yourself, are charged with the responsibility to educate and convince customers of its value proposition.

You feel pressure to meet your sales targets for this month. Two deals that you thought you would be able to close fell through, and you are just short of your monthly target. Today is the last day of the month, and there is one more customer that you may be able to close a deal with.

You've been talking with the customer's director of product for two months and understand their needs well. They are a venture-backed start-up working on developing their first game, and as coding progressed, they realized that the analytics software that they had originally adopted was insufficient to meet their increasingly complex needs. This mistake in judgment has introduced unnecessary delays, and

(Continued)

(Continued)

they now need to find a suitable replacement as soon as possible. Every day that passes is cash burned for this pre-revenue start-up. To your knowledge, this customer has considered other vendors, but none have been able to offer adequate solutions to their complex requirements.

The previous week, you brought your technical partner to meet with the customer and had a productive conversation that seemed to convince the director of product that your software will meet their needs. She made a few additional technical requests and said that she needed to check on some budgeting issues before deciding. You two agreed to hold a follow-up meeting today. You have checked with your technical team and have full confidence that you can meet her needs. Your company is prepared to dedicate the necessary resources and is ready to start the project. You hope the fact that everything is in place and ready to go will convince her to give you the deal today.

As you step inside her office, you can tell that she is visibly agitated and stressed. She apologizes and says that today may not be a good day to have this follow-up conversation because she needs to handle a host of other issues. You are surprised that she didn't call you to cancel the meeting.

Now that you are here in her office and this is the last day of the month, you are reluctant to just leave. You want to close this deal to make your numbers. At the same time, you hesitate to pressure her in her current state. Perhaps, you can offer her some help and

(Continued)

(Continued)

support. You have encountered agitated customers struggling with a variety of issues before, so perhaps you could offer her some perspective. She is now waiting for you to either leave or say something.

Analyze: What are five ways to seize the moment to get the customer to give you five minutes (rather than leave right away)?

Principle 8. Engage Your Being

As we started to discuss in Chapter 5, our being is central to +influence. To effectively +influence, we need to use the right words, align our being with those words, and ensure both words and our being are in alignment with our +influence objectives.

Words are like the surface of a lake: it looks calm, but underneath the water there are many plants, rocks, and other organisms. The being within us is what is in the lake, and some developments in the lake will surface that could affect our +influence. We may not be able to control what shows up and when. That's why it's valuable to engage the inner being and, over time, improve access to those qualities, *i.e.*, harness what's in the lake more and more. Chapters 10 and 12, on aligning the being and development, will shed more light on this.

To +influence what others think, feel, and do, we first need to influence how we ourselves think and feel so we can do the right things. This is basic but hard to do. Think back in the last two weeks: When was a time when you felt conflicted about something you needed to do, where one part of your brain knew that you should do it, but another part of your being held you back? Maybe it was as simple as wanting to work out to lose some weight, but you didn't have the motivation or energy, or you just wanted to take it easy. This inner conflict also happens when we try to influence others. We know that we should be trying to get our direct report to step up his or her performance to avoid being fired, but another part of us dreads relaying the hard message, and so we dither. That will cost you both later. In both cases, it is our own being — the conviction and our inner qualities, such as courage, compassion, and discipline — that we need to activate before we can compellingly try to talk to someone else and/or take the desired action.

Given the importance of the being, we devote an entire chapter to it. Chapter 10 will examine how we might align our being with the +influence in the moment and improve that alignment with practice over time. Chapter 12 adds to Chapter 10 by delving further into how we can best develop ourselves, +influence, and our leadership.

9

Habits to Raise Proficiency in +Influencing

We are the sum total of our experiences. Those experiences — be they positive or negative — make us the person we are, at any given point in our lives. And, like a flowing river, those same experiences, and those yet to come, continue to influence and reshape the person we are, and the person we become. None of us are the same as we were yesterday, nor will be tomorrow.

— B.J. Neblett

Our experiences shape who we are, almost as much as our nature. A rare few are born influential in certain, limited ways. Many, like Tsun-yan, were not.

+Influence Personal Story:
Overcoming Denial, Inspiring Self to Change

Six months after he was elected as a director[60] at McKinsey, he was put in the penalty box. He had a year to change things or risked being fired.

Despite his client development and leadership prowess, he was seen to be too tough on people, didn't get along with his colleagues, and was excessively ambitious. From the fastest associate to principal, and principal to director, Tsun-yan went from heaven to hell. It bewildered him and made him angry. Life became very dark. He felt misunderstood and unfairly treated. He even thought it might have been professional jealousy, unfair practices of his peers, or something even worse.

But he also knew he had a real issue to deal with. When people disappointed him, he had difficulty controlling his anger and had episodes in which he lashed out at people. These episodes became seared in people's minds and got in the way of people working with and getting to know him, regardless of how brilliant he was and how much business he brought in. He was also very demanding — of himself and also of others. His standards were high, and his dedication and devotion to them relentless. He expected others to feel the same way he did: it was a privilege to be let into McKinsey, so you gave it everything you had. He felt this discipline and devotion would help younger consultants grow up faster, realize their potential, and live up to firm and client expectations. Much to his surprise and dismay, most didn't understand or appreciate it.

So, he undertook personal reflection and coaching with a vengeance. He took all available leadership assessments to understand himself better. He hired himself a coach — the first senior partner in McKinsey to do so. He tried to slow down, to become more relatable, to work on modifying his behavior.

"Tsun-yan, you have already arrived and yet act like a young man trying to get somewhere in a hurry," Joe Keilty, one of his early assessors, summarized his takeaways over dinner.[61] "You have a big gap between your good intent and the effects on people." Tsun-yan took this to heart and would later repeat it to many ambitious leaders he counseled.

The setback opened Tsun-yan up to a whole new side of himself, as well as how to +influence others, that he would have never known if he didn't go through this trial.

We will all face profound setbacks and must choose how to respond. After much inner struggle, overcoming his anger and frustration, Tsun-yan chose to learn and grow out of his worse instincts, to discover the better aspects of himself and to help others do the same. Denial is the more common response by executives facing similar setbacks — choosing to wallow in pain or give in to cynicism. "Denial is not just a river in Egypt," as Michael Murray,[62] as one of Tsun-yan's colleagues, famously said.

Many years later, we worked with a Scandinavian CEO who was put in the penalty box by her board after a period of denial and externalization. Tsun-yan's own story gave her hope that she, too, could get out of the hole. She did eventually climb out of the hole by freeing herself to live a different life, after righting some wrongs with her team.

Many readers will intuitively know there is more to proficient +influencing than going with native ability and well-practiced execution ("doing") by applying the principles in Chapters 7–8. You are right. There is a lot more.

Power of Conscious Practice

You've likely been to a powerful workshop or training program where you felt you learned a lot. A few weeks after, though, you can't remember much and start thinking the workshop wasn't that impactful. What drives the gap between your immediate feeling at the workshop's end and a few weeks later? It's the attitudes and habits you need to adopt and internalize to consistently practice and apply what you've learned.

Developing proficiency in influencing, like becoming good in any skill, has four stages:[63]

1. Unconsciously unskilled
2. Consciously unskilled
3. Consciously skilled
4. Unconsciously skilled

To go from *unconsciously unskilled* to *consciously unskilled* is primarily logical. Hopefully, reading this book and logically considering its ideas, anecdotes, cases, facts, and principles will help you to better appreciate the importance of +influence in your life and contexts as well as see how anyone can improve their influencing. If you find yourself rejecting what is in this book, perhaps you can examine to what degree you have an open or closed mindset.

To go from *consciously unskilled* to *consciously skilled* is all about practice. Improvement comes with conscientious practice. Practice leads to habitualization. What habit will you adopt to use the principles day in and day out? Who will practice with you? What or who will enable you to call on these principles during times of anxiety and stress when you most need them? The five attitudes and habits in this chapter offer some starting points.

To go from *consciously skilled* to *unconsciously skilled (mastery)* is mostly about your being — not just what you can access today, more about going outside your comfort zone, and integrating what you have experienced and learned into your being. Becoming more conscious and calling on the inner qualities needed for the +outcomes requires at first a lot of effort, but will over time become more automatic.

So, how consciously do you try to align your being with your influence attempts? Are you constantly working to uncover more of your personal qualities, use a variety of strengths, and minimize your negative instincts? Are you able to break through some inner barriers that hold you back from seizing the moment and bringing your fuller being to bear? The attitudes and habits in this chapter will give you a start on how to involve your being in +influence more, and Chapter 10 provides a more detailed guide.

The following five habits and attitudes will enable anyone to become more proficient in influencing:

1. **Care about others**: Raise others' productivity, growth, and satisfaction — not just your own.
2. **Stretch yourself**: Pause your reflexes and go outside your comfort zone to uncover and apply the inner you, along with approaches new to you.
3. **Be present:**[64] Notice what is going on in yourself and in others during influence attempts.
4. **Get feedback**: Get feedback on how you did against set goals at every opportunity.
5. **Reflect (after action)**: Reflect periodically to improve your influence attempts and update your assumptions and beliefs.

With these habits, you can join the many professionals and leaders who have improved their influence skills. In a LinHart survey of 189 American professionals and leaders, 41% described themselves as having "significantly expanded my influencing repertoire over the years," and 15% more strongly agreed with this statement.

Care about Others

Nobody cares how much you know, until they know how much you care.

— Theodore Roosevelt

From caring comes courage.

— Lao Tzu

When you show deep empathy toward others, their defensive energy goes down, and positive energy replaces it. That's when you can get more creative in solving problems.

— Stephen Covey

To care about others is not only a virtue in most spiritual and moral traditions worldwide but also highly pragmatic.

Chapter 3 discussed how higher productivity, satisfaction, and growth for everyone in the situation and/or organization are more likely to get everyone involved to change and evolve in a positive direction.

To figure out what is greater productivity, satisfaction, and growth for others, logically and mechanically applying the principles from Chapter 7 (doing) is not enough; you must genuinely care about others. When doing and caring come together, all of yourself can see into the other person, his or her relationship to you, and the larger situation, and discern how it would benefit the other person and how best to +influence the other person. If you are just mechanically applying the principles, the chances of gaining insight are much lower, and any resulting influence attempt might feel contrived, for reasons you and the other person can't necessarily articulate but are real.

Caring about others comes naturally to some people, but not to all. Shaping experiences compound personality inclinations in known and mysterious ways; for example, some people experience great violence in childhood and thus vow to show kindness to others of which they were deprived, whereas some wreck the same violence on others, closing off their heart to others' suffering and their own pain. It is also hard to care deeply about others without caring deeply about ourselves, which requires people to work through self-shame, self-respect, and self-love issues. Caring is foundational to human existence, but it is a foundation we need to cultivate and preserve — not a foundation to be taken for granted.

———————————— ✝ ————————————

+Influence Personal Story:
Uncovering Her Capacity to Care

Huijin would not be described as a highly caring person, but she has put in 15 years of conscious effort to uncover the caring and emotional side of herself, in service of her personal mission to help others find their whole and true self and channel that toward better decisions and actions in their career, business, family, and society.

Leaving her home country to immigrate to Canada was traumatic.[65] Her parents struggled economically and emotionally, and 10-year-old Huijin repressed her pain and fear. It was the only way a child could cope. She reached into her natural aggression and strove to survive, first excelling academically and then being single-minded in her career. While she reached the pinnacle of the world's best schools and companies quickly, she still wasn't happy; in fact, she didn't even know what it felt like to be happy. All this changed in her mid-twenties when her inner self caught up with her. She reconnected to her feeling side and to her soul and spirit that was crying out for expression. She gave up her first career as a strategic consultant, jumping into the risky open sea to pursue her mission to help others, no matter where it took her — success or failure. Caring still doesn't come naturally to her as it does for Tsun-yan, who is a Helper[66] in the Enneagram personality profile,[67] but she consciously reaches within herself to care about others in her own way, with her unique value-add. She will never be a warm and fuzzy big sister kind of helper, but she is a warrior on your side who will help you face the reality and tumult with courage and inner strength. Many people helped her on her journey to uncover her true self, and she vowed to do the same for at least one million people throughout her lifetime.

> *It is an absolute human certainty that no one can know his own beauty or perceive a sense of his own worth until it has been reflected back to him in the mirror of another loving, caring human being.*

> — John Joseph Powell

With caring, one can then be curious about another person's way of thinking and feeling about a situation or organization, respect the difference between yourself and the other person, and use that knowledge to design influencing paths that respect each person's different starting point. A big mistake of many well-intended people is assuming, or even insisting, that other people think and feel the same way. This fallacy has no logical basis but comes from deep within us, a combination of ego, wishful thinking, and expediency. The more deeply we believe in ourselves and our purpose and intent, the more deeply we could be susceptible to this misperception that everyone is like us, or should be like us. "Should" is a dangerous word in +influence, since the world and human beings don't work on "should." Curiosity is the antidote to "should" and is something all serious +influencers need to cultivate and deepen.

Case 9.7 CEO dealing with underperformance of mentor

As a CEO who has been encouraging a higher-performance culture in a national oil and gas company, it has become an embarrassment that the VP of engineering, long tenured and who hired you into the company, has struggled to solve many problems in the engineering function. These issues have resulted in missed production targets and higher maintenance costs and have impacted the company's reputation. In your culture, this is a hard issue to confront; elders and seniors are highly revered. However, the situation has become bad for the VP; people are talking behind his and your backs, and you can see he is also increasingly anxious about what people may be saying about him. His health is also noticeably not as good as before. Perhaps he wants a dignified way out?

You must find a potential role for him. One possibility is to mentor the project leader of a major new upstream project in Nigeria, where the company holds its largest exploration and production acreages outside its home country. This could really use his experience, but it is a big move, and he would have to leave the top management team. You are nervous but know you've got to get on with it. All the great triumphs he has had and how much he cared for you when you were a young engineer add further to the burden. You also remember something he said to all young engineers: show people your heart, let them feel your sincerity, and they will follow.

(Continued)

(Continued)

Analyze: How do you open the conversation in a way that shows that you care for him? How do you tell him he needs to redeem his legacy?

Stretch Yourself

You can't change nature, son! Change IS nature, dad, the part we can influence. And it all starts when we decide.

— Kitty Richards, *Ratatouille*

In caring about ourselves and others, we must not only care about our current self as we know ourselves to be, but also the deeper, potential self within.

For each of us, some influencing situations will be easy, while others will be difficult. This is as true for the beginner as for the experts among us. New challenges always have a way of finding us just as we have mastered a certain level. Some challenging situations are hard for most, if not all, of us, such as telling a loved one that the relationship isn't working and needs to change. These moments of truth call on us to dig deeper within ourselves, beyond our usual reflexes, to find personal qualities and strengths that will guide us on what to say and do and how to be. In such cases, our brain alone won't have the wisdom to find its way to greater productivity, growth, and satisfaction for all. Our heart and soul must help us rise to it.

Expanding our influencing ability is a self-fulfilling prophecy. If we think we can only influence in the way we have always done it, we won't try other methods and hence will rely on our reflexes and stay in our comfort zone. If we are open to trying other methods, we will find that some methods work better than others and that we might need to work on our being, too. While there is no magic bullet that will turn a novice into a master +influencer overnight, we have seen so many people successfully stretch outside their initial comfort zone. Year after year, we have observed most of the MBA students transform their influence range and effectiveness at the end of the course, and a survey of alumni confirmed this to be true.[68]

A well-rounded basket of influence tactics, like the repertoire of a musician, is learned, not inborn. Most people have notable instincts and preferences that show up as a natural zone of effectiveness. No one can be effective in all circumstances with all types of people. Effective influencers work on improving their repertoire rather than accepting it as "unchangeable."

Lou Gerstner, the famous IBM CEO in the 1990s who saved IBM from bankruptcy and revitalized the company, found his leadership and influencing skills severely stretched when he first entered IBM. He realized that instead of relying on rational ways of influencing, which had been his hallmark and comfort area, he needed to relate to the feelings of the customers (*e.g.*, anger) and employees (*e.g.*, anger and pride) to get them to give IBM another chance. This was critical to avoid bankruptcy. His book, *Who Says Elephants Can't Dance?*,[69] describes in detail how emotion-filled his key communication was and why that was effective.

The above is a powerful example of not going with your reflexes but instead inquiring on what people need to think, feel, and do to move toward the desired +outcomes. Reflexes are "actions performed without conscious thought as a response to a stimulus."[70] They help us act quickly and are efficient in the sense that we don't need to go through a conscious analysis to decide what to do. They are great when the reflex is appropriate for the situation at hand — for example, when a new situation is similar to past situations from which the reflexes were formed — but highly dangerous when the new situation is very different. In the VUCA world[71] of the 2020s, it is prudent to assume a situation is different, pause your reflexes, and examine the situation from afresh, applying the principles from Chapters 7–8 step by step. Assuming the current situation is the same as before is foolhardy and dangerous.

Going beyond our reflexes and trying the required influencing pathways inevitably leads to venturing outside your comfort zone.

Pushing yourself outside of your comfort zone has a four-stage process, as illustrated through Tsun-yan's penalty box experience earlier in this chapter. At first, you will have trouble accepting you have a weakness, which is a significant problem. Then, you will struggle with yourself on whether you want to shore up that weakness. Whatever seemingly rational reasons you come up with for not taking action is typically your defensive mechanism at work. The third stage is a (reluctant) decision to work on your weakness and actual attempts to overcome your weakness. The fourth stage is recognizing that you can and will overcome your weakness. Persevere through to stage three, and you will most likely be successful.

This process requires faith — that whatever you have experienced of yourself in the past is only one part of all that which you are capable. We are conditioned to think we are fixed. No. Each person has a deep and broad range of qualities and so much untapped potential. Pressures often bring out hidden ones like courage. We can also uncover additional qualities; for example, after a setback reveals that we have overused certain strengths and need to apply underused ones. For instance, Huijin has worked hard to uncover compassion and humility to balance out her strong tendency to judge others.

Be Present

There are books on techniques to improve one's presence,[72] but the presence we are talking about is deeper: presence is the undivided attendance of the whole being in the moment. By being present, you are paying attention to your own — and the other person's — thoughts, feelings, and influences; noticing the non-verbal signals; sensing the energy in the room; keying into the tone of the conversation; and interpreting their implications for your influence attempt.

How to increase your presence tactically?

Take the next upcoming in-person meeting you have in your calendar. Let's say it's with Joe, your immediate superior. Meditate before the meeting for 30 seconds, long enough to visualize Joe when he is at his best. What were the usual indicators on his facial expressions (*e.g.*, his eyebrows are raised when he is positively energized)? Get a fix of that along with the usual way he dresses including items like eyeglasses, the shoes he often wears, *etc.*

In the first minute of the meeting (60 seconds is a long time), notice the same items (eyeglasses, shoes, *etc.*). Is there anything unusual? (*e.g.*, The way he put them on, adjusted them, *etc.*). Pay attention to his facial expressions. How are they different or the

---

same as when he is at his best? Take note of that and keep monitoring that whenever you feel your energy is waning, distracted or disoriented on the matter you are discussing with Joe. By focusing on Joe (the subject in English grammar) as a separate entity from the topic of discussion (the object in English grammar), you have more streams of attention tied to the same unfolding interaction. All things equal you would have more data on the interaction quality and direction ("what's going on" in simple words). More importantly you will have come across to Joe as being more present, more "there".

There are two fundamental benefits to being present in this fashion: you gather a lot of data that you could have missed, and the attentiveness signals your sincerity, bringing you and the other people closer.

With presence, you can learn in real time how you and the other person are thinking and feeling and wish to act on the big issues, whether you have the same or different view on what could be the pressure points and outcomes. There will invariably be moments in the interaction that open up new possibilities, unforeseen beforehand, that the present person can pounce on.

Paying full attention with all your being — mind, body, heart, and spirit — also signals your positive intent of wanting to listen, understand, and respect the other person, which will encourage the other person to reciprocate. This reciprocation is instinctive, so it doesn't depend on the person's emotions or intentions.[73] This movement toward each other changes the tonality of any interaction to something more mutual and positive, facilitating +influence.

Being able to continually pay attention throughout a lengthy interaction is really hard; all sorts of noises get in the way: we start judging ourselves and others, react emotionally, get distracted, or doze off; voices come into our head (about this situation or others); or the conversation gets so intense that it takes on a life of its own. In conflictual or adversarial conversation, tensions multiply.[74]

Therefore, being present is a muscle that one needs to strengthen daily — not a switch to be flipped as and when you wish. When you notice noise arising in your own head and heart, you need to pause it and try to return to a place of being open-minded and open-hearted. More noise will come, so you need to keep returning to the place of being open, centered, and grounded. It overlaps with mindfulness, so practicing meditation and having a spiritual practice (*e.g.*, prayer) will help you develop the muscle of being present.[75] Simple techniques of breathing and visualization before an important meeting also help.[76]

Caring about others and the other habits and attitudes in this chapter will also help you to stay present. They all promote some distance from your own feelings, beliefs, and assumptions, so you can uncover more about others and yourself. When you have this distance, your mindset will be more open, and you will be more able to take in what is happening without judgment and repression. Then, you will see a lot more. With this greater seeing, you will have more insight into setting your +influence objective and how to move others.

Case 9.8 Last chance to retain a seasoned sales leader

You are the co-founder of a digital media company that has large consumer goods, fashion, and retailing companies as main customers. You and your co-founder started this company three years ago in your apartment, and the company has been growing rapidly, with sales doubling every year. Both you and your co-founder are engineers who have developed proprietary algorithms matching advertisers to innovative e-advertising or marketing products and services that deliver significantly better returns (on marketing dollars) than competitors. You don't have a lot of experience managing people.

Your sales leader, Tim, has just resigned after only one year with the company. You have been happy with his performance so far and want to retain him. Tim has worked for large companies all his career and was responsible for a business with USD 250 million in sales in his last job. Since joining your company, he has successfully closed many deals with large corporate customers. Your company has only 5% market share among large corporates, so you need Tim to capture more share. You also value Tim's broad management experience, especially as the company takes on more employees, and operations get more complex. When you recruited him, Tim was excited about the opportunity to contribute to the broader development of the company.

You have observed Tim get increasingly frustrated over the last few months. He has been vocal about what

(Continued)

(Continued)

---

should be done with many aspects of the company that don't report to him. He complained about the customer service team — that they don't know what their job is, and they should report to him so that the sales team (which already reports to Tim) and customer service team can work together to better serve clients. He also seems to be frustrated that he is not involved more in the decision process for deciding which new products to pilot or not. Perhaps there is more to his frustration.

Tim is walking toward your office. Now you wish you had followed your instinct to talk to Tim earlier. But your time has been consumed by fundraising and coordinating new product launches in the last three months.

Analyze: How did the co-founder's lack of presence contribute to the resignation? What should the co-founder do now, and how could he maximize his presence for the conversation with the sales leader?

Giving, Receiving & Inviting Feedback

Only with feedback do we know for sure whether we have achieved our influence objectives and why. The sooner we get feedback and the better quality it is, the faster we can try alternative methods and improve our +influencing efficacy.

Feedback is grossly underappreciated because it is often not done at all, done very badly, or seen as something only for performance reviews. Good influencers make feedback a daily occurrence, not one to two times a year. To give quality feedback, we need to deeply care about both the task and the individual.

Quality feedback is specific and timely, and it addresses both the observable behavior and the impact of the behavior on the giver of the feedback. When feedback has these three characteristics, it is non-judgmental and useful to the receiver. This applies to both positive and negative feedback.

Examples of high-quality feedback:

- When you cut me off just as I was starting to explain my ideas, (the impact is that) I felt that you were not interested in my ideas.
- Last week during the project meeting, you avoided key stakeholder Y's challenging question. (The impact is that) it made me question your willingness to address key stakeholder concerns.
- I notice that when discussions get heated, you can stay calm under pressure and reframe the issue in a way that helps all of us find a path forward. (The impact is that) it makes me think about seeking your advice on difficult issues.

Examples of low-quality feedback:

- (Angrily) you are not interested in my ideas!
- You dislike tough questions.
- You made me angry.
- You were too aggressive.
- You were very difficult to work with.

When giving negative feedback, it is not necessary to jump in with suggestions on what to do differently. It is emotionally difficult to give and receive constructive feedback, and recognizing this through words and body language will strengthen the relationship between the feedback giver and receiver. Even when you have formal line management responsibilities for the person to whom you are giving constructive feedback, it is worthwhile to pause after giving the feedback. This will enable the person to digest the message they have just received — often, people are unaware of the (negative) impact they have on others. In addition, they may come up with, by themselves, the same improvement ideas you are thinking of and hence feel more committed to change. They are less likely to feel attacked if the feedback and improvements do not follow one another immediately.

For feedback to lead to positive change, the receiver needs to care about the impact of his or her actions and have the desire to improve. It is easy and (sadly) common to get defensive when receiving constructive feedback, which erodes the relationship with the person giving the feedback. Therefore, the recipient should focus on asking clarification questions and not defend past actions ("Oh, I didn't mean to do that"). It is also worthwhile to thank the other person for the feedback; after all, they are sufficiently interested in improving you or the business to give feedback in the first place!

To achieve meaningful change in yourself, feedback is necessary to help you see how much you are improving. However, because giving feedback is perceived to be difficult or is likely to be negatively received, many people shy away from giving it. Therefore, you may need to invite feedback from others. There are different options:

- Invite others to let you know what impact you have on them.
- Let them know you are trying to improve a specific skill, and ask for one or two suggestions on what might help you to achieve the desired change.

The latter approach, known as "FeedForward,"[77] was coined by Marshall Goldsmith to help leaders focus on the future, which they can change, rather than the past, which they cannot.

Reflection

Reflection is the most time-starved activity in a world crazed by too much doing.

— Tsun-yan

Try this simple exercise. Go to a quiet place with nothing but a notebook and a pen. Nothing electronic. In 45 minutes or less, jot down the answers to the question: "Where am I in my life?" Those of you who have done a similar exercise before would have noted that for the first five minutes, you had a hard time finding answers. You get distracted by other things coming to your mind. Or you may be writing down a jumble of thoughts. Then, after persisting, you discover a subtle shift to a certain mental flow, starting with one or two thoughts which lead to some others.

Put simply, reflection is making sense of where you are in life or in a situation, what is happening, why it is happening, and how it affects you and others. By understanding what is, we can better imagine what could be (better). Reflection involves thinking, but also sensing, understanding what drives feelings in ourselves and others. This includes deep diving to understand a critical detail and getting on the balcony to see how different pieces fit into a whole.

To reflect, you must quiet down until your deeper thinking and feeling capacities are activated. This is a different energy than the energy of data gathering, choosing, and doing things. Spiritual and meditative practices are good examples of deep reflection. The same practices can be used to reflect on yourself and the world around you, how you are affected by it, and *vice versa*.

To reflect, you must also stay *down* to get to the deeper, underlying issue. Reflection is like peeling an onion. For example, if you lost your temper today in a meeting, you might reflect on why. Out of two reasons — you are naturally impatient or you were having a bad day — you could reflect further and ask why. Is it common for me to lose my temper? When was the last time I lost it? If so, what does it say about my state of mind?

For reflection as a learning process, one should also have a takeaway. It could be something you learned about yourself, something you learned about what motivates the other person you were talking to, or something you want to learn and may be a new direction you want to chart. Some of these takeaways may take time to crystallize, but the discipline of deriving takeaways gives reflection forward momentum.

Reflection may come more easily to some at the beginning (*e.g.*, those with high intrapersonal intelligence[78]), but everyone can and should do it. The key is to get into a routine of reflection, be it daily (*e.g.*, every night before sleep), event-based (*e.g.*, on flights), retreat-based, or people-based (*e.g.*, done with a coach). Methods and aids, like music, can also help. There is no one right way to reflect. It's the outcome — whether or not you are getting deeper insights that inform how to get to positive outcomes better and sooner — that matters. Deeper insights of ourselves, of others, and of our business and organizations will shed light on what can be done and how many different steps it will take to get it done.

―――――――――――― ✝ ――――――――――――

+Influence Personal Story:
From Doubt to Coaching Leader

Naithy Cyriac is an example of how dedicated, sustained practice of the +influence principles has had a deep impact, raising her +influence skills and excavating the leader in her.

Attending the LIFE2 program in November 2015 helped her to overcome fears and see herself as someone who could pioneer the Myanmar business of her firm and unleash the entrepreneur in herself — a vast departure from the shy girl from India who took her first-ever international flight in 2012 to study at the NUS Business School. This is her story: how she stretched and owned her true self and leveraged +influence principles and her being (see Chapter 10) to help her clients and grow her team. "*Being able to step back and focus on strengths shifted my approach, and my being. I moved away from a 'what could fail' mentality.*"

Naithy and Huijin would joke about the time she wanted to drop out of the pilot +influence course at NUS Business School. She kept going for some reason, and neither Huijin nor Naithy could have predicted she would become such an avid practitioner of +influence.

Upon her graduation, Naithy surprised Tsun-yan and Huijin by going to Myanmar with her consulting firm, and when she came to LIFE2 in November 2015, she brought the question of whether to take up the leadership role for that office. Myanmar was growing rapidly in 2015, a Wild West of sorts. Naithy's pioneering spirit was in full swing.

Through deep reflection and intense peer high challenge high support, Naithy realized that the key issue she needed to address was her own inner struggles related to self-doubt or self-worth. Her fears led to a debilitating hesitation to embrace the responsibility wholeheartedly, to stretch herself.

When she asked herself more deeply "Can I do it? Do I want to do it?", she realized the answer was yes and yes.

Shortly after, Naithy became the country manager of Myanmar for her firm and went to build a vibrant business and team there from scratch.

> *LIFE2 helped me to be more confident. Less self-doubt on how to execute and follow through. More self-leadership, willing to step up to do more. I took the risk of asking for a promotion/more responsibility and received an immediate and positive response. The influence approaches I learned before helped me secure both the support of the partners and the company founder, which I am very grateful for. As I embraced the new role, I embraced situations that would stretch my "sense of being," pushing me toward my better self.*
>
> *LIFE2 also helped me hit my sales targets by establishing trusted relations with new clients. It took a while for me to get comfortable. LIFE2's principle of "defining your own apex" — doing what you are best at — was a great help. I love meeting people and hence, instead of adopting an aggressive sales approach, I focused on establishing a meaningful relationship with potential clients, taking time to build rapport, which is what I am good at.*

Tsun-yan and Huijin were especially delighted to hear from Naithy on her efforts to coach her team and help them grow. Out of all the LIFE2 alumni, she has probably done the most on this front. Again, unexpected, especially considering her young age and the tough demands of growing a business from scratch. Her seriousness and sustained intention and action in coaching others is unusual even for far more mature leaders.

> *Hi Huijin, hope you're doing well. I was promoted again last Thursday, and the unique factor that influenced the decision*

as per the partner's feedback was my coaching/training of the juniors, especially the new hires and their comparative performance after their first project with me. This really touched my heart, so wanted to share this with you and thank you, Tsun-yan, Anna, and especially Rohan and Dany[79] for inculcating this quality in me and, more importantly, giving me multiple opportunities to experiment with my leadership styles and observe the students... I still want to do better, e.g., in equipping others with the influencing skill set I have now, in a customized way.

We are always a work in progress in becoming our best self. Sometimes, we may even become our worst self, when we have had a huge setback, or the environment brings out our worst qualities. All of us will fall into a ditch at times. What differentiates people is how fast they get out of it and where they go after the ditch. Self-leadership makes or breaks people's response in a ditch moment:[80]

- The deliberate practice of influencing your thoughts, feelings, and behaviors toward your objectives.
- A learned discipline to access your inner being and motivations to deploy for that influence.
- A habit of mind.[81]

There is a saying that you can't change what happens to you, but you can control how you respond.[82] This applies to even the most powerful CEOs and politicians.

In an uncontrollable VUCA environment, equipping ourselves as best as we can to do the best in more contexts can give us a sense of purpose, of having some influence over our life instead of being at the mercy of circumstances or other people. This sense of agency can be like night and day to our inner life, whether we have positive energy every day versus feeling like a victim drowning in anger and despair.

10

Aligning Our Being to +Influence

Man's nature is not essentially evil. Brute nature has been known to yield to the influence of love. You must never despair of human nature.

— Mahatma Gandhi

Dorian Lo, a senior leader in the health care industry,[83] has a favorite story about Tsun-yan delving deep into his being to +influence others.

About a year into my time with McKinsey, Tsun-yan gave me the opportunity to observe a dinner with a senior management team of a North American bank. I didn't know what to expect, since I was a doctor before joining McKinsey, with little experience of business, and no exposure to senior management teams. I was astounded by what I saw Tsun-yan do. Since then, it has inspired me to push myself constantly beyond what I am capable of.

Tsun-yan is a well-known introvert, but in the dinner, he was anything but! He gave a rousing, passionate speech which energized the team to cheer, literally cheer at the top of their lungs for the better future they will have together. 'Phoenix rising from the ashes' was how Tsun-yan described this team, and they believed in him. They believed more in themselves because of him.

We left the meeting, and as soon as we were out of sight of the client, Tsun-yan's shoulders sagged, and he looked so tired! Only then could I see how much energy he harnessed in service of that cause and how much of himself he gave.

I didn't say anything to Tsun-yan then, but this episode stayed with me. He dug deep into himself to give the team what they needed to do better. It takes a lot for an introvert to perform at that level.[84] If Tsun-yan can push himself far beyond the comfort zone, surely I can too! This has inspired me to dig deeper into myself.

Disconnect Between What We Say, Feel, and Our Being

We encounter disconnect between what people say, feel, and do all the time (see the examples below). This disconnect disempowers everyone involved. It makes us question and judge the person while not buying into what that person wants us to think, feel, and do. It weakens our own intent and makes our +influence objectives fuzzy, resulting in confused influence objectives and poor execution.

- The CEO gives a speech at a town hall meeting with 300 staff. She encourages people to speak up about problems in the company but doesn't take any questions. She seems to be in a hurry to leave.
- The leader of a project asks senior management for a USD 3 million top-up investment on a risky project but was nervous and fidgety when he made the request in a presentation.
- A husband and wife have grown distant. The wife says she wants to help the husband deal with his life issues but

withdraws from the conversation when it gets heated. Her face becomes visibly taut, seemingly resentful.

- A salesperson used to selling products is now asked to uncover customer needs and create solutions that benefit the customers. His initial five minutes with the client are still about the latest product upgrades and features.

Aligning disparate aspects of our being with a target +influence objective and strategy is hard work. As mentioned in the last chapter, doing so requires both the conscious accessing of our being "in the moment" and the ongoing uncovering of our being. The two require and enhance each other. In challenging influence situations, we run against our inner limits, be it our fears, long-held values, and entrenched power relationships. Some people let the limits stop them in their tracks, while others reach deep and spontaneously into personal qualities to break through those limits — on the spot.

There is a universal and constant struggle to devote ourselves to the high road of productivity gain, satisfaction, and growth instead of taking an easier, lower road. This struggle is waged in our being. We all have individual needs and wants or see others act out theirs. It is tiring to always make the effort. The CEO in the foregoing example was working 18-hour days prior to the town hall meeting. We also get demoralized — the best of intentions leads to poor outcomes, while those who are self-centered and better self-promoters seem to get ahead.

Work, lest we forget, is merely a part of our life journey. It is up to each of us to choose in whose interest we serve and toil. This choice is made in many moments every day; not a directional one that is made once and forever. For example, the chief of staff could have given the CEO a pep-talk before the town hall meeting, encouraging her to take a few questions.

We believe it is joyful and pragmatic to devote our being to our collective +outcomes. We will all be psychologically and practically richer for it. Life is too dreary otherwise.

Below are the four aspects of our being that we need to work through to align our being with any +influence attempt. Once aligned, there is unity and congruence in your +influence attempt, and the other parties will feel you are authentic and true to your intent. Without this alignment, we would be "faking it," and not likely to "make it" for long. We can all sense when someone's heart is not in it.

- Personal qualities
- Emotions
- State of being
- Conative

A majority of professionals and leaders are aware that beyond logic, emotions and other aspects of their being are powerful weapons in +influence. Not surprisingly, non-logical levers are used less, though in our personal experience, far less than this self-assessment from LinHart research involving 189 American professionals and leaders indicates. What is your answer to this question? Just imagine how much more effective our influencing attempts will be if we are always able to bring not just logic, but also our emotions, principles and values, and our full presence?

For each influence attempt, ask yourself what personal qualities, emotions, state, and conative you need, to effectively influence yourself and others to think, feel, and act according to what is required for +outcomes. In the second disconnect example, senior management needs to see a good rationale for the USD 3 million top-up investment and, more importantly, a confident project leader who believes in it.

Table 3. Bringing different aspects of ourselves to bear when influencing others.

Question: When I influence others, I bring the following aspects of myself to bear.

	Occasionally, seldom, or never (% of respondents)	Often (% of respondents)	Always (% of respondents)
• Tight, compelling logic with facts, analysis	34%	49%	17%
• How I feel, and how I'd like others to feel (emotions)	42%	38%	20%
• My being (*e.g.*, principles, values, spiritual truths)	40%	38%	22%
• A grounded, centered, present state of being	39%	48%	13%

Source: LinHart research involving 189 American professionals and leaders.

Notwithstanding his nervous energy, the project leader must demonstrate conviction and courage to get anywhere with that request.

In one of our MBA HOP[85] sessions with a senior executive,[86] where he played himself as the then CEO of a large consumer-facing business, his immediate feedback to the student marketing team was, "Even before I get to your final recommendation, I have trouble with your conviction. You came across as if you don't believe in it!" The students' being, specifically their convictions, betrayed them.

Winston Churchill's personal fearlessness inspired the same in Britons during World War II,[87] because empathizing with fears can stimulate courage in others. He was inspiring even when he was brutally honest about the reality. "I have nothing to offer but blood, toil, tears and sweat." That was what he told the House of Commons before he asked for a vote of confidence in his government.[88] You need to uncover what the influencee needs to think, feel, and act in a desirable manner; dig into your own being for the needed qualities, emotion, and mind-state; and express them in a way that will be well received.

For the husband and wife talking about life struggles, the husband may be comfortable talking about his emotions, whereas his wife may be flooded with emotions and need time to process before continuing the conversation.

Case 10.9 Failure to dissent makes everyone look bad

You (Vaibhav[89]) — the project manager of a well-regarded consulting firm — feel ashamed that you let your client down and didn't contribute to the discussion regarding how extensively to launch a new product of your client company. The CEO of the Asian consumer goods company who hired your consulting firm had asked you what you thought about an important assumption underlying the recommendation to launch a new product across Southeast Asia, and you froze and said nothing. Your client, Andre, the head of product development, tried to defend the assumption, but the CEO ended the meeting early and asked Andre and you to not come back until you had a unified and robust recommendation. The CEO walked out shaking his head and seemed disappointed.

(Continued)

(Continued)

The meeting was to get the CEO's go-ahead for the recommendation to launch a new product across Southeast Asia, instead of the alternative of launching the product in one country, *e.g.*, Indonesia first. This meeting was the culmination of four months of hard work. Andre and you had debated the issue of a regional versus one-country launch extensively, and you reluctantly agreed to go with Andre's recommendation of a region-wide launch.

Though you have a good working relationship with Andre, you find his style difficult to deal with. Andre is 20 years older and the most aggressive senior executive you have worked with. With Andre persistently pushing you to go with the regional launch option, you started to doubt whether your concerns were valid. You struggled to voice concerns you had. The partner for your project, Chang Lee, had been out of action for two weeks right before the review meeting due to health issues, so you had no one else to turn to for help.

As an MBA grad from a top school, this is the kind of project you dreamed about working on, and you are not going to let this end on a horrible note. You feel disappointed in yourself that you haven't risen to the challenge, so far. In the meeting, the CEO asked the same kinds of questions you had, but you couldn't articulate them with enough strength and confidence like the CEO had.

Everyone except Andre has left the room, and you can see that Andre is angry and wants to talk to

---

(Continued)

(Continued)

---

you. You realize you need to admit your mistakes(e.g., not telling Andre how strongly you felt about the regional launch, failing to be a "high-challenge" thought partner). At the same time, you need to give Andre feedback.

Analyze: What has contributed to the fiasco so far? How does Vaibhav need to align his being and the influence?

Personal Qualities

Because everything we say and do is the length and shadow of our own souls, our influence is determined by the quality of our being.

— Dale Turner

Are only a few leaders born with special qualities, or can all of us uncover these qualities in ourselves? Nature versus nurture[90] is a reductionistic debate. Research has decisively shown that both matter.[91] There are many music composers, but there is only one Mozart. That said, we can make good enough — if not beautiful — music by taking lessons, nurture whatever talent we are born with, and devote ourselves to deliberate practice.[92] Deliberate practice is not mindless repetition; rather, it is purposeful and systematic practice conducted in full presence to connect the activity with our inner being, processing the result with the goal of improving performance. People attributed genius to Pablo Sarasate, the great violinist, and to Joe DiMaggio, the New York Yankee baseball legend. But deliberate practice connected their being and gave them their breakthroughs.

All human beings have and underuse the basic human qualities, though a few may have higher quantities of them. Commitment to uncover and use our qualities varies greatly from person to person, and those who put in the work are richly rewarded.

Qualities are unleashed when situations call for them. The basic human qualities that support +influence are below. There are obviously other human qualities that might give you power over others, but LinHart focuses on seven qualities that are likely to encourage you and others to work toward greater shared +outcomes.

Care for others: This is a key driver of +influence efficacy discussed in Chapter 9. The capacity to care is within all of us, so we just need to care so that others can care for us. The greatest test of care is still being able to care when the other person has hurt us.

Courage is the capacity to act purposefully despite fears. We have many fears — physical, emotional, and spiritual — and rightly so; many bad things happen. We also have hopes, aspirations, and goals that influence us to act despite those fears. When we stand on the edge of a cliff, dare we leap off the cliff, not knowing if we can fly? Courage empowers us to leap, even when we don't know the outcome. History and everyday life abound with acts of small and big courage, from Ukrainian President Zelensky staying in Kyiv to fight[93] to the firefighters and doctors who put themselves on the line every day.

Curiosity is the desire to understand the world and others as they truly are, rather than staying in the comfort of our own perceptions and judgments. People can sense if we are seeking to understand them or just waiting to "reload" and reassert our rigidly held views. Being curious about people and endeavors with different value systems is especially hard, and we need to constantly draw on our commitment to shared +outcomes to keep up the effort. The payoff is worth it. Like caring, it may encourage reciprocal openness to what we care about and the finding of common ground, even for transactional reasons. It also helps us to understand the pressures and issues others face and what their assumptions and beliefs are, both essential to crafting the right influence strategy. Ron Heifeiz advises us to spend more time with people that resist us — not those who already agree with us.[94] Sun Tzu, the great Chinese philosopher, was even more emphatic: "Keep your friends close; keep your enemies closer."[95] How can you keep them close if you are not curious?

Humility. Humble people do not believe they are superior to others and do not feel the need to praise themselves. Helping others and showing compassion come naturally to them. A marker of humble people is that they are down to earth, modest, and won't seek favors in return for their support. Humility neutralizes our own arrogance and sense of superiority, which is off-putting, making others less open and receptive to any influence attempt. It puts the focus on the shared productivity, satisfaction, and growth, rather than any specific person's self-interest, helping to enhance common ground. Humility includes acknowledgement that there are always far superior beings in the universe, awareness of the blinding consequences when pride or arrogance got the better of us, and compassion for the human conditions that befall others.

Compassion is the ability to empathize and sympathize with people's struggles. It is a powerful weapon against strong negative emotions and behaviors — both ours and others. When someone is yelling, instead of yelling back, ask yourself what is driving the person's pain, and inquiring the person about what is wrong. Strong emotions, like anger, are rarely just about the task issue. Instead, it is often about the person's relationship with the task; about that person or others in the situation; or about a violation of his or her deep needs, values, or identity. Therefore, do not react to the emotions of others; feel and acknowledge them and remember the isolation you felt when you last needed compassion from others.

Persistence motivates people to continue their influence attempts despite the many obstacles or setbacks that may be in their paths. Showing up despite repeated rejections is a powerful way to demonstrate conviction and seriousness — that setbacks only serve to stiffen the resolve to continue pursuing a worthy goal. For example, the project leader asking for the USD 3 million top-up investment is fidgeting because he was eviscerated in his last meeting by senior management, where they grilled him on the mixed results from the project. However, by showing up again well prepared, passionate, and committed, he earns their listening.

Drive through passion, intensity, and a strong work ethic. To elicit strong followership, +influencers need energy, fueled by their passion for their cause and a strong work ethic, which creates an infectious intensity in building greater allegiance to their cause. Therefore, drive is an internal push within oneself, a motivation, to accomplish long-term goals. Ambition is related but different. It refers to the desire to achieve individual success as the primary source of that drive. In the purest sense, ambition serves self-centered ends, whereas drive serves both ambition and +influence.

What might good use of qualities look like? +Influencers deploy a combination of the above seven qualities in the moment. They are centered and at ease with themselves, not easily perturbed or rattled, and thus calm under pressure. They do not feel an urge to prove themselves, yet remain persistent in their cause. Persistence, together with humility and a drive for the greater good, makes it easier for them to handle rejections, which merely strengthen their resolve to come back to press the cause. +Influencers know when to lead and when to follow, confident of the value they can add through knowing themselves well. They have great courage in making decisions that may be unpopular or fly against prevailing views of how things should be. When confronted with better solutions or new information, they are willing and able to alter course. They will usually have strong followers who often go the extra mile for them. +Influencers always balance performance and compassion as they seek a greater good for all.

+Influence Personal Story: Competing Fairly

Horst Kremer was the CEO of retail banking in a two-horse race for Group CEO-ship of a major bank. At several junctures of the 12-month race he had the opportunity to play to his advantage (*e.g.*, withholding product economics and deep operating data from his rival). His sense of fair play led him to instruct his senior staff to openly share this sensitive information with the other candidate. His humility (and humble familial background from Hamburg, Germany) was mistaken by the Board to be diffidence. Sadly, he lost the race. However, his courage and magnanimity in accepting defeat impressed the Board, so much so that within a year, the Board regretted their decision. The new group CEO was floundering, whereas Horst was persistent and unstinting in sharing his domain knowledge with the new leadership with no rancor whatsoever. By the time the Board put out the feelers to see if Horst would come back and replace the teetering group CEO, Horst had gone on to become an influential trustee and trusted advisor for a top Asian billionaire with an impressive global footprint. Truth and light ultimately shone forth from the constancy of Horst's being.

Emotions

In any interaction, we are affected by our own and other people's emotions, whether we like it or not, conscious or not.[96] Intentional influencers are highly aware of how others feel and how those feelings affect thoughts and actions. They are also aware of how their emotions affect their own thoughts and behaviors. Especially during difficult conversations, strong emotions need to be acknowledged, if not addressed, before people's thinking capabilities can engage fully.[97] Sadly, too often, strong emotions are driven underground, resulting in circular conversations that leave real issues unaddressed. To address strong emotions in others, we must address strong emotions in ourselves as well.

Many task-oriented business leaders are not fully aware of emotions, in themselves or in others. This is an inner limit that can be overcome through conscious practice and reflection, as Huijin has experienced.

+Influence Personal Story: Embracing Her Emotions

Her classmates from Wharton and Harvard Business School and colleagues from McKinsey will all attest to her extremely developed left brain (*i.e.*, the logical side). As if she needed any confirmation of her weak emotional side, out of a total 34 strengths, empathy ranked as 33 on her CliftonStrengths assessment results.

Thankfully, we are not just numbers and our psychographic profiles. The capacity to feel and make sense of emotions is within all of us. Even for Huijin. The only barrier was herself — specifically, the protective barriers she had put around her own heart.

In her twenties, constructive feedback and falling in love got her to embrace her emotions. When she was an analyst, she received feedback that she was too task-focused and should also work on building relationships. Relationships means feelings. Begrudgingly, she started to connect with others and their emotions. Then, later in her 20s, when she fell in love for the first time, she learned more about emotions. Because of these negative and positive forces, she began to embrace emotions, instead of repressing or ignoring them.

Once she let herself feel the emotions, she started analyzing them. A colleague and friend, Avital Carmon, a veteran coach, noticed: "While others empathize with others emotionally, you mentalize (empathy)." Huijin used logic and keen observation skills to derive what people should be feeling and why, and how they needed to feel differently to think and act in a certain way. She found that she could tell how people felt by examining their eyes and paying attention to shivers in her neck and back that signaled the presence of strong emotions in others.

Her mentalizing ability helped her to understand what drove her emotions and what they were telling her she needed to deal with, enabling her to influence herself more effectively; this "channeling" works equally well when influencing others. Channeling requires space where people can become aware of the emotion, understand what is driving the emotion, and express it.

After sitting through three days' worth of intense emotion during *Coming into Your Own, a Women's Program*,[98] Huijin realized she didn't have to be afraid of strong emotions. She wasn't permanently overwhelmed. Emotions are like waves: they come and go and leave us with important information.

They only become a problem when we let them dominate narratives and feed our worser instincts. Just as Huijin did, we can all learn to work with and befriend our emotions.

Emotions are powerful doors to +influence. They often indicate a bottleneck that must be addressed and can be constructively influenced. For example, people who stubbornly refuse to listen to negative feedback could have strong fears of not being a good or worthy person. By acknowledging the person's identity need, the person is more likely to receive feedback on his or her actions more objectively, and not as a personal judgment.

Mastery of anything comes from consistent and constant practice, but also from the willingness to go deep. EQ (emotional intelligence) is no different.[99] There must be a willingness to befriend the intense emotions instead of shying away from them. Intense emotions can come from painful memories, but we must not let our past, origin, strengths, or anything else define us. There are many tools to help us gain an understanding and mastery of our past, even trauma.[100]

Case 10.10 Overcoming past failures

The leader of a project asks senior management for a USD 3 million top-up investment on a risky project but was nervous and fidgety when he made the request in a presentation.

The project leader has bad memories of a failed project 10 years earlier in his career, where he advocated for an expansion only to be derailed by a global market downturn due to a financial crisis. This damaged his career then. He is deathly afraid of this reoccurring, just when he is getting some recognition again.

(Continued)

(Continued)

Analyze: How should he coach himself to think, feel, and do, to prepare himself for the meeting with senior management?

State

> **Case 10.11 CEO persuading Chairman to improve governance**

You are about to go into a challenging discussion with the controlling shareholder representative (non-independent chairman) to tell him that having 10 out of 12 board members be non-independent goes too far, to the point that the minority shareholders might rebel and make everyone look bad. You expect the chairman to get intense and insist that you go with what he wants. You know you cannot, because the opposition would be too severe. You have already tried to talk the minority shareholders down, and they have agreed to some concessions, like not calling for the resignation of the non-independent chairman.

You are aware that your own ability to retain your composure, not react, and be open to the chairman while encouraging him to see the bigger picture is key. This is not easy; you also find the situation highly discouraging. However, you know you need to do this and can do this.

(Continued)

(Continued)

Analyze: How might you best influence the controlling shareholder to see the wise action in his own interest? What state of being do you need to be in to best execute this, and what must you do to maintain that state?

State refers to "the particular condition that someone or something is in at a specific time."[101]

For +influence, the overall state of a person — especially the coherence between mind, body, and heart in the influence moment — impacts its efficacy the most. We cannot help but pick up others' state of being and make rapid, unconscious calculations of what it means. Significant misalignment will dent any +influence attempt.

Why is the overall state of a person so consequential? The state of the influencer we observe in our work impacts the state of others who are being influenced and their thoughts, emotions, and actions. We intuitively interpret the overall state of a person as signals of the person's intentions, motivation, emotions, capabilities, and attitude.[102] For example, everything else being equal, a project leader that is calm and collected will be perceived to be more confident than one who is fidgeting and noticeably nervous. However, calmness isn't the all-weather state. For a couple having intense discussions about their life challenges, one spouse's calm state is likely to be interpreted as not caring, whereas being worked up might signal caring.

When shaping your influence attempt to achieve +objectives, you must ask yourself what state would most likely encourage the other person to think, feel, and do what is necessary for +outcomes. Then, you need to meditate and work on yourself to embody that state during the influence attempt. This requires constant practice of tuning into and channeling your own energies and emotions to bring out what is needed at a particular time. This self-mastery is the holy grail of +influence.

Common states you should be able to call upon or identify in yourself and others include:

- Calm
- Intense
- Agitated
- Nervous
- Tired
- Excited
- Emotional
- Open/closed
- Withdrawn/disengaged/doesn't care
- Interested

Case 10.12 Leadership presence in a town hall

The CEO gives a speech in a town hall meeting with 300 staff. She encourages people to speak up about problems in the company but doesn't take any questions. She seems to be in a hurry to leave.

Analyze: What state would be consistent with the CEO's stated objective of encouraging people to speak up? What other actions, words, and feelings are necessary as well?

Conative

As long as the reason of man continues fallible, and he is at liberty to exercise it, different opinions will be formed. As long as the connection subsists between his reason and his self-love, his opinions and passions will have a reciprocal influence on each other, and the former will be objects to which the latter attach themselves.

— James Madison

We define conative as a proclivity (*i.e.*, a bias, a tendency) to process emotional and rational stimuli in a way that results in actions in a preferred, often intuitive direction.[103] Often, we observe that a person's conative lands behaviors in a certain way even when our thoughts and emotions may point differently on their own. When we have a strong conative, we find it much easier to make choices and act on them. It does not mean we are making the right decisions, just that it is easier to come to a decision. Those with a weak conative tend to be swayed by what others say, often having unstable (flip-flopping) decisions or inconsistent algorithms for landing on emotional versus logical calls. You can see from how they interpret what is right versus wrong, and what is right versus expedient. Therefore, developing a strong, clear conative helps in being an effective +influencer.

While it is impossible to describe one method to determine an individual's conative, there are some generalizable aspects of developing one's conative that apply to most people.

The first aspect is to move from a reactive to a creative orientation, a framework codified by William Adams of the Leadership Circle group.[104] A reactive orientation avoids bad things out of fear, keeping yourself safe and secure against failure, displeasure of others, and being overwhelmed. A creative orientation, motivated by hope and love, is about taking action and making sacrifices in service of a positive future that you think is important, even though it may be uncomfortable and risky. Reactive orientation is directionless, whereas a strong creative orientation has a clear north star. People can sense, through words and body language, whether you are operating from a reactive or creative orientation and will respond accordingly. A reactive orientation is likely to engender reactive reactions (*e.g.*, control, self-protection), whereas a creative orientation will encourage more openness to behaviors (*e.g.*, caring, relating) required for +outcomes. This creative-reactive ratio will strongly hint at the person's conative.

Another aspect is moving from meeting other people's or society's expectations and standards of what is good to developing our own internal locus of what is good and worth fighting for. While the latter does involve an individualistic, potentially self-focused phase, it equips people to address external pressures (*e.g.*, societal pressures) on their own terms, expressed in what is higher productivity, satisfaction, and growth for both organizations and individuals. While social and family pressures can be powerful influencers of behavior, they are not necessarily aligned with +influence, which allows people to freely choose to be influenced in a certain way.

A third aspect of conative is whether you are working mainly for your own individual achievement (as in "ambition" discussed earlier) or are focused on the success of a larger collective. In other words, are you focused mostly on yourself or on others? When people sense you are working for the whole, they are also more likely to do the same and make sacrifices.

Carl Jung says that one key life task we all have is individuation, when we develop our own sense of what we want to aim for in life, what we're willing to do to get it, and how we uncover inner resources to make it happen.[105] This becomes a powerful lighthouse for our actions and choices, enabling us to constructively deal with the pressures and demands of others and society. Without this lighthouse, we have multiple lights flickering in the distance and in ourselves, making it difficult to decide what to do and where and how to influence in any situation. This lighthouse is both to be found and built, in the sense that no one can build one for us to merely discover, but we cannot make up this lighthouse out of nothing either. We must uncover enough of our true selves to see what the lighthouse could be, in our society, family, and organizational contexts.

+Influence Personal Story: Turning Down the Call to Become a CEO

Tsun-yan's conative revealed itself unaided over two decades and crystallized through pivotal choices he made, such as whether to become a CEO himself. Unlike most professionals who want to move to the "buy side," he was more ambivalent. He was never one to follow the conventional path.

In his late forties, Tsun-yan got three offers to be a CEO and turned them all down. The first one was in Canada, followed by two in 2000, the year he returned to Singapore. These were prestigious, tempting offers for a consultant. Finally, when he retired from McKinsey at 55, he got another surprise offer. He agonized over these decisions but finally said no to them all.

These were hard decisions for him. One gets far less respect as a consultant than as a CEO. But the point of life isn't just about prestige; it is to be of service to society while simultaneously being true to oneself. Those two deeply held beliefs are part of Tsun-yan's character and hence worth making sacrifices for. He knew his maximum service to society was and continues to be helping others, especially CEOs, reach their best potential.

Tsun-yan has looked back at these choices and mused out loud that they were the best choices he could have made. Though he and LinHart continue to thrive, he has paid a price for those choices, in terms of prestige and stature, but he has also gained the freedom to be true to who he is and to his unique gifts. His conative continues to be affirmed.

+Influence Personal Story: From Too Many Choices to Clarity and Courage

Finding one's conative takes experience, reflection, and also courage. Joseph Mocanu's story shows how each element builds on one another, and how targeted, intense inquiry by a skilled mentor can catalyze the breakthrough. As his story shows, finding one's conative is hard; choosing to live according to it is even harder. We come across many high-potential leaders who come so close to crystallizing their conative, only to move away from it because they fear the unknown, don't want to leave their comfort zone, or get absorbed by life's challenges and disruptions. As former Medtronic CEO and author Bill George talked about in his book *True North*,[106] it is essential and so hard to find one's compass.

> *"LIFE2 completely changed my career. Getting clarity of purpose was essential. It was a huge weight off my chest. Having the courage to do something was the medium-term impact: I went ahead and did it."*

Across 120+ LIFE2 alumni, Joseph Mocanu had his breakthrough the fastest, before the three-day intensive part of the program started. "Tsun-yan and Andy (Andrew Clay, LIFE2 faculty) triggered the process during my deep-structured interview[107]... it was 90% done by the time I started the three days. After that, it was more refinement and iteration." This was a surprise. Ahead of the deep-structured interview, Huijin had informed Tsun-yan that Joseph was fairly confused, with too many good choices. This made Joseph's breakthrough and his lightning-fast and sustained actions post-LIFE2 amazing.

When they met for the first time in the basement of a Robinsons department store café, Joseph struck Huijin as highly talented, energetic, and scattered. She sensed immediately that he was different from the usual consultant. He had a PhD in medical biophysics, invested in early-stage technology companies on the side, and exuded positive though nervous energy. He was close to making full partner at his consulting firm but seemed unclear whether it was something he truly wanted. He seemed like a scientist at heart. Joseph said he wanted to improve his presence and capacity to influence senior client executives. *"LIFE2,"* Huijin said, *"can definitely help you, and maybe you can also use the opportunity to reflect on your path before going further down the consulting partner track."* What Huijin didn't say (but thought) was that there was an awkwardness in Joseph that might inhibit him from becoming a great consultant. Huijin hoped LIFE2 would help Joseph work through that and allow him to own his true and whole self.

In the two-hour deep-structured interview, and then confirmed in the three-day program, Joseph realized that his purpose was to help radically extend the human health span.

Tsun-yan helped me realize that I was burning the candle on both ends — spending a lot of time on start-ups while

*pushing for partner [in the consulting firm]. It was clear
that I was more passionate about the start-ups than my job.
Hanging onto the job to make money to support the start-
ups was inefficient and might risk me doing both poorly. I
started thinking about focusing on the start-ups full time
and started to hear the inner voice saying I guess I could.*

With that emerging clarity, it became obvious to Joseph
that he should change from the consulting path to doing
health care technology investing. He quit his job a few
months after LIFE2 and started preparing to launch his own
early-stage health care technology venture fund.

This was not an easy path. First-time funds are fraught
with risk, and early-stage funds even more so. Nonetheless,
Joseph knew it was the right thing for him — an expression
of his true self — and set off on this adventure. *"Two years
later, I have never been happier. I consciously did it and made
a decision. I was really happy I made a decision."*

A few years later, when Huijin saw Joseph at the 2019
LIFE retreat, the awkwardness was gone. His true and whole
self shone through with comfort, confidence, and conviction
in what and who he was. *"Before LIFE2, I thought I needed
to improve my presence, persuasion, superficial stuff. What
it ended up being is having all those things through clarity of
purpose and creative energy, with which everything just falls in
place naturally."*

Joseph closed his first fund during the COVID-19
pandemic, in 2020, over two years after he had embarked
on the journey. Tsun-yan and Huijin are amazed at his
perseverance hundreds of investor meetings later. With his
conative clear and pursued vigorously, his natural talent
and joy in finding health care technology entrepreneurs,
especially those with deep technology backgrounds like

Joseph, came into full bloom. In 2022, he started raising his second fund, together with heavyweights he had attracted to his team.

When asked how he keeps himself going, especially when the going gets tough: *"I am grounded by purpose. Once you find it, life is too short and too precious not to realize it."*

Joseph also keeps learning, a hallmark of LIFE2 alumni: *"For the people I meet for the first time, I would like to improve my efficiency in discerning if there is a synergy of purpose and if and how I can meaningfully help the other person advance their vision or agenda."*

11

+Influencing Through the Written Media

Case 11.13 Confirming starting a project

You and a potential business partner started collaboration discussions three months ago. Initial enthusiasm has faded away, and you are concerned about several issues and doubt whether the key success factors for a partnership really exist. You wonder, should you call for a meeting to discuss the issues, WhatsApp him to call you back ASAP, or write the person an email laying out your concerns? You are not sure what the best next step is.

One could make a compelling case that written media is more challenging than a live dialogue.

While the overall principles of positive influence apply to written media, written media (*e.g.*, memos, emails, SMS, and other messaging apps) have unique characteristics that require extra anticipation of what is on the minds of the people you are seeking to influence, the pressures they face, and also the dynamics from the evolving context. As opposed to a live conversation, you cannot see the person's reaction nor intervene in real time to correct a misimpression or manage a strong reaction. People's reactions can range wildly, from silence to forwarding it to somebody else, or even posting it on the Internet; immediate, open feedback and exchange is not to be assumed. Compared to live interactions, when using written media, your own and the other people's being are more opaque, making it even more challenging to determine if what is written is how people feel and if it aligns with their being and how they feel about the underlying issues (*e.g.*, how a project's outcome affects the person's sense of identity). Lastly, you must pay extra attention to pace, via consciously deciding when to reply, wait and see, or go silent, since you don't have the other person's response to pace you.

Our complex world today brings additional challenges, as we observed in our working with top executives. These risks of written communication can be reduced but never eliminated with firewalls and other security measures. First, top executives are often surprised that parts or all of an email are sent to other 'unintended' audiences. Second, written materials intended for 'internal' recipients are leaked by insiders to external audiences. Third, social media offer multiple platforms for spreading half-truths that unsuspecting outsiders might fall victim to malicious intent to damage top executives when these postings were read without nuanced contexts.

While these are often complex issues that experts in corporate communication, legal and public affairs might add value in solutioning after the fact, it might help before the fact that leaders ask themselves the following questions even before composing the writing:

- Who else might eventually 'see' this writing?
- What is the voice, tone and boundaries I might need to adopt if x and y might see this?

- What are the "white spaces" the draft writing will present a reader? By "white spaces" we mean areas left unaddressed in the narrative. How might audiences (intended and others) fill in with their own "imagination" or "content" that once added will dramatically change the thrusts and/or impact of the narrative?
- How might the communication be tightened up so that the narrative remains as intended if some parts are lifted out and quoted without the rest for context?

Some people might think the above questioning may be redundant or onerous in a harried world busy enough. Well, if the stakes are high enough, not considering the above is dangerous. The context could very well include hostile parties with malintent or forces (*e.g.*, long-time, pent-up frustration) that could explode negatively. To secure +outcomes, the writer has no choice but to take another pass through the writing with these questions in mind.

In practice, we have found an efficient way to afford such precautions simply by setting the writing aside or parked in draft overnight. Start a new day reviewing it with fresh eyes, or have someone else read it with explicit request to consider specific extra-audiences in mind. Both will go a long way to reduce if not eliminate the likelihood of "blow-ups" from unauthorized or unintended circulation.

When there are challenges, there are also opportunities for the conscious +influencer. When you have found the powerful framing and words that hit the bullseye in addressing the central issue on the minds and hearts of the relevant people, they will keep "reading," thinking, and feeling, giving you more space to make the case in a more structured and comprehensive fashion than live conversations allow. In an era of declining attention spans, written media still has the power to get people to settle down and dive deep into issues.

The starting questions to lean into written media are:

- When do you use written media versus calling someone up for a live two-way dialogue?
- What process should you follow when writing to hit the bullseye?
- What other key success factors of written media are there?

When to Use Written Media

When you do not need to or cannot reach the other person easily, written media is good. While there are constraints, the written form has one time-tested advantage over the spoken word: written messaging gives influencees time to read and absorb it and reflect on the substance and the implications of your message. Whether it is 160 characters in a typical SMS from the dumb-phone era or an email or memo, recipients can revisit and reflect on alternative views before replying. Length isn't a constraint for substance. For CEOs we work with, we use both 15-page essays, WhatsApp, and other things in between. The limited length of text messages forces us to really hone in on the key issue and what we want the person to think, feel, and do.

Selecting the issues you want others to reflect deeper on, and which issues benefit from immediate reactions and two-way dialogue is the next consideration. Distinguishing the need for individual reflection drives the choice of the right mix of media, assuming timing works. More complex issues typically have multiple influence moments and, therefore, the opportunity to use a combination of media. Cases 11.1.F–G earlier in this chapter are good examples.

Pre-reading to lay out the key issues, get focused inputs on issues on people's minds via WhatsApp, and invite voluntary reactions are some good uses of written media to prime for an in-person interaction later. Having served on boards, for-profit boards across six stock exchanges, and not-for-profits in essential services, Tsun-yan has learned a few good practices to share:

- Pre-reading, including thinking about the contents, should be limited to no more than one hour for every half-day meeting in-person for board directors; 1.5 hours for advisory boards and 2 hours for management. This may sound counterintuitive, but based on our experience serving on boards, board of directors need more time to deliberate and debate decisions that come to the board.
- Use a one-page summary upfront to tee up whether this agenda item is for information, discussion, or decision making at the upcoming meeting. If for discussion, what inputs are sought? If for decision, what is being decided?
- Limit the general surveying of participants to before or after the meeting. People are fatigued by excessive surveys. If needed, keep it to three questions and say upfront for how the inputs will be used.
- Targeted inputs are better with selected participants of pertinent backgrounds or expertise.

A similar discipline applies as well for simpler interactions — including a job interview, a feedback session with your boss, and a life expectations conversation — which will pay dividends. The process forces you to think: For the influence objectives to be achieved, what are the key issues that require airing, what are your and other people's incoming assumptions and beliefs, and what remains to be addressed following an in-person meeting? For a job interview or feedback session, dropping the interviewer or the boss a note is usually a good idea. Thank them for taking the time and emphasize one or two messages. Give them a question or something to consider.

Lastly, there are some situations where writing is essential, such as when there is no recourse (*e.g.*, confirm results of negotiations), you have one last chance to rescue a relationship (and the person refuses to talk to you), or to reach closure. Lastly, when the other party has far more power, writing can also be better in leveling the playing field.

Writing to Hit the Bullseye

With written media, you cannot elaborate on or change what you've written based on the other's response. Therefore, you must get it right the first instance and land the points by being more thoughtful and disciplined — and then adjust as you go in a more interactive in-person mode.

Prior to writing, questions one must consider include:

- Influence objectives: What do you want the recipient to think, feel, and do? Toward what task and relationship objectives?
- What are the key issues to be addressed to achieve the influence objectives, from your perspective as well as the perspective of others you are influencing and other relevant stakeholders? Issues could be logical and/or emotional.
- Timeliness: Understand the window within which you can still influence. When is it still timely? "Timely" means the other person remains open, and a reasonable influence attempt can be made. Things that required immediate, urgent attention might be more suited for a message, whereas documents for an important meeting should be received a few days early, but not too early, which could have unintended consequences (*e.g.*, people gossip about it).
- What is your own state of thinking and feelings on the matter? This is especially important if what you are

writing could trigger a strong reaction or emotion. Many people have developed the habit of not sending an angry reply right away.

Writing has traditionally been a good way to convey relational messages. It remains true today. In writing, emotional messages can also be more easily calibrated — such as through tone, degree of formality, and action words (edgy or less) — avoiding getting caught up in emotions and dynamics. If need be, words that convey a gradation of emotion can be "tried on" to see which is closest to how you think and feel and thus be genuine and congruent.

Case 11.1.F New service launch

As the executive sponsor of the new product launch, you (Sue-Ann) write biweekly reports to the CEO documenting progress made and issues to be addressed. Having had heart-to-heart chats with the project manager, Vik, and the team in the last week, you feel it is important to quickly address the performance issues of the launch so far and how the project team wants to pivot the approach. You also wonder if you should address your distractedness, and how you plan to correct that. Thankfully, the next report is due in 10 days, so you have some time to make a judgment. While you want to be honest, you don't want to look bad, especially since the project of your competitor, Henrique, is doing far better.

Analyze: What should you include vs. exclude from the report? How much of the project issues, and how your leadership of it should be revealed? To what intended task and relationship objectives?

Conciseness and Clarity

We are all apprentices in a craft where no one ever becomes a master.

— Ernest Hemingway

People have limited time and attention. Unlike with friends and family, in business, politics, or community service, there is often no opportunity to have the same conversation again. Unclear and unconcise communication is not just poor writing; it often betrays unclear thinking. Regardless, it creates doubt and confusion and muddies the influence attempt.

Conciseness is expressing ideas effectively without redundant words (or sentences).

Clarity is when the intended idea is conveyed and easily understood by others.

Clarity requires knowing what you want to say and conveying it using sound logic. Sound logic refers to the argument making sense logically and being the best explanation (solution) of an issue. Conveying what you want to say using sound logic requires using a suitable structure to organize and convey your thoughts. There are two classic structures that can work across most situations: governing thought backed up by three supporting thoughts,[108] or the story (situation, complication, and resolution). While the governing thought structure is seen more often in business (*e.g.,* in presentations), the story structure can be a more compelling way. For example, Sue-Ann can talk about the fundamental opportunity behind the new service, complicated by challenges of its launch and how she and the team propose to address them.

The Elements of Style, by Strunk and White, has classic tips on clear and concise communication:[109]

- Convey one idea per paragraph.
- Use short sentences.
- Use simple words.
- Cut out superfluous words and sentences.

We have a practice of writing the central thought in 160 characters (SMS length) because it forces us to get to the essence of the issues and influence objectives. Give it a try. Allow yourself only one message — not a string of messages. This can help you tighten up a longer writing.

One way to check whether your communication is clear is to read your communication from the perspective of the receiver. Imagine you have no further opportunity beyond this attempt. Would the receiver get what you are trying to say? How would the receiver feel? What would he or she want to do? In the process, you can check your assumptions of what the receiver knows. Getting feedback from others on your writing is another way to assess and improve the conciseness and clarity of your communication.

Going from unclarity to clarity is normal for written media — if you are willing to put in the work and address the issues the feedback process surfaces. If you are sometimes not clear, it may be useful to see where the problem lies. It could be your inner conflict or muddled thinking. Are you crystal clear on the influence objectives? Are you clear about where you stand on the key issues? In high-stakes situations, it is normal to be afraid and anxious of the consequences — what happens if we're successful or not successful. If we don't work through these fears and anxieties, our conviction and confidence will be affected, and execution of the influence commensurately poor. You can refer to Chapter 10 on how to work through such fears and other tensions as part of aligning your being with the influence.

Pace

Many people don't think for a second about when to respond to or initiate a written message. They may assume that a message should be replied to immediately to show that they are on top of things. That is especially true when replying to an authority figure such as a boss. We have found it useful to ask the question: Within what time frame should I respond to give the right impression of urgency, cadence,[110] thoughtfulness, and intensity of emotions?

Try experimenting with each and see what you take away from them:

- Urgency: the time of day and how soon a reply is expected or made. Sending a message late at night with an explicit ASAP request is full of urgency. This should be rarely used lest the sender is seen as unreasonable and insensitive.
- Cadence: relevant when a series of written messages are sent back and forth discussing a matter. A consistent frequency (*e.g.*, once a day) is suitable for daily updates, whereas once every five minutes sets a different urgency if an update or information sharing is needed for a quick resolution. Format introduces another variable to influence the depth and formality of messaging. Therefore, a full written report twice a year, interspersed with informal monthly email updates, could strike a balance of how much effort goes into formality versus timely updates.

- Thoughtfulness: some issues require a deeper reflection or data acquisition prior to a response. You could send an interim response saying, "These two issues could use some evidence gathering; let me get back to you after I have the data." Otherwise, you risk confusing a well-founded view with a visceral opinion if you reply with a position on all issues.
- Emotions: the same words could accompany vastly different emotions and intensities of feelings. So, take care to use additional words to convey specific feelings.

There is a saying attributed to Einstein, "*We cannot solve our problems with the same level of thinking that created them.*" This applies to the issue of pace as well. To figure out the ideal optimal pace for a response, you need to have the bigger influence game in mind, and then break that down into different steps of influence that can then be executed via written or live media.

Case 11.1.G New service launch

While you (executive sponsor Sue-Ann) have 10 days until you must submit your next biweekly report to the CEO on the new product launch, the ringtone of your phone just went off and you have a WhatsApp message from the CEO, Jane, with an innocuous question, "What is the latest with the new service launch?" You don't get messages from the CEO very often. So this message makes you sit back and wonder whether and what you should tell her in response via WhatsApp, and whether you should write the next biweekly report earlier and send it earlier. You feel anxious about both actions since you

(Continued)

(Continued)

---

may have to own up to what has not been going well and your own distraction. However, you are resolved to address the issue and feel liberated with that prospect. You want to make sure you do it in the best possible way for your career and for your project — to get her support for both.

You are worried about your career prospects, especially since Henrique's project of expanding into the Middle East has been going well. He has delivered 120% higher than the initial one-year goals, at a lower cost against a challenging macro environment. You and Henrique started at the company together and have always been rivals of sorts. The two of you are probably the top contenders for the next big executive job that will become available; the CEO of Europe is due to retire in two years. In addition to performing well, Henrique is also active in promoting himself, calling many of the top executives of the company his mentors. You've always felt that he has had many advantages over you, such as his gender, which makes it easier for him to relate to the mainly male top executives.

You wonder how the Henrique factor should affect your response to the CEO, Jane, and how you lead the project.

Determining the time frame in which you should respond to such a big question from stakeholders depends on your understanding of the pressures that they face, what they would do or need to do with the response that you give them, and also what impressions you want to create.

Regarding the new product launch scenario, if the CEO is being questioned by a board member versus just wondering, the urgency is very different. The style of this CEO also matters: Does she like to take a lot of time to think through things and reply, or is she someone who responds right away and expects others to do the same? While you shouldn't mimic the other person all the time, you need to consider how your pace of response comes across to the other person, relative to what is demanded by the task.

Given Sue-Ann's distractedness and issues of the new product launch, everything else equal, she might be better off replying sooner to create the impression that she is on top of the issues, which is different from before. Replying immediately does not mean giving the whole story, though. To the contrary, it is a great way to acknowledge the central issue on the CEO's mind, convey the central message, and set the expectation of when greater details will be shared. The message must not be too much or too little — conveying too much might cause alarm, while conveying too little might reinforce fuzziness about Sue-Ann's leadership of the project.

Tone

Get it down. Take chances. It may be bad, but it's the only way you can do anything really good.

— William Faulkner

With written communication, people can't see any non-verbals or experience your being; the written words are all they have got, along with their preexisting impressions.

There are many ways to think about tone; for example, formal or informal, distant or intimate, business or personal, general or specific. There's no one tone that always works for a particular type of influence situation. Instead, you need to consider your relationship and task objectives. What do you want to influence the other person to think, feel, and do? What kind of tone would be most conducive to achieving these objectives?

For example, if you want to have more relational objectives, you might use a more informal, intimate personal tone versus a more formal, distant business tone. However, be aware of overstretch. If you're writing to a stranger, you can't sound like you're writing to your best friend. Similarly, if you are writing a formal confirmation of important agreements that people need to be held accountable to, an informal tone would be jarring.

You can also use tone to acknowledge the pressures that people feel. If your stakeholders feel immense pressures, a grave tone is not appropriate to acknowledge the gravity of the situation, while an airy, light tone might make you sound tone-deaf. However, no one wants to dwell on problems alone; providing a silver lining in storm clouds is a must for effective +influencers.

Case 11.14 Attracting talent via LinkedIn

You are the chair of the new talent development taskforce in a global oil and gas company and a frontrunner to be the next CEO. Big efforts on ESG have not changed the company image as a big "polluter" in the war for talent, especially in fast-growing Asia where young talents have a lot of better options. There is also a dearth of Asian women in the middle to upper ranks, hollowed out by attrition to greener pastures in the last decade.

(Continued)

(Continued)

You have heard that a Singaporean American female leader in her mid-30s is hustling to get backers to start a clean-tech fund. She has already approached a number of your contacts. They like her gumption and ambition but question whether she and the team she has built have enough commercialization experience to bring good clean technology to the market effectively. This is a common failure point for clean-tech ventures and investment funds. You feel you can help her, not only through the resources of the big oil company, but also because you have personally built large businesses using innovative technologies in your last job with a big industrial company. You are also a keen mentor of younger folks.

You find her profile on LinkedIn and proceed to write her a five-sentence email.

Analyze: Think about the best tone to use in this message: what you would like her to think, feel, and do as a result of this message. Then write this email.

We don't have to be Shakespeare to improve our use of written media. Writing to hit the bullseye with conciseness and clarity is not easy. It took us a long time and with a lot of help and challenge from others, thus we encourage you to write a lot and get feedback. If you don't get a response from somebody, ask yourself why that is. And ask in a different way. This kind of learning reflection and constant practice turns an average influencer into a good influencer.

Section III

Becoming Your Better Self Through +Influence

Overview

Section III Becoming Your Better Self Through +Influence
is about how your development as a person is intimately
linked to your craft of +influence. What you care about
and what you will sacrifice for, your unique strengths and
foibles, and the degree to which you master yourself all affect
the speed at which your +influence efficacy increases. The
obverse is also true; your outer behaviors affect who you are
inside. +Influence is also the first and last mile of leadership,
across shop floors and boardrooms, and across different
cultures. It all comes down to connecting with the underlying
human being inside each and everyone of us, and channeling
primal emotions into a force to rise above tensions and
conflict and achieve +outcomes. The ultimate payoff for your
pursuit of +influence is that you hone a personal craft —
your own unique blend of conduct and character built upon
the principles, practices, and insights in this book vested
with your inner being through sustained longitudinal effort.
This is the healthiest expression of our inexorable human
desire for higher ground. This section advances learning with
seven cases that get at the deeper dynamics of influencing
situations where there must be a personal and interpersonal
breakthrough to enable a breakthrough in the task.

12

From +Influence to Development

Our own individual effort will take us only so far in improving our influencing effectiveness. In our experience of working with thousands of leaders, 5–10% of professionals are drawn to self-development;[111] for the remaining 90–95%, some external stimuli and support are required to kick-start and sustain any continuous improvement. This chapter will deal with the attitudes that predispose us to be a part of the former, *i.e.*, work to develop ourselves — from our +influence attempts to complementary efforts in developing ourselves. Chapter 13 is about how we can surround ourselves with the high challenge high support of others.

The historical[112] account of how a piece of abandoned marble became the world-renowned statue David in Florence shows there is a gem in each of us, often hidden for a long time — only glimpses have been seen by a few — and can only be revealed through the great effort of others.

The story of the statue of David begins before Michelangelo's work on it from 1501 to 1504. Prior to Michelangelo's involvement, the *Overseers* of the Office of Works of Florence *Duomo*, consisting mostly of members of the influential art of wool guild, or the *arte della lana*, had plans to commission a series of twelve large Old Testament sculptures for the cathedral. In 1410, Donatello made a figure of Joshua in terracotta, then Florentine Agostino di Duccio completed Hercules in 1463, perhaps under Donatello's direction. Eager to continue their project, in 1464, the *Overseers* contracted Agostino to create a sculpture of David. A block of marble was provided from a quarry in Carrara, a town in the Apuan Alps in northern Tuscany. Agostino only got as far as beginning to shape the legs, feet, and torso, roughing out some drapery and probably gouging a hole between the legs. His association with the project ceased, for reasons unknown, with the death of Donatello in 1466, and ten years later Antonio Rossellino was commissioned to finish the job but was terminated soon after.

The block of marble remained neglected for 25 years all the while exposed to the elements in the yard of the cathedral workshop. Such a large piece of marble[113] was costly, made exorbitant by the labor and arduous haul to Florence. In 1500, an inventory of the cathedral workshops described the piece as "a certain figure of marble called David, badly blocked out and supine." Thus, the search began for an artist who could turn it into a finished work of art. The giant stone was "raised on its feet" so that a master experienced in this kind of work might examine it and express an opinion. *Though Leonardo da Vinci and others were consulted, it was Michelangelo, only 26 years old, who convinced the Overseers that he deserved the commission.*

Here's the punchline: "The sculpture is already complete within the marble block before I start my work. It is already there. I just have to chisel away the superfluous material." Famously, Michelangelo was attributed to have said this about his masterpiece.

The moral of the story is that there is already a "best" version of a person within each of us; the role of development is to remove the superfluous material, and let the best self come out. Each of us is a unique combination of personal qualities, strengths and frailties, operating in different contexts with unique pressures; we all have fears and anxieties that make us small, but how that fear manifests is different. Just like each marble statue is unique, each person's journey to uncover his or her best self is also unique. As we master our fears and anxieties, use our +personal qualities more, we become more effective +influencers.

The VUCA nature of the 21st century demands that we develop ourselves; staying constant, in our comfort zone, relegates us to irrelevance. We change contexts when we change jobs or become an entrepreneur, or our contexts change on us, disrupted by forces with little notice. We find ourselves having to deal with new and greater challenges we never sought, stretching us to the limit. Some challenges we rise to, but others overwhelm us. Whether you like to introspect and develop yourself or are pressured by external forces, you will find yourself in need of and benefitting from self-development. As Chapters 9–10 showed, this comes through consciously reaching into our being to deploy what we can, as well as coping with the often unconscious and messy unleashing of qualities.

Regardless of how conscious we are of our being, our awareness and ability to harness, deploy, and unleash our being inevitably grows over time. The more we are deliberate (see Chapter 10) in putting to use our being, along with our skills, the more we develop — becoming more conscious of what is in our being and how it can be harnessed to combine with our skills into a higher level of proficiency.

Having examined thousands of leaders' journeys, we find seven factors that accelerated their development as described below. The more factors are activated to work in your favor, the faster you will progress in +influence.

Role models: Most of us had role models when we were growing up. These were people who inspired us for who they were and things they could do and had done. We wanted to be more like them or at least emulate some parts of them, so we followed in the footsteps of these positive role models. For example, Huijin's first two engagement managers in McKinsey (Yi Wang and Fritz Nauck) inspired and challenged her through their combination of being intellectually rigorous and caring about her development.

Other people vow they will never inflict trauma on others like their parents or bosses did to them for having, for example, poor emotional control or failure to dissent. Negative role models are powerful, reminding us that we must consciously take charge so we don't act out the same negative behavior pattern.

For the most part, though, we are typically far less involved in learning actively with role models than we would be with our mentors (more on the latter in Chapter 13). Many of us are just content admiring our role models. For example, Tsun-yan's childhood role model was a family doctor who looked after his family, a caring and calming figure who helped others in need. He inspired Tsun-yan to consider taking up medicine as a profession. Even though Tsun-yan changed his mind later, it kindled in him a lifelong desire to help others.

That said, role models don't always need to be older, wiser or more senior. Stephen Bear, a South African mentee of Tsun-yan, was a case in point. While Steve was an avid learner and absorbed a lot of what Tsun-yan had to offer, his craft surpassed Tsun-yan's in several important areas, such as his legendary ability to create personal followership with client executives he looked after. As these executives grew up thanks to his counseling, Steve would be the first one they'd call as and when they got a big promotion or moved onto another company. Tsun-yan very much saw Steve to be the role model on this he learnt from and told all other mentees stories of Steve's great exploits in this regard.

<u>Reflection question</u>: Who are your role models and how do they inspire you to develop yourself in a specific way (versus "up-there" role models, such as Gandhi or Steve Jobs)? What did you do with the inspiration?

Opportunities: Most people's development is in response to a demand — how much opportunities and challenges stretch you and make you apply yourself impacts the speed and extent of your development. On a trip to the Canadian Arctic, we noticed that the polar bears that populate tributaries of the Georgian Bay are certainly livelier and in better physical condition than their counterparts in zoos. Because of their late summer diet of beluga whales that come into the bay and the berries that carpet the tundra where the polar bears hang out, they are a lot better fed than their brethren elsewhere. "You are what you eat," so the saying goes. Actually, how hard you have to work to get your "food" also matters a great deal. In the polar bear case, their diet means they thrive or perish.

Sometimes we hear people are frustrated by some invisible ceiling, that other people get all the opportunities. In such a case, you might examine how clear the stakeholders are about your desire to grow and develop yourself, including both risks and rewards. During the last three times you were offered a challenge beyond your pay grade, did you take it or shy away? When you had to put yourself on the line for something, did you bravely show up or put someone or something in its stead?

When Tsun-yan had just been elected a principal[114] at McKinsey, Ron Daniel, the then global managing director, came into his office during a visit to the Toronto office, shut the door, and told him: "I've got to tell you, your partners in the Canadian practice thought you were plenty smart but didn't think you would last — they didn't think you could survive in Canada as a 'fish out of water,' attracting and retaining enough clients." Tsun-yan thanked Ron for his candor and resolved to find his own clients through his own unique method; for the rest of his career, he never had to look to the office to "assign" him clients. You might also find inspiration in the story of Shaw Voon Hau, at the end of Chapter 5.

Reflection question: Do you feel your bosses or employer has given you enough opportunities to grow well? If yes, what have you done to develop those muscles yourself? If not, what are you doing or willing to do to find the diet you need to survive and thrive?

Willingness to leave your comfort zone: Little gets done if you and everyone else stay within their own comfort zone. If someone starts to move away from the comfortable, others may follow, so you might as well be the initiator. Just imagine: would you prefer to jump off a cliff or get pushed by someone from behind? Jumping off ourselves allow us to visually aim at a place and choose your moment after you have taken a few breaths. You can also equip yourself with tools to make a safe landing, e.g., bring a parachute. There is no chance to collect yourself if someone pushes you at a time of their choosing.

To get out of our comfort zones, we must first deal with the thing that holds us back: fear. And for most people, it's the fear of the unknown. A general orientation for trying new things and experiences comes easier by asking the questions: "What is the worst that could happen?" and "How bad is it if the worst did happen?" Many professionals, because of their upbringing, lack self-confidence to leave the safety of their comfort zone. Once they have had a successful experience of going outside their comfort zone, they realize it is not necessarily unsafe. This is one of the key impacts of LinHart's work, both with graduates and senior executives.

Reflection questions: What has been your openness to new experiences? Is your natural inclination to stay in your comfort zone? Why? What would you like your attitude to be (the same as or different from your natural inclination)?

———————————— $+$ ————————————

+Influence Personal Story:
Suspending Pride to Learn and Grow

Fear is not the only thing that holds us back; pride also does.

Leaving the comfort zone of being an expert to learn how to be a manager and leader is an extremely difficult and impactful departure a person can make. In adult development terms, according to "Seven Transformations of Leadership,"[115] an expert crosses developmental stages when he evolves his action logic, from being an expert to being an achiever. An expert focuses on "logic and expertise and seeks rational efficiency" and is good as an individual contributor. An achiever is "action and goal oriented" and better suited for management and leadership challenges.

This change is not just embracing new responsibilities but also leaving the safety and pride of being the expert. One must brave not being (yet) good at influencing people and working through people. Though code and academic papers can be dense, there is at least a known rationale one can learn to decipher them. However, people — why they do what they do, think a certain way, and get stuck in feelings — are mysteries to even the best experts of +influencers. Therefore, the transition from technical expert to expert leader takes a lot of courage. Joydeep Sarkar is one such leader.

Joydeep had gotten promoted in a US-Singapore health care analytics firm, two or three times in his first 18 months with Holmusk until he reached the position of chief analytics officer. This is a very important position in Holmusk, driving the entire company's ability to develop products that meet customer needs scalably. Whereas others couldn't keep up with the rapid developments in the company, Joydeep rapidly learned how to relate to the clients' needs and their business considerations. He also found himself in foreign territory while managing a large team of 20–30 data scientists.

When Joydeep joined LinHart's LIFE2 program, it became clear that he hadn't thought deeply about what it meant to be a chief analytics officer managing a large team. He was still very much operating as an expert, relying on his own ability to solve problems and create new solutions. Hearing that being a leader is about getting other people to do something better, faster, and newer than they would have done themselves — Tsun-yan's definition of leadership — was a lightbulb moment. He really embraced that this was a separate role from what he did as an individual expert, and that this role as a leader was something that he needed to get good at.

While it took some time for Joydeep to get his arms around how to change his behaviors, how he spends his time, and gain new skills, his determination never wavered. He followed up regularly with his LIFE2 faculty, Mathia Nalappan, who became a mentor to Joydeep, and got into a habit of action-reflection, drawing on Mathia for High Challenge High Support (covered in Chapter 13). The relationship has been very rewarding for both. According to Mathia, *"my motivation to stay engaged with Joydeep beyond the LIFE2 program was his high self-awareness and his willingness to make the shift, which many senior leaders who are successful in their current roles aren't willing to do so.*

I have seen the shift in his scaling as a leader over the years and assuming bigger roles including being a Board member."

Willingness to ask for and receive help: It takes a confident, self-assured person to ask for help. Everyone knows the help of others can make a big difference when tackling a challenge. Yet few people actually ask for the help they need. Why? Is this hesitancy to ask for help a part of human nature or a learned construct? For one thing, people underestimate others' willingness to help.[116] They are so caught up in their worries and concerns that they don't see the "prosocial" willingness of others to help, according to Xuan Zhao, a Stanford research scientist. They are reluctant to burden and inconvenience others. In Western societies, after all, people are supposed to be independent and self-sufficient. So asking others to go out of their way appears selfish and likely to evoke negative feelings in the person who needs help. Furthermore, people fear that asking for help will make them appear weak, incompetent, or inferior, and the fear of being rejected makes them feel inadequate and even shameful. Reframing these fears to develop a positive relationship with asking for and receiving help is a key element of self-mastery. It helps to note that research[117] has shown that seeking advice could even boost how competent the help seeker is seen by the help giver.

Our experience concurs with these scientific studies: the best leaders in our database ask for help because they are honest on what they don't know and what they need to know. The worst-performing leaders, by contrast, are defiant in the face of certain failure, confident to the point of hubris that they can "figure it out."

Reflection questions: What is your natural inclination regarding asking for and receiving help? What is the source of this inclination (*e.g.*, your personality inclination, formative experiences, or role models' inclination)?

Willingness to keep trying: This is a character-defining strength. We see two important aspects that nourish +influence and are nourished by it. One is perseverance and the other is resilience. Perseverance is our ability to pursue a goal or passion over time, sticking with it, especially when we encounter resistance, obstacles, and setbacks to seeing it through despite pain and discomfort.[118] With the greater instant gratification delivered by modern media, perseverance is a less-celebrated virtue as some people confuse it with persistence and obstinacy. Just look at the timeworn saying of Thomas Edison, "Genius is one percent inspiration and ninety-nine percent perspiration," and you'd understand. Yet, the difference is real and productive for getting +influence outcomes: perseverance calls for our ability to postpone gratification and exercise self-control in service of an unceasing drive to reach our goals. So, intentionality and goal orientation serve +influence and perseverance.

Two contemporaries underscore this point: J.K. Rowling and Richard Branson. Rowling wrote her first manuscript of the Harry Potter series in dire poverty, dependent on welfare payments as a single mother. She used every spare minute she had writing, even while numerous agents rejected her. She did not give up, believing what she wrote would be her deliverance. Eventually, she found a publisher who saw the gem in her work. Branson probably failed more tests as a student than our readers have passed. Rather than dwelling on his failures, he focused on his entrepreneurial skills and laced them with a big dose of grit and creativity. Grit, a related quality, according to Angela Duckworth, is perseverance plus passion.[119] James Dyson famously went through 5,127 handmade prototypes in four years of his Dual Cyclone bagless vacuum cleaner before settling on the model that made him a billionaire.[120] Our take on perseverance certainly has passion and therefore grit in it.

We have all heard about resilience during the pandemic, if not before. It is the ability of some people to pick themselves up, recover, and bounce back quickly. We know some of the factors that help people who have this quality: how optimistic you are, how purposeful your conative is (*e.g.*, devote yourself to a mission or just get through the day), how you make sense of and learn from failures, how your environment supports non-success, and how self-confident you are. All these factors are not set in stone, but are shaped by our own thoughts, feelings, and choices.

Reflection questions: When faced with setbacks, how long does it take for you to get back up and try again or keep going? What or who helps or hinders you from a faster return to your former resourceful self? Upon a setback, does your goal gets fuzzier, stay the same, or get even clearer?

Willingness to manage tensions and face conflicts: Tensions exist in every living organism, waiting to be channeled. Without tension, our muscles would be limp and unable to do any productive work. Even the humble rubber band is useful when it has tension: it holds things together. Tension is maligned as a word. People avoid using it unless they use the word synonymously with strain and conflict. In reality, some tensions are unavoidable, and productivity lies in how you manage rather than eliminate them. Tensions between the long term and short term and between the whole and its parts (*e.g.*, of a multi-line business) are examples of perpetual tensions in business. The desire for both individual expression and acceptance by others is a perennial tension in the personal realm.

Conflict of any kind is up another level in challenge. Be it conflict of interest or conflict in allocating scarce resources (*e.g.*, talent), executives experiencing conflict take different postures, ranging from confrontational (*e.g.*, zero-sum game) to confronting (*i.e.*, not avoiding it) and problem solving.

Effective +influencers learn to deal with tension and conflict in constructive ways. By becoming aware of tensions and conflicts within ourselves, as well as with others and with our environment, we understand more of the underlying issues that need to be addressed and influenced for +outcomes. We gain insight into how others' values, beliefs, and histories shape their preconceived notions. We register respect in how they think and feel without delegitimizing the +outcomes that benefit everyone.

Holding things that seemingly oppose each other makes conversations challenging, escalating into the zone of tough conversations as illustrated in several of the cases in this book.[121]

Case 12.15 Colleagues making fun of you

You just found out that some of your co-workers in your department have set up a WhatsApp group without you in it. They have been making fun of you in terms of how you are struggling in your job.

Your boss is part of this WhatsApp group. You had what you thought was a good working relationship with your boss. He has given you some feedback, but not a lot. You keep feeling he is uncomfortable somehow and there is more he wants to say. You have been meaning to talk to him. You don't know what to make of his participation in the WhatsApp group.

(Continued)

(Continued)

You have been struggling in your programming job. Although you studied programming, you are not the strongest programmer. Colleagues say your greatest strength is communication. You took the programming job to challenge yourself. Now you wonder if you made the wrong choice.

This hurts. Not only have you been doubting yourself, but this also makes you feel isolated too. How can you look them in the face again?

What should you do? You and your colleagues are in the midst of an intense phase of a project. You are barely keeping up. Do you act now? To do nothing doesn't feel right.

Reflection questions: What are the top two to three tensions you must manage in your business and life? In your organization? What is your attitude toward managing tensions, and how is it the same as or different from your disposition toward conflicts? How do you experience these attitudes within yourself? What are the contributors to this?

Comfort with yourself: Early in our careers, most of us are awkward, uncertain, and uncalibrated — too much or not enough of something in various circumstances, which made us uncomfortable about ourselves. As we mature as professionals, we have opportunities to become more self-aware, to grow, and to develop. Some of us stay uncomfortable with ourselves. But others gradually grow more comfortable in their own skin, thus when interacting with others, they are calm, centered, and self-assured, regardless of which parts of them — strengths or warts — show up. Beneath the surface, they have become conscious of a good amount of their inner being,[122] knowing when some of it will surface, how to deploy it when it does, and understanding how it informs and nourishes their ability to influence. A major contributor to this comfort is the acceptance of themselves as is, especially their weaknesses. It is only when we accept ourselves as is, that we can accept others as they are.[123]

Others may remain uncomfortable well into their late thirties and early forties. Even under the veneer of success and wealth, discomfort rises when they feel the need to display calmness and confidence while their inner being indicates otherwise. To make matters worse, they are often afraid of facing themselves and the voices inside, of what would happen if they "let it out" — that it would destroy the frail peace that keeps them sane and able to go through everyday life in some semblance of calmness and normality. People who interact with them can sense this discomfort: they detect an abnormal level of tension, spot the incongruence between body language and voice (*i.e.*, content and tone), and judge that something is askew or, worse still, that the person is disingenuous.

When we are not comfortable in our own skin, we deny ourselves the prospect of having this fundamental centeredness with ourselves, which imbues our choices and influencing attempts with a natural presence and authenticity that is powerful. Facing ourselves can be painful but ultimately liberating.

Reflection questions: To what degree do you accept yourself as something good to be uncovered rather than trying to be something or someone else?

Chief among the seven attitudes to be an effective +influencer is being comfortable in your own skin juxtaposed with the disposition to go out of your comfort zone. Whether doing martial arts or playing tennis or golf, returning after each move to a position of balance and centeredness is key. That combination of centeredness and then, in an instant, reaching out for the next move is analogous to the combination being referred to here.

Across the seven attitudinal dispositions, how many are in favor of your development or hindering it? You can reflect deeply on this. There are so many things we cannot control — the rise of more extreme climate episodes, whether countries live in peace or go to war, how far the interest rate will go up and how rapidly it will decline — but our own attitudes are something we can shape through reflection and critical questioning, and adapting our mental model.

It is a great joy to be able to update our attitudes to deal with challenges more constructively and with more positive energy. We wish this aspect of "evolving self"[124] for you.

Case 12.16 Inspiring staff to develop themselves

You are the managing partner of a regional accounting firm that is undergoing a major AI implementation. The implementation promises to cut down the grunt work the associates must do, freeing them to do more value-added work, like interpreting the AI analysis, discussing the results with the management teams you are auditing, and looking for weak signals of issues in the company. You were thinking this is great for associates, who would always complain about the drudgery of the work. On the contrary, they have resisted the AI implementation, complaining the system is difficult to use, results are not reliable, and clients are pushing

(Continued)

(Continued)

---

back on using it. No implementation will be smooth sailing, but the defensive, almost rejecting, attitudes of the associates worry you. You went to some of your mentees (younger partners) to understand what's going on. They told you that you have missed something, that the associates' mindsets and fears (including layoffs) need to be addressed, along with building their skills to do the new higher value-added activities with their freed-up capacity.

You have called for a meeting with the key associate representatives, elected by the associate body, to discuss how to adjust the AI system implementation. You can see them now, walking into the conference room across from your ginormous office. Your busy schedule had prevented you from talking to some associates directly to get a feel for the issues.

Analyze: How could you excite the associates about the opportunity to develop themselves following the AI implementation and persuade them to take advantage of this opportunity to be at the forefront of the industry rather than remaining stuck in the past?

+Influence Personal Story:
Telling Client he is the Problem

Early in Tsun-yan's consulting career (with McKinsey), the late Marvin Bower, one of the early pioneers and legends in management consulting, shared an inspiring story. He told Tsun-yan that he had decided to write a letter that challenged a CEO to consider that he might be at the heart of his company's prolonged performance problems. Marvin's forthrightness succeeded in inspiring that CEO to change course. Since then, Tsun-yan has often reminded himself of Marvin's frankness. Human nature most often pushes us toward conflict avoidance, but Marvin inspired Tsun-yan to have the courage to speak directly about tough issues, even if it meant risking his relationships with clients and colleagues.

Not everyone felt inspired about Marvin's actions at the time. Some considered his behavior reckless, disruptive, and undiplomatic. For those inspired by his values, the important question is: What to do with that inspiration?

Inspiration only begins its useful work when our spirits are moved to thought and action. The self is the weak link between all things inspiring and resultant thought and action. Blaming others for not inspiring us when we are not inspired externalizes the problem. And we cannot inspire others if we are not inspired ourselves.

To become self-inspired, Tsun-yan has found it useful to build three reinforcing processes within oneself: the evolving self, congruent self, and courageous self.

The evolving self is the first step in the process of achieving inspiring self. The evolving self occurs when you seek to push forward to your full potential by shedding elements of your old self and inducting new (and better) elements into your inner core. Ask people who are in their 50s or older, and they will tell you how they have changed in some important ways while remaining otherwise the same in the last 30 years.

Some people change because of their responses to life events; others put in the hard work to evolve to become a better person and/or leader. Yet, many remain stuck well below their potential because the tensions between the comfort of staying with the familiar and the pain of shedding the skin in which they have grown accustomed are often unbearable. The evolving self is the recognition, desire, and action toward continuous learning about yourself.

The congruent self begins with the unwavering drive to be true to yourself. It results in a deep self-awareness and an unbroken flow from being and thinking to feeling and expressing. In other words, congruence is "I say what I think, what I think is how I feel, and how I feel is who I am." Incongruence dampens the full emotional response to an inspiration and blocks the urge to act on it. It takes inner strength and hard work to resolve the tensions among conflicting desires in favor of truth about yourself and what increases productivity, satisfaction, and growth for yourself and others.

The courageous self is the resolve to act consistently with your congruent self, even in situations that harbor significant risk. Consider whistleblowers reporting corporate wrongdoing: they know that by speaking up, they risk being discredited, oppressed, and made unemployable. But their will to abide by their own values in the face of adversity inspires them to act for the greater good. It also applies to the choices we make in our own lives and careers, which are equally risky since they sometimes require us to give up all that we have known, recognition from others, and our confidence and identity.

Inspiring yourself is integral to the never-ending journey of becoming a better person. Without it, the inspiration we receive from others does us no good.

13

How Others Can Help You Develop

Our chief want is someone who will inspire us to be what we know we could be.

— Ralph Waldo Emerson

Having a positive attitude toward +influence and development is foundational. Doing something to help yourself and allowing the right people to help you will certainly accelerate that trajectory. This chapter introduces two things that have worked well for LinHart in client and graduate programs. The first is to create a learning environment, and the second is to get yourself into a true mentorship with someone who could accelerate your development.

> "The ingredients for you to reach your best potential and tall legacy are all there. I sensed your potential for that greatness. You just need to work on your repertoire of influence to equal your best potential.
>
> Today, if you please forgive me for saying so, based on your narrative, you are a sophomore in influence when your leader gifts should put you up for a doctoral. If you improve your influence, it means less resistance from others, and learning full spectrum 'seeing' from others' perspective, not taking noises at face value. People mean something

else whenever what they say doesn't make sense. Above all,
work on harnessing the beautiful human qualities that are
already within you to influence positively, towards realizing
your true potential.

I shall remain a fan of that great leader that is already
in you!"

While Tsun-yan wrote this to encourage a senior leader who was facing resistance in an organization he was struggling to understand, the same encouragement could apply to all of us. We all need help, can help each other, and occasionally need professional help.

Demands of life, business and indeed societal forces all create tremendous influence challenges, every day and especially in certain critical junctures. Our constant frustrations, mental health issues, and task failures are all symptoms of our +influence ability not being at the level required to ace those challenges. While +influence is not the be all and end all, it is something we can do about, versus other uncontrollable factors, *e.g.*, ChatGPT (the highly intelligent AI chatbot which can write essays on any topic) automating large parts of our jobs.

The choice is therefore ours: will we apply ourselves to the hard work of developing our +influence ability and, in the process, uncover our best and whole self, individually and together with others? It's absolutely one of the best choices all of us could make in life, irrespective of field of work, level of ambition, and place of residence. We all must contend with people who are different from us, contexts that change on us at a moment's notice, and disruptions that upend our pre-existing coping mechanisms. We might as well approach this unshakeable reality of human life with curiosity, courage and compassion, and not let our fears, fatigue, and desire for easy answers get the better of us.

Create or Immerse Yourself in a High Challenge High Support Environment

Throughout Tsun-yan's four decades of helping people, unleashing people to do something faster, better, and new — beyond their own preexisting capability — has been a central theme. He does it with individuals through one-to-one counseling and many leadership teams and groups, and he has taught CEOs how to create such an environment in their companies, to raise business performance, uphold people's pride[125] and raise skills through a combination of inspiration, challenge (sometimes a "forced march"),[126] and support. In all cases, there will be a strong challenge for the individuals — with opportunity, the need for change, the consequences of not changing, *etc.* There will also be strong support — encouragement, resources, advice, and guidance where appropriate.

Huijin had separately discovered the importance of having both challenge and support via an American teaching manual about how some inner-city teachers created a unique classroom environment to enable disadvantaged inner-city kids to perform well academically, much better than the norm.[127] LinHart has coined the term "High Challenge High Support" (HCHS) to meld the two streams of experiences into a reliable, repeatable methodology.

Our environment shapes our sense of what is normal, good, and bad. Across the wide gamut of influence experiences and influencer profiles, we have observed that we learn a lot faster and improve our +influence efficacy if we are not just challenged or just supported, but when we experience both together.

In the HCHS environment LinHart has shaped, stretching yourself will be the norm, and you will be well supported without much conscious effort on your part. You will welcome being pushed outside your comfort zone because, without exception, everyone will have their turn at being challenged. LinHart typically asks participants to grapple with situations far from their experience. You will look forward to suspending your existing beliefs long enough to consider some new ones. You lean in and engage constructively precisely when your tendency might be to move away, dismiss, or tune out because your peers will encourage and nudge you to do so. The high-quality feedback and suggestions will make it hard for you to not face your weak points, and the encouraging and supportive atmosphere will neutralize your anxieties about looking bad. People will cheer you on when you challenge yourself to tackle a tougher challenge. You learn from how they overcame their own weaknesses to succeed in high-pressure environments and see that you are all on the same learning journey.

In a low-challenge, low-support environment, people judge each other, so people feel they are safer sticking to their refuge and are uncomfortable with stretch efforts. Preconceived notions about people persist and never seem to fade away. People are cautious toward each other, giving nice-sounding but banal comments instead of constructive feedback. And they watch their backs. You worry about getting your head metaphorically blown off if you dare to peek above the parapet. Risk taking in service of the greater good? Don't even think about it lest people think you are acting above your pay grade, grandstanding, or are too naïve and stupid to trying something out of the ordinary.

However, even in low-challenge, low-support environments, you can shape an HCHS subculture. You can find a handful of kindred spirits who want to do the same thing and resolve to provide HCHS to each other. That's a cabal for change. Over time, your success will attract more people to be a part of the HCHS culture.

The power of a high challenge and support environment can be seen in the real-life experiences LinHart has had in its programs. The table below arrays the impact measures from four runs of an undergraduate-level leadership influence program (~50 participants each run), along with the stable long-term (across 10 different runs, 200+ participants each run) average experience of our MBA-level leadership influence program.

You can develop HCHS muscles at the individual (Table 4) and group levels.

Table 4. Key High Challenge High Support behaviors at an individual level.

High Challenge (Stretch the person)	High Support (Strengthen the person)
• Show them the gap between their intent and impact • Challenge the person to reflect/think deeper and differently • Show the person how much more potential they have, but aren't owning/acting on • Help the person face up to and remove blockers (*e.g.*, fears, limiting beliefs, identity) • Share your own challenges and stretches • Volunteer someone for a challenge • Hold someone accountable for the change/improvement goal they set	• Teach/coach the person on a specific challenge • Affirm the person for progress made, stretches attempted • Encourage, enthuse, and energize the person • Have and show faith and belief in the person's intent and ability to change/grow • Accompany them to a "challenging" meeting • Change stakeholders'/organization's perception of the person

Table 5. Role of High Challenge High Support in driving development of influence skills and leadership.

Impact measures (out of 5)	Undergrad program run 1	Undergrad program run 2	Undergrad program run 3	Undergrad program run 4	MBA level program
% of students who pushed themselves out of comfort zone	70%	25%	11%	55%	60%
Learned useful communication and influence skills	4.9	4.4	4.1	4.5	4.5
More aware of the broader skills a leader need	4.8	4.2	3.9	4.4	4.4
More aware of personal qualities I want to develop	4.7	4.2	3.9	4.3	3.9
Increased my aspiration to be a leader	4.5	3.8	3.4	3.9	4.1
More confident	4.3	3.9	3.7	4.2	4.2
Increase in the level of knowledge on the topics taught	+1.5	+1.3	+1.4	+1.7	Not tracked

Source: LinHart program feedback from participants over a decade.

Exercise: Reflect on the frequency (on a scale of 1 to 5) to which you practice each of the behaviors in Table 5 and sum up the scores to get a sense of how much you are providing HCHS to others. You can also do the same exercise in relation to yourself (*i.e.*, how much others exhibit each of these behaviors toward you).

Failing to grow together

HCHS doesn't just occur in the workplace, but is equally important in our most important relationships, in our families, and among spouses, as the following case illustrates. Growing together is hard, and growing apart is painful. The pivotal question is how we deal with those closest to us changing, hence changing our relationships with them. While a good outcome can never be guaranteed, a HCHS approach can make a difference in tackling the issues and in saving the relationship, albeit in a different, evolved form.

Case 13.17 Failing to grow together

Chilin has a wonderful career in China as an upcoming senior executive in Procter & Gamble, one of the leading consumer goods companies globally. She is the chief marketing officer at the relatively young age of 37, makes a high salary, drives a Ferrari, and lives in a penthouse apartment with her husband Lee Fung and their poodle. But all is not well in Chilin's seemingly fairytale life. Her marriage has been unraveling for some time. Lee Fung and Chilin met when they were both getting their Master's degree at BeiDa (or Peking University). Back then, they shared a lot of the same ideals and passions for life. Lee Fung is a historian and joined the university's history department; his career never took off as much as Chilin's. As Chilin got more and more successful, the distance between them increased further and further. They found that they had less to talk about, and Lee Fung would get quite resentful of the time that Chilin spent at work and on business trips. He

(Continued)

(Continued)

has even asked her to stop working a few times which makes her angry. There is similar pressure from both Lee Fung and Chilin's parents, which didn't help the matter either. In her heart of hearts, Chilin knows that her relationship with Lee Fung is not really working — not for him and not for her. She yearns to have that old Lee Fung back, the idealistic, passionate person who had a joy for life, who had ambition, and who understood and encouraged her ambitions. Now it feels like they are on two very different planets. But the prospect of separation and divorce is very daunting since it's still frowned upon in her social circles in China. Chilin doesn't know how she could possibly explain it to her own parents as well as to Lee Fung's parents. But she knows that she has to talk to him because this current state is not sustainable. They have had another big fight, and Chilin is fed up.

Analyze: What should Chilin's influence objectives with Lee Fung be in the opening conversation?

High Challenge High Support among Groups

The HCHS environment is a core and distinctive feature of all LinHart programs and leadership counseling. It is the water level that lifts all boats.

There is a high correlation between the percentage of participants who do HCHS out of their own volition and the collective impact of the program felt by all participants. The HCHS attitude to learning and leading will propel participants to aspire for more, go beyond their comfort zone/past success, be okay with not knowing the answer, and embrace steps — not just incremental changes. People egg each other on positively, not leaving anyone behind.

While the expectations and behaviors of the appointed leader (*e.g.*, the faculty of a class) play a disproportionately important role in encouraging HCHS, only participants can be committed to making the HCHS environment happen.

To catalyze this commitment, in every LinHart program, we prompt the relevant group, 5-6 peers or a class of 25, to consider and reflect on:

- Why is an HCHS learning culture important to each of you, as a learning group, and as a class?
- What mindsets and behaviors will you adopt to support an HCHS culture?
- How will you address divergence from agreed norms?
- How will you give each person space to contribute, dissent, or engage silently?
- How will you create an emotionally safe culture where everyone can be vulnerable?

In the process of reflecting and discussing these questions, the participants make the HCHS environment on their own, and take ownership of their own learning experience and development.

The above questions, and the concept of nurturing an HCHS environment, can be applied to many different contexts (*e.g.*, family, community service groups, leadership groups, and sports teams). The best natural leaders do some form of this already. When consistently applied, and coupled with a personal willingness to challenge oneself, the average leader can also bring a group together quickly and get more from each individual group member.

LinHart's programs believe in multimodal HCHS learning, meaning participants get to learn through a variety of interaction modes, including paired peer coaching, small group learning, and cohort learning.

Seek/Shape Mentorship

———————————— ✝ ————————————

+Influence Personal Story:
Creating Opportunities for Mentee

In 1998, Tsun-yan went to Aldo Bensadoun, the founder of a global retail shoe chain based in Montreal, to help Stephanie, Tsun-yan's highly talented associate, find a retail client. She was passionate about retail and didn't want to settle just doing the banking and "rock and paper" work of which Tsun-yan had a lot. It was get retail work or see her leave. Tsun-yan was inspired by her passion and determination, so he started to look for a retail client in Canada that could use some help. Ron Oberlander, his mentor and client, suggested he go and meet Aldo Bensadoun.

Tsun-yan's approach was bold and risky but paid off. He said to Aldo, "I don't know anything about retail, but I want to help you, so I don't lose a good talent who is passionate about retail."

After a stunned silence that seemed to stretch into eternity, Aldo responded, "What can you do for me?" Tsun-yan replied, "I can get one of my colleagues to make you some money by reducing stock-outs in stores and overall inventory levels, and you can invest some of that money you are about to make in international expansion, which I know how to do." Not sure whether he was intrigued or dumbstruck by his *hutzpah*, Aldo said after another pause, "But we are already international. We have a store in New York City's Times Square and one in Jerusalem." Tsun-yan interrupted him,

"You don't understand. You need to go big or go home." With the help of Tsun-yan, Stephanie, and colleagues, Aldo grew into a 2,300-store worldwide chain at its peak. Stephanie stayed and made partner.

What motivated Tsun-yan go out of his way to make Stephanie's dream come true, instead of influencing her to do the rock and paper studies? Or to just let her go?

In his darkest hour, when he was in the penalty box[128] for "poor people leadership," Tsun-yan discovered that his own struggles made him want to invest in and help people more — not less. He wanted his mentorship of people to be the distinguishing characteristic of his McKinsey career; not his ability to get business by which he became famous in McKinsey Canada and globally. "If McKinsey had a hall of fame and I were to be fortunate enough to be inducted into it, I would like the caption underneath my portrait there to say, 'The best mentor that ever walked the halls of McKinsey.'"[129] He was perfectly serious though no one else took him seriously. Few looked beyond his intense and thundery style to see a mentor's heart. "Put it in the appendix," his evaluator intoned. He did, but never swayed from the commitment he made to himself. Tsun-yan always held this goal deep in his heart and continued to mentor people in his inimitable HCHS fashion. According to Dominic Barton, recently retired McKinsey global managing director and Tsun-yan's mentee, he has mentored over 450 mentees.

There are many different definitions of mentors, and most are transitory and transactional relationships. We see mentorship differently.

Mentorship is a deeply personal, trusting relationship between two people, in which the more conscious, experienced one sees unique potential in the other one (mentee); creates challenging experiences between them to help the mentee develop the knowledge, skills, qualities, and intrinsics to fulfill that potential; and becomes vested in that mission of unleashing the mentee, with no other objective than the satisfaction of seeing the other person succeed as the reward.

"I saw the angel in the marble…" so began Michelangelo, one of the most famous quotes of possibly the most famous sculptor, "and carved until I set her free." Being a mentor is a bit like being Michelangelo. You don't shape the stone into an image that you want, but into the beautiful statue that is already there.

Mentors differ from others whose help you need along your journey:

- A mentor is not just an **advisor** who doesn't get involved in the doing.
- A mentor is not just a **teacher** who may teach skills or techniques but is NOT vested in the long-term wellness and success of the mentee.
- A mentor is not just a **sponsor** who creates opportunities that are also in the interest of the sponsor in return for the mentee's dedicated services. A mentor will help even if he or she has little to gain.

On the surface, it is hard to tell a good mentor from one of the other types of relationships. They work on the same projects together, they have feedback sessions, one's success seems to elevate the success of the other, *etc*. However, there are subtle differences.

There are five markers for a true mentor:

- *Genuine interest* in the person — what makes the mentee tick, what his or her passions are.

- *Constant vigilance*, alert to telltale signs of hidden strengths and innate talent. Some of these are weak signals or nascent, thus needing close attention.
- *Continuous thought* to determine how these strengths could be nurtured, expressed, and tested; how to build awareness and self-confidence; and what might be the next doable stretch to challenge and develop the mentee.
- *Timeliness* — be present when the mentee deals with challenges and opportunity. Importantly, are you there to encourage them when there is setback and guide them to pick themselves up? Mentors are also there to step back and interpret progress made, the next frontier, and the journey ahead.[130]
- *High challenge and high support* — to have the trust to give unvarnished feedback yet the unstinting support to help the mentee make his or her own progress.

A mentor must be unceasingly patient, relentlessly faithful, and forever hopeful.

What makes a good mentee? According to Tsun-yan, drawing on his experience with hundreds of mentees over his 40-year career, "Good mentees are deeply committed to the mentoring relationship. This gets tested at moments of disappointment. Never give up." Good mentees also have the following habits:

- Volunteer to do things for and with mentors. Tsun-yan was willing to do almost anything to be mentored by the greats.
- Over time, create opportunities so your mentor can see you in action.
- Take risks in stretching yourself, but set it up with your mentor first so he or she can catch you when you fall off the trapeze.

---- ✝ ----

+Influence Personal Story:
Learning from the World's Best

Over a two-year period around 1985, Tsun-yan set out to spend a day or two with the greatest consultants in McKinsey in the field of organization he could learn from at that time. He didn't take "no" for an answer and won time by volunteering to create client situations or simply by doing the legwork for them. Through efforts like this, he was mentored by greats such as Jon Katzenbach (*Wisdom of Teams*), Kenichi Ohmae (*Mind of a Strategist*), Ed Michaels (*War for Talent*), and Rajat Gupta (*Mind without Fear*).

On a cold, wintry day in February 1985, Tsun-yan finally got a chance to sit down with Bob Waterman,[131] of the *In Search of Excellence* fame, in the breakfast room of a motel in Boise, Idaho, where they stayed overnight for a day visit to Ore-Ida,[132] a client of his with whom he worked on an innovation project several years back. Bob was there to follow up on implementation. Tsun-yan volunteered to take notes and write the report so he could spend the day learning from Bob, a giant in the field of organization. Bob didn't have much use for Tsun-yan initially, but relented when Tsun-yan persevered, making his learning purpose clear. Over ham and eggs that morning, Tsun-yan learned more about how Bob became a giant in consulting. A golden nugget that guided Tsun-yan's own development for decades to come, Bob shared that: "I did not have one career, but related careers of 5-6 years each, building on each other. I forced myself to renew, and not become stale."

Mentorship is a rewarding activity. Tsun-yan speaks from personal experience: "I saw in my mentees potential they often didn't see in themselves. At my 60th birthday bash, this came up unrehearsed as one of the themes among three generations of mentees. And seeing them realize that potential has been some of the most rewarding moments in my life. Equally rewarding has been mentees returning to visit to update me on their progress."

Like any deep relationship, some mentorship relationships will disappoint. A mentor may even be betrayed by mentees who decided to trade in mentorship for immediate gains like advancement. In Tsun-yan's career as a mentor, he was betrayed twice. Both times, the hurt was deep, but Tsun-yan sought them out to forgive them. That forgiveness was essential to keep his heart wide open, to give to other mentees who would come later, and he did not want them to be shortchanged by any fear of betrayal. The lesson is to give without the expectation of something in return and to accept that some relationships inevitably evolve from what one wished them to be. Tsun-yan speaks from his experience:

> The world is changing rapidly. Bosses, clients, and colleagues come and go, knowledge you build has a short half-life, but the people you mentored will be your lasting legacy. So, be genuine in acting in your mentee's interest, let their journeys take you along at least partway, even if their ultimate destiny will take them elsewhere. Don't give up so soon. You would have some of the most rewarding human experiences possible if you let them stick with you for a while. Then, learn to let go so they can indeed grow, even in ways that would surpass or be different from your fondest dreams for them.

We can rely on serendipity in our walk through life's many forests, or be far more intentional in ensuring we have the high challenge and high support of others, from peers and mentors. Chance meetings of a caring senior every now and then, who might pass on some pearls of wisdom, may help along with the learning by osmosis that comes with our experiencing challenges. However, without intentional effort and investment of our heart, we get a low percentage of the maximum learning benefit from a situation because the intensity, cadence, and balance of challenge and support are too low. The two facilities shared here from our experiences — HCHS and mentoring — have proven invaluable to the thousands of people we have touched professionally and personally. Like them, by finding, joining, or shaping and then making the challenge and support happen for yourself and others, you will go faster and further in realizing your potential as a person, +influencer, and leader.

14

From +Influence to Leadership

Perpetual optimism is a force multiplier.

— Colin Powell

Lead with influence, not job title and authority.

— Rohan Belliappa

Case 14.18 Leading a difficult transformation with low staff trust

You have recently taken over as the CEO of a large underperforming health care system in the United States. Morale is very low and performance similarly so, with the system ranking in the bottom 10% in pertinent industry association lists. The IT system implementation is half done, resulting in glitches in electronic medical records and operating issues that have led to medical errors and several patient lawsuits. In your initial discussions with hospital CEOs, senior clinicians, nurses, and admin people, a depressing picture emerged. The last CEO was on a relentless cost-cutting drive and cut to the bone of the company.

(Continued)

223

(Continued)

Many of the best doctors left. Compensation for the remaining was squeezed to the point that some nurses had to take on additional jobs to make ends meet. Trust in management is very low. While they can sense you are different, they have also been hurt for too long.

Your three-month review with the board is coming up in a week, and you need to send a pre-reading soon, along with a heads-up discussion with the chairwoman in an hour. You are debating what to say to her. She was there seven out of the nine years the last CEO was around, including the five years of relentless cost-cutting. Was she aware of what was happening and the intended and unintended consequences? How about the nine out of 12 other board members who have been around the last five years?

You sigh and think to yourself: First, no matter how much they knew or didn't know, you need to air the whole situation and persuade the board to think about how to win the hearts and minds of the people. Failure to do so would result in more patient lawsuits (with multimillion-dollar awards), rising staff attrition, and further damage to the integrity of operations. Second, the regulators have already warned you that unless they see a material change in the situation, they will take stronger action than the last three warnings given. Third, extraordinary energy is needed behind the change initiatives, well beyond the enormous tasks of day-to-day operations.

Analyze: How do you want the chairwoman to think, feel, and act? What are the key parts of the conversation you need to have with her, and in what sequence? What might you sense in the first three minutes to guide you in which part of the conversation to have first?

Once you have internalized the truth that influence is ubiquitous and you are using it, well or poorly, in your life, you are already well on your way to accepting the next profound universal truth: Everyone is a leader. You are a leader. Like +influence, everyone can deploy their leadership in service of collective benefits. This chapter takes you through an abbreviated discovery.

Leadership is the social influence of getting people to act faster and better and to create a new reality that benefits, beyond themselves, others in the collective to which that influence applies. Since everyone is involved in influence and capable of +influence, everyone can be a leader. It's as simple as that.

If a work meeting drones on and achieves little, whose fault is it? It's the person sitting at the head of the table, our reflex says. He or she runs meetings poorly, our judgment continues, and likes to launch into monologues that kill time. But wait, what's your contribution to the low productivity? You failed to seize the moments, even as a junior person, when there are openings to move things along either by introducing humor or a gentle reminder to all that, at this point, you all are an hour behind schedule in the agenda. You, too, can +influence.

---------------------------------- ✝ ----------------------------------

+Influence Personal Story:
Interrupting a Powerful Person

Dominic Barton, a former McKinsey three-term global MD, once told Tsun-yan at a gathering in Chicago, "Stop pontificating! And sit down! I'd like to hear what others have to say." Stunned and embarrassed, Tsun-yan sat down quietly. Tsun-yan remembers this incident vividly because, get this: At that moment, he was an awe-inspiring, dragon-slaying, big senior partner and Dominic was merely a proverbial aspiring associate.

If it is so simple, why do most people still view leadership to be the preserve of a few powerful people? To start with, the word has gone deep into our language and therefore culture: people are conditioned to equate leaders with those few in charge at the top. Holding it firmly in place is another notion, that people who are holders of high office are powerful because they are vested with great authority to act. So, leadership, power, and authority are all words that bleed into each other in meaning and anathema to the empirical truth that everyone is a leader and can be a better leader.

Authority is the *potential* power embedded in a role or position. Therefore, the president of the United States has the authority to impose martial law in times of civil disorder, suspending all civil laws and authority. How effectively and frequently this power, the ability to produce compliant behaviors in others, is applied depends not only on the circumstances but also on the president's mastery of influence on his or her constituents. A current example is French President Macron's exercise of a power to push through raising the retirement age by two years without a full vote by the legislature. It is legal but seen to contravene democracy, resulting in massive, angry protests, possibly even greater unrest. An important corollary of this lies in the reality that all things equal, the more powerful top anointed leaders are, the more the constituents ascribe influence to the office holders.

A fascinating example of this power balance and mutual influence is the phenomenon of returning to work after the pandemic. Despite decisions by some CEOs that employees must return to the office in September 2021, return dates were repeatedly delayed, not just by the actual infection data but by employees' reluctance to give up work from home (WFH), conveyed in one form or another to their CEOs. Simply put, the actual power is played out by mutual influence and is seldom one-sided.

+Influence as the First Mile of Leadership

Case 14.19 CEO candidate with fixed preferences

Stan, a successful CEO who has completed an IPO for his start-up, is being headhunted for a CEO job of a U.S. hospital chain. He is people-oriented and easy to relate to. A pre-interview group lunch with members of the top team (that would work for him, should he get the nod from the board) perceived him as a good boss to work for and conveyed the same to the chairman of the search committee. Sensing that the job was his, Stan met the chairman after lunch and began to lay on his expectations, including WFH two weeks a month and limiting time at HQ, in Chicago, to no more than one week a month. That was before the chairman had a chance to explain specific issues with the current organization's performance, which required stabilization right off the start and what Stan might do to dig into the root causes for those issues. Stan did not get the job.

Analyze: Was the chairman, who is a bit old school to begin with, right to turn Stan down? What was Stan's contribution to this unfortunate outcome?

Look back on your career and reflect on the occasions when you just received word of a promotion, an important new assignment, or a posting. Or accepted a job with a new employer. How much effort did you expend to influence the trajectory toward success before you said "Yes"? LinHart's experience and research suggests that only a third of workers go past the hygiene factors (*e.g.*, pay, appurtenances, and benefits) to dive into mutual expectations of achievements, timing for delivery, and alignment on specific support and resources above the status quo. Recent research LinHart did confirmed this.

Table 6.   Frequency of first mile leadership.
Question: Think back on the last time you got a promotion, big assignment or changed job; before you said 'yes', what did you do to increase the probability of success beyond hygiene factors (such as pay increase, benefits and appurtenances)?

	% of respondents who took this action
Clarify your superior's expectations	37%
Ask generally for advice (*e.g.*, on what to do and not to do)	41%
Ask boss to grant you time to consider what's required for success and your ability to supply same; request a second meeting to discuss your insights	34%
Call out gaps between boss' expectation and your own sense of what's doable and find ways to close expectation gaps	22%
Be clear with your boss what are the must have's vs should have's to close the gaps and the impact on likelihood of success if the must have's are not met	46%
Ask for specific support from boss to close remainder of gaps	30%

Source: LinHart survey of 189 American professionals and leaders.

In Stan's case, +influence suggests that he should explore with the chairman the organization dynamics that gave rise to the perceived need for stabilization. Depending on the likely causes, Stan could make a better judgment of how he might need to immerse himself in the organization to validate the chairman's views and build his own conviction of how he, as the new CEO, might stabilize the organization. Of course, Stan might be wise to work at the office in-person for a month or so before he throttles back to a mix of WFH and in-person work. That's what LinHart means by "first mile of leadership" — sensing what the context really demands, people's explicit and implicit expectations, and manage stakeholders' expectations towards what is aligned with reasonable outcomes (*vs.* wishful thinking).

----------------------------- *+* -----------------------------

+Influence Personal Story:
Courage to Ask for Debt Relief

A European executive was considering whether to take on his first CEO role in a debt-laden telco. Tsun-yan was struck by what he did to +influence the trajectory of success beyond talking to his usual sounding board about the industry situation and the company's position in it. The executive visited the top three creditors of the telco (with the permission of its chairman) and enquired what their reaction might be if he were to take on the CEO role. Upon hearing favorable to very favorable responses from the senior bankers, he asked whether they could consider rescheduling the debt repayment and/or relaxing one or two of the loan covenants so there would be more breathing space for him to transform the business.

"Look," he told Tsun-yan afterwards, "I'd otherwise become part of the problem the moment I sign on as the CEO."

He added, "It will be mission impossible if I, as sitting CEO, requested the banks to go easy on the debts." No doubt the creditor banks were aware of the precarious situation the telco was in and probably gauged this leader to be the best available candidate for getting their money back. If they had said no categorically to his "unreasonable" requests, they believed he mostly likely wouldn't have signed up and the banks would have to try their luck with the other lesser candidates. The first mile started before the executive signed up because he had the greatest influence before he did. "I am not a magician, and I know what I can and cannot make happen. I would not have signed on the dotted line if there were no gives from the creditors." He didn't get all the changes he asked for but just enough that made all the difference in space to maneuver.

To Tsun-yan, this is one of the most inspiring examples of +influence at work in the first mile of leadership. Beyond his business insight and credibility, this CEO had a radical openness and courage to engage his stakeholders. Other leaders in the same situation typically go with their self-limiting assumptions: "Oh they would never go for that", "That would make me look weak as a CEO", even though the bankers may be contemplating the ugly scenarios of rescheduling debt and have their preferences mapped out. It is dangerous to leap to judgment in complex, ambiguous circumstances, based on untested assumptions. If you don't see and look for degrees of freedom, you will never find them.

Case 14.20 JV partners work out conflicting expectations

You feel the 40/60 (you/your partner) profit sharing for the first year of your venture is not fair, given the current division of labor. Your partner, Tiffany,

(Continued)

(Continued)

designed and launched a leadership summer camp program for youth in Hong Kong last year, and you two are partners in a venture to bring this program to China. Your partner's 60% share of the profits compensates her for having done the proof of concept (in Hong Kong), supporting you in the sales and marketing effort, and delivering the program for a year. Knowing that the profit sharing will change to 70/30 (you/your partner) in the second year helps, but only marginally, since that change feels far away.

You share your partner's vision for the program and believe it is valuable to Chinese youths. This is a labor of love for you. You don't expect this venture to make a lot of money. You and your partner were classmates, so there is more than business at stake.

You feel frustrated, isolated, and unfairly treated. At the back of your mind, you are afraid that you won't be able to get any customers for the training program, and your partner will blame you. You have been working so hard on this venture and other work that you have barely had a chance to talk to your partner in the last few weeks. The sense of camaraderie, though high at the beginning of partnership discussions, is fading. The negotiations on profit sharing have taken far longer than either of you anticipated, wearing both of you down.

You are about to meet Tiffany to resolve this issue and want to get back the sense of partnership you once had. You told Tiffany there is something important you need to talk to her about.

+Influence as the Last Mile of Leadership

Intuitively, we know from experience that we can plan and prepare a PowerPoint document so all the facts are arrayed properly, but an important meeting can still go awry once it gets underway. That's high-stakes interaction when leadership is made or broken by the dynamics that unfold immediately as the meeting begins. How do you otherwise get your counterparts to do something you wanted, faster or better, something they would not otherwise have done? That is what is meant by "the last mile."

Recently, Tsun-yan ordered a plain white teapot for $17 from a popular online shopping platform. One click, and it was on its way with delivery promised for the next day. It arrived as promised but chipped badly. Sure, no problem for return or replacement. So, he pressed the "Get a replacement" option. The button was there so it couldn't be bad, right? Regrettably, this was a bad choice. What ensued in the following three months was an ordeal where unimaginable things went wrong before receiving the outcomes he humbly sought — a plain white teapot for $17 and not being charged twice. Tsun-yan did not write in to complain, preferring to follow the process and persist in resolving the eight consecutive problems that the process threw up. He waited two separate days for the outsourced pickup firm who failed to show up, bought a new printer to print the return label when the pick-up option clearly failed, and talked to an outsourced customer service agent to get his second $17 back because, according to their world-leading system, he had failed to return the damaged pot within 21 days. Sure, he chose to persist so he could learn what *else* could go wrong in the last mile. You got the point: *A lot can and do go wrong in the last mile!*

The +influence basics in Chapters 7 and 8 will go a long way in helping you reduce some of the things that would not go according to plan. Having taught executive leadership programs and thousands of business school students and coached many CEOs and senior executives in their first and last mile in their leadership influencing, LinHart has come to treat +influence as the most basic building block of leadership. Put another way, if leadership is a social influence resultant from all influence attempts on the pertinent people and situation, then the most basic measure of leadership is one's ability to produce +influencing outcomes. In more challenging, higher-stakes situations, the following higher-order skills empirically play a vital role to deliver consistently more and better +outcomes.

Presencing (or Being Present)[133]

Peter Senge first coined the term to denote the ability to "act in the service of what is emerging." LinHart's experience suggests that you could start even earlier than that. Just look around the next time you and your significant other have a date night; the most obvious is a Valentine's Day dinner. How many couples are "present with each other"? Or do they appear bored, occupied with their cell phones or looking past each other at the other diners? Physically, they may be sitting at the same table, but are they emotionally there for each other, thinking loving thoughts, and spiritually appearing as one? Being present with someone means being fully there, the whole being — physically, rationally, emotionally, and spiritually. When you do, more of what's in your inner being becomes conscious to you, a vital step toward harnessing qualities like empathy and courage and putting them "in service of what is emerging."

Sensing (versus Seeing)

In an important interaction, most of us would have picked up on the more obvious visual cues. For example, they are late for the meeting, they appear quiet and are not engaging much in small talk, or they seem hurried. But if we are present and alert, we will sense — that is, become aware of — a lot more of what is going on, even before the meeting gets going. Underneath the surface, are you picking up restlessness, higher-than-normal nervous energy, weariness? When you hear people say, "I smell a rat," they don't typically mean the odor of a rodent; rather, they are referring to what their sensory organs are telling them about all the information from the external world, summing up images, sounds (including tonality of voice), touch (*e.g.*, clammy or cold hands, firmness of handshake), feel and, more rarely for business, smell and taste. Sensing, in short, allows us to experience the world around us.

When you are leading, your role typically allows you to sense certain things before you see them. They may come across as weak signals[134] in a flood of data and noises.[135] Even if you can't put your finger on it, you sense it — unless you are distracted or overly focused on what is being said. You could choose to dig for more intelligence or ask someone who's closer to the source. But it's your choice as a leader to amplify those weak signals to see if you need to act and, if so, when. The challenge for leaders is to address the problem or opportunity when they sense it, not putting it off until they see more undeniable facts. "Seeing is believing" may be too late. By the time all the irrefutable evidence is in hand, the problem could be exponentially costlier to fix, or the window of opportunity may have closed. That's why we must be more conscious of and better at perceiving.

Perceiving (versus Sensing)

If we liken sensing to letting the flood of data speak to us and pick out the essence of what's going on, then perceiving is interpreting the sensory information absorbed. To cross a road, we look in both directions, pick out any changing traffic lights, and listen to the sounds of oncoming traffic to sense the interaction of our choice of crossing with the traffic conditions. Perceiving allows us to select the relevant data (*e.g.*, the traffic light is about to change, how fast cars are moving), organize, and interpret it so as to decide whether and how (fast) to cross the road.[136] Importantly, perceptual skills are higher order, and not something most of us are born with. They can improve with learning, not only in selecting and organizing the data acquired but also combining it with broader information about the environment and with what we already know about it from the past. In LinHart's work we often encounter problems in influence attempts due to incorrect perceptions. We perceive the other party is ready to sell a puppy, for example, at $700, when the seller is willing to sell at a lower price to the right buyer who shows a genuine willingness to take good care of it. A common root cause is too much noise (thus a low signal-to-noise ratio) in data acquisition, looking only for singular confirming data based on (faulty) assumptions and jumping to conclusions prematurely. The latter involves judgment.

Case 14.21 Misaligned views of the future

You and a fellow colleague are two of the most senior partners in a large asset management firm with $100 billion in assets. This year, the market is tumultuous due to central banks raising interests rapidly (from 0

(Continued)

(*Continued*)

---

to 3–4% depending on the market), sucking liquidity out of the market everywhere. This has a severe impact on everything — fundraising, what new funds to launch, and what bonus amount to give to people this year.

During the last few years, the alternative asset categories — private equity, venture capital, and real estate — have been the darling, but now the valuations are tanking. You lead those. The public markets asset categories — simple equity funds, bond funds, and money market funds — led by your colleague have had mixed performance but are now receiving net inflows. Now, LPs (limited partner investors) are forced to rebalance, away from alternatives to public market assets, which also have the benefit of liquidity.

As you enter year-end compensation and strategic planning discussions, you know it will be intense and conflict-ridden, since you and your colleague have different beliefs of what's important now, along with the structural changes in the market. However, you could both be wrong; the world is undergoing disruptive changes that no one can predict. So, it's illogical to think he or you know the answer. You know the most productive discussion is to acknowledge the cyclical shifts, focus the discussion on the long-term future of the firm, and encourage a discovery problem-solving mindset. But your senior partner entered the meeting room with a deep frown on his face and crossed arms and avoided eye contact when

---

(*Continued*)

(Continued)

you tried to engage him in social talk. You sensed a lot of negative energy coming across and are deeply worried that the meeting will be conflictual.

Analyze: How do you frame the discussion in a way that encourages an open exchange of beliefs?

———————— $+$ ————————

+Influence Personal Story: Giving Up Too Easily

Nothing is more frustrating for a subject-oriented consultant than when the client is not helping himself or herself. It is the greatest test for one's professional tenacity.

A project to rescue an automotive plant in Ontario, Canada, taught Tsun-yan a profound lesson about perseverance despite non-change. He was the project manager assigned by the automotive company to turn around a car manufacturing plant. It was very tough because the plant manager was resistant. Everything Tsun-yan did to influence the plant manager failed. It was so frustrating for Tsun-yan that he couldn't take it anymore. The plant manager looked away to somewhere distant and said: "Consultants are like dark clouds, they come and they go. This too shall pass."

Eventually, Tsun-yan went to the plant manager's office and told him, "We are leaving. Unless you are replaced as the plant manager, there is no point for us to be around." The plant manager was never replaced, and the plant continued to struggle. A few years later, the plant lost its product mandate and 5,000 people lost their jobs, the only good job in a town which grew up around the plant.

Tsun-yan blamed himself. He had abandoned the plant because he couldn't persuade the plant manager that fundamental change was needed. "I didn't try hard enough. I didn't stick around long enough." From this incident, he resolved that he would learn to +influence better and be a lot more patient with clients, good and bad.

Much of our schooling and upbringing has to do with learning how to evaluate and judge, so we are not about to reconstruct that education. Rather, there are three aspects of judgment that come into play in determining the effectiveness of +influence and thus leadership. The first has to do with being judgmental, an attitudinal issue. Judgmental people make sweeping, generalized, yet far-reaching pronouncements often on scant or unverified information. For example, "Private school students are all spoiled rich kids!" or "He takes a long time to get to the point, so he must be stupid!" They alienate people on contact because they decree their views categorically and definitively on what is right and wrong or good and bad. As shown in the second example, there is the telltale "therefore" embedded in their view. Of course, we form opinions and make judgments constantly. Effective judgments don't have moral overtones, and stop short of drawing inferences about the person's character or worthiness.

Immature leaders also make the second kind of mistake, which is to judge others with finality and behave according to that judgment, with or without stating it. If you think someone is not trustworthy, you will not entrust the person to do anything that has a modicum of risk. There is often some kind of incidence or story justifying this judgment. But by adopting the unchanging, final position, the judge closes off receptivity to change and the possibility of a better, more productive relationship with the judged. The judge shortchanged his or her ability to produce better outcomes and is a less effective leader because of it. Psychologists[137] have pointed to this reactionary behavior as emanating from fear. A definitive judgment, to the judge, is seen to close off any recurrence of loss, hurt, and other harm incurred or perceived to have incurred in an earlier episode. Discerning people ask themselves, "Even if this is valid, what *else* could also be true?" They assume they can never know enough about the person or circumstances to claim that their perspective is the *only* truth. By being open to other possibilities, they foster a more constructive stance, which often invites, in our observations, a reciprocal openness for better outcomes from the other person.

The third mistake in judgment by maturing leaders is leaping out with a judgment that is surely before its time. We were all reinforced in school as problem solvers to quickly come up with the right answers, putting up our hands so we could share them, presumably with the slower species in class. Real life does not reward speed in every circumstance. We all know many issues, especially those that value long-term relationships (such as business partnerships, parent-children relationships), require the right timing. Being timely is often more productive than merely being fast. In LinHart's work, therefore, we explicitly teach people to gauge the time frame within which a reasonable influence attempt can still achieve the desired outcomes. We have termed this time frame "moment" (see Chapter 8 for full treatment of the topic of moments), which could be a few seconds (meaning you must act now or lose it) or years. Being conscious of the likely duration of the moment in question, allows us to take the time to do the right things, including plan the right influence, gather some additional data to test assumptions, bring some stakeholders along, and launch trial balloons.

CEOs and younger leaders alike can train your mind and heart to avoid the three pitfalls in Judgment above, to experience people and situations not as fixed, immutable objects but as ever-changing entities. Avoid generalizations by checking your assumptions, judge more the situation than people, and validate your judgment by checking whether new data are consistent. Finally, assess the best moment to jump in with your judgment.

Seizing

Catching the right junctures during the influence episode to go for it, to produce the desired outcomes, is what seizing is all about. Look for that moment when things and/or people shift, however slight or tentative it may be. It could be an expression of doubt on someone's face, a change in tone of voice, a shift in energy in the air. All these potential signals of a change from the past are gifts to the +influencer to lean into the ambiguity and gather more real-time data to better inform the Judgment: Is this a moment to seize by an +influence attempt?

The challenge many leaders face is that they sense the emerging moment but don't pounce. Or they wait too long and botch the execution in a rush for the last mile. In essence, the inner barriers for good seizing far outweigh any external factors (*e.g.*, fluidity, ambiguity) confounding the required judgment. Sensing could be a problem in not picking up the stimuli from weak signals that are below the sensory thresholds. By being distracted and not present in the whole being, we sense a lot less than what is there, for example, miss vital clues from body language. Our disposition to weak signals may also be to wait for more evidence, with some people more prone to wait and see than others. The delayed response could also be due to unresolved inner tensions that hold us back from timely judgment. We can spot this phenomenon often as suspended animation or restlessness. One common phenomena seen in younger leaders is their tension between sensing that something needs to be done but perceiving that it's above their pay grade to act on it until told to do so. In this case, LinHart has taught them to ask themselves, "What is it that I could do to improve the situation while I draw the attention of my seniors to the issues?"

Case 14.22 Family business leader with conative issues

The CEO and COO of a pan-Asian educational company are cousins, the third generation of the family that founded the company 45 years ago.

The CEO is slightly older, in his late forties. He has been distracted lately, missing meetings, and not focused on the next five-year plan that is being developed.

The COO is younger, in her early forties. She is responsible for developing the next five-year plan, first with the senior leadership team, and then getting the sign-off from the ownership group. The ownership group consists of 15 people from across three generations: grandmother, wife of the founder, three 2nd generations who are not active in the business anymore, seven 3rd generations, and two 4th generations. While the majority of the ownership is passive, three to four are quite actively engaged in the direction of the company and have strong views.

(Continued)

(Continued)

The COO is getting antsy: there is only one month left for the leadership team to finish the plan. It is only 30% done, and the CEO's input is the key bottleneck. There are important decisions to be made: should the company and family aim for more incremental growth, slow and steady, or push into China and India in a big way? A Chinese business group has proposed a joint venture for the Chinese market that could quadruple the top line in five years; the risks are commensurately high.

Analyze: What could be going on with the CEO? How could the COO find out more? What does the COO need to watch out for to avoid over- or under-judging?

As you might have sensed by now, the five higher-order skills build upon each other. Much deliberate practice and apprenticeship are required to master them to your best potential. However, you can get started with the following behaviors that, with practice, will habitualize to serve you well in a 10–15 minute ritual (additional to the regular content-driven business preparation):

1. Meditate before a high-stakes meeting beyond the normal preparation. Think about the +influence objectives that will serve all stakeholders well. Bring your being into presence with those objectives by visualizing what you will think, feel, and do that will best support all participants in achieving the outcomes. Crystallize in three single words what might guide the presence of your whole being with the stakeholders and a mental posture

that might heighten your sensitivity in your sensing of what will unfold.

2. As you step into the meeting place, look around the setting and pick out one or two things: a piece of decorative art, perhaps, that could help center and ground you.

3. Meditate on mental images of past experiences with the key participants (if there is no prior meeting to draw on, image searches online may provide some sense of the human beings you are about to meet) that would relate to or reinforce those key words.

4. As meeting participants arrive at the meeting space, dedicate a part of your being to observe and listen to the non-verbal cues of their state of being. Let that stream of data flow continue as you blend it with the content of the meeting and any pertinent occurrences in the broader surroundings or environment to prime your sensing further.

5. Check your incoming perceptions based on background preparation and past experiences to see if you need to change any of your incoming assumptions and beliefs.

6. Land these perceptions in your choice of how to start the meeting within the context of your role in the first 90 seconds or so of your participation (that's the first mile). Go down to the specific choice of words and tone of voice you feel are most natural to you and that are aligned with the three guide words you chose for the meeting.

15

Shop Floors, Boardrooms, and the Great Cultural Divide

What does it take for someone to +influence on the shop floor of a unionized manufacturing plant or in a boardroom of a listed company? What does it take to +influence in work settings across these and other cultural divides? The East versus West, sociopolitical allegiances within a country,[138] high-growth entrepreneurs/founders of young ventures versus professional CEOs of large listed companies?

One would assume these are very different environments, each with disparate cultures, languages, domain knowledge, and social dynamics, even before factoring in the impact of current geopolitical tensions. These are all good reasons to turn to specialists in each of these domains for perspectives on how to navigate them.

Tsun-yan came to this subject *after* accumulating immersive experiences that worked in many of these cultural domains, including, notably, shop floors and boardrooms. Not by design to specialize in a grand transversal take across the divides (too many variables!) nor by accumulating domain experiences one after another (even 40 years were not enough sequentially!); rather, by his curiosity about all the players in their basic human forms — men and women with their hopes and fears, triumphs and setbacks, capacity for human agency,[139] and (self-)limiting frailties. And that curiosity, powered by the irrepressible desire to help and make a difference, is the common denominator across all these cross-cultural experiences.

Oddly enough, another insight that came while writing this book is that the receptivity with these attempts at +influence is far greater in situations with higher stakes.[140] The guardedness around confidential commercial interests and sensitivity to impacts on stock prices are real — the walls go up when the stakes rise. But the human issues often seem intractable as attempts to solve them internally have been found wanting, making people thirst for connection and help.

The founding chairman of a global family-controlled MNC in East Asia had only one son to inherit the executive chairmanship, but the divisional chiefs of each of the giant business units were loyal only to the founder. "Junior can inherit the shares and be a non-executive chair. But it's unlikely he'd be a credible executive chairman like his father." This view, socialized among the top echelon of professional executives, troubled the founder enormously, threatening his strong preference for family values that would sustain, he believed, the rising global brand equity that would outlast him in the conglomerate.

The founder had about a decade, he figured, before his son reached the age of 45, before that the die might have already been cast. In this case, it was a "single pass, no fail" process[141] to get the son to become a "credible" executive owner. There was no going back once the decade was up, other than turning the reins over to a professional. What made a big difference was our connection at the human level to the chairman's heart as a father and as a highly successful founder. He understood that we understood and were committed to the mission: help his son build his own high-performing team to succeed the professional top executives that surrounded the founding chairman.

The challenge to cross strong ethnic and, in this case, intense corporate cultures is magnified in the microcosm of assembling the right team for his son. Competence is par for the course. The new team members must also have enough CULTURAL fit with the pre-existing family and ethnic values, while also having the leadership mindset and skills to help the son carry on an enterprise that would in his career be more global and less ethnically homogeneous.

Ironically, the richer and more famous the family is, the harder it is to find the right people with requisite leadership, business know-how, and values to fit a far more complex set of needs[142] than a typical professionally led company. "There were plenty of talented 'mercenaries' who would jump at such an opportunity to be a part of the team but for the wrong reasons," said another patriarch who had to tread lightly in guiding the glacial transition from his generation to the next.

+Influence Personal Story:
Sensing the Energy for Change

A second anecdote that illustrates this human connection across cultures hailed from a 2010 top management conference for Bharti Airtel,[143] in Delhi, India. Tsun-yan was invited as a guest speaker to follow remarks by the executive chairman, Sunil Mittal, whom Tsun-yan had never met before. And Sunil had only heard of Tsun-yan when he asked Chua Sock Koong, the then Singtel Group CEO and an Airtel board member, for an "inspirational speaker" for his annual management conference.

When Tsun-yan got up to the podium, he didn't say a word but trained his eyes on the 300 people sitting around their tables in the room for a minute, which seemed interminable as far as public speaking goes. He then started his remarks by observing the energies in the room, something like: "I wasn't in the room when Sunil spoke, so I have no idea what he said or asked of you. But I sense there is about 40-50% of you who are enthused about the discussion just now; a quarter of you seemed excited but vibrating in a manner that might suggest to me you are unsure or unclear of some parts of the message or what to do about it. Then there are less than a tenth of you who seem to be skeptical of what's been said. So, if change is likened to a summation of forces in a preferred direction, are you signed up enough, aligned enough, and charged up to make a concerted go at it?"

After Tsun-yan's speech, Sunil stood up and said: "All of you know I have never found any use for consultants. But this guy just now opened my eyes to the possibility that he is different. And I want to find a way to work with him." Within the year, Sunil let Tsun-yan help with leadership renewal at the telco, and appointed him to the board. Sunil, years later, thanked Tsun-yan for his uncommon "spiritual[144] gift" of connecting with people's energies and linking that to a collective purpose. This anecdote reminds us that making a connection isn't about a technique or a tool; rather, it is primarily about connecting to people through their thoughts, beliefs, and — yes — energies.

Working with Huijin, Tsun-yan has crystallized his philosophy, experiences such as the foregoing, and skills into a craft for LinHart to connect reliably and repeatedly to the human forces in these higher-stakes situations to effect an inexorable move toward the best human potential of the pertinent people. We are all at our personal "best" sometimes, when we are inspired by the right people and surrounding conditions. What if we can be at our best two or three times more often than we are now? When people are (more often) at their personal best, they are more inclined to harness their inner being, learn to +influence others, and embrace +outcomes.

In this chapter, LinHart's guidance on +influence across cultural divides is summarized as follows:

- Connect to human beings behind their appointed roles, accepting them as they are.
- Harness the inchoate[145] emotions, pre-existing often not fully formed, as a force for change.
- Pursue +outcomes with passion and value-add.

While value-add requires domain skills, expertise, and insight, all of us are capable of the first two elements, if we don't limit ourselves in how we see ourselves and the other person(s).

Case 15.23 Turning Around an Automobile Assembly Plant

The St. Marguerite[146] plant, which has assembled automobiles for the last 15 years, is in trouble. Performance in meeting the production schedule within quality standards and cost targets had fallen steadily in the last five years, so much that St. Marguerite now ranks 26 out of 30 plants in the company's portfolio, with an overcapacity of more than 30%. Not surprisingly, the head office has rejected the plant management's application for a new mandate to assemble another vehicle in St. Marguerite beginning 16 months from now. Plant manager Bob Whitehead has also just learned that the current production model will not be renewed due

(Continued)

(Continued)

to falling demand, poor quality reviews, and supply constraints. This means, without a new mandate, St. Marguerite will be shut down for good at the end of the current production year in May. While finger-pointing is going on between management and the autoworkers union, the livelihood of 2,600 workers is at stake. Being a car company town, St. Marguerite does not have much re-employment prospect to absorb the workers who will be laid off.

Joe Calderone, a young production engineer with three years' experience, has been assigned by the head office as a (half-hearted) response to Bob's cry for help. Officially, Joe is supposed to report back on what, if anything, can be done to save St. Marguerite. Joe has with him Vikram and Anna, two fresh graduate engineers, and Paul Smith, a veteran plant manager, who has been reassigned from manager of a now defunct plant to a miscellaneous desk job at the head office so he can retire with pension by December of this year.

You are Joe, having arrived at St. Marguerite at 10 am yesterday with the words of Jack, the VP of production planning at the head office, still reverberating in your head: "Look, Joe, this is an open-and-shut case. Don't waste your time beyond going through the motions for two weeks the most up at St. Marguerite. The union is hostile, and Bob, he knows the score, and there isn't much anyone can do in one production year to turn around their performance." You studied the plant performance record for the last three years on the flight over and have met with a cross-section of the supervisory staff, including one of the

(Continued)

(Continued)

two shift supervisors and body shop and paint shop superintendents.

Your meeting with Bob is at 3 pm the next day. What might you do at your first meeting with Bob? What might you do to prepare for the meeting?

Tsun-yan faced situations like the above case many times in his career. In 1985, a much younger, hotheaded Tsun-yan told a car assembly plant manager in Ontario (the same one as in Chapter 14) he would "not set foot" in his plant so long as he remained the plant manager. The plant manager was recalcitrant and unconvinced that the transition from manual to robotic assembly would go badly given poor preparation, according to Tsun-yan's diagnostic. Sadly, that prognosis came about, causing plant shutdowns and the loss of jobs. While vindicated on his moral stance, Tsun-yan has faulted himself until this day for not being more effective in +influence to save the livelihood of the autoworkers. Because of this episode, he vowed to himself to never give up on people. In a plant similar to the case of St. Marguerite, he seized the opportunity to convince the plant manager and the chief of the local autoworkers union to work together. He managed to help the plant turn around its performance and earn not just one more vehicle mandate, but another 15 years of livelihood for its 2,500 workers, by applying the below three key principles.

Connect as Human Beings

Connection and caring may sound basic and innate to all human beings, but they aren't easy to bring to bear in every work situation or for every type of person, especially those who look or talk differently from us. LinHart's database on leadership assessment indicates one common contributing factor to senior leaders who are failing[147] in their roles: a poor "caring connection" and "high distance" experienced by their peers and subordinates.

Tsun-yan encountered the challenge to connect in a highly personal way, being the first ethnic Chinese to join McKinsey's Toronto (Canada) office in 1980. He stood out as a very odd duck on the shop floors in Eastern Canada and in the American Midwest among multiple automotive (assembly and component manufacturing) plants, paper mills, and power utilities. Earlier still, he worked in food processing plants in Southwestern Ontario, where all kinds of tomato products and vegetables were processed into canned food. Devoid of a familiar background and other affinities his American and Canadian colleagues were born with,[148] he initially had to find deeper, more universal ways to +influence others to survive in his job. He was called names including, memorably, "the Iron Chink."[149] As his track record built in the eyes of his clients and then his colleagues, he started to gain confidence in blending his analytic skills of soft people issues with his own philosophy of helping others:

> When I focus on what they are supposed to be there to do (*e.g.*, the board is there to govern, the CEO is there to lead, plant managers are supposed to care for their workers and make quality products), when I see them as primarily task doers, I fail to connect with them as human beings, limiting my influence.

While factory workers and CEOs live very different lives, in different homes, in different neighborhoods, they do share certain passions; for example, the great North American outdoors. Tsun-yan could not relate to any of the sports and was greatly handicapped in the social banter that inevitably accompanied post-game. Marvin Bower, McKinsey's founder, once told him, "There is no chance you can become a CEO counselor. Not only did you not go to the same schools as them, but you also can't even do small talk about the games to get them comfortable. Why would they tell you their innermost fears and hopes that they won't even tell their spouses?" Undaunted, Tsun-yan resolved to overcome his enormous handicap in becoming a CEO counselor. Years later, he caught on to fishing when Ron Oberlander decided to take him to Labrador in Newfoundland for salmon fishing as a gift to help him "loosen up and relax." Once Tsun-yan hooked one on the fly rod and felt the spirit of life through the majesty of a fighting fish, fishing became a lifelong pursuit of his that also gave him another way to connect with clients as humans.

Factory workers and CEOs alike all struggle in life — some have health problems, others have broken dreams, money problems, or marriage issues. But family issues are the most common. Tsun-yan also experienced firsthand how a CEO's personal life can impact the business he or she leads: When a bank CEO in the middle of a multi-year transformation confided in Tsun-yan that he was having an affair with a female subordinate and thinking of divorcing his wife and quitting his job altogether, there was really no point in discussing any business objects — like performance targets, transformation plans, and strategies — until the human issues were addressed. And addressed properly.

Even the greatest leaders are fallible, imperfect human beings who are navigating their own urges, reactions, and motivational ups and downs while making vital decisions and showing up as whole persons for meetings with stakeholders. By "whole person," we mean not just rational but also emotional, physical, and spiritual. The more one can connect to that person, empathize with that person's struggle to stay on track, and desire (however fleeting in some) to have a positive, lasting impact, the more one is able to +influence.

During one of the years Ron worked with Tsun-yan closely, their dinner discussion always started with Ron talking with him about Yixin, Tsun-yan's then teenage daughter. After discovering that Tsun-yan was challenged in his relationship with Yixin, Ron stipulated that every dinner discussion begin with an hour-long conversation about the progress he was making with her. No business topics were allowed before the hour was up. Deeply moved by Ron's caring friendship, Tsun-yan not only learned about the depth of Ron's humanity but also learned about himself — his own whole being — in the process. The ensuing chat about business became richer as they factored in the whole-person considerations of the players involved.

In connecting with other human beings, we have seen that curiosity about the other person as a human being really matters. But curiosity coupled with unconditional regard is a superior winning combination. One without the other is less powerful. Carl Rogers, America's pioneer of a person-centered approach to psychology, popularized the idea of unconditional positive regard.[150] He believed that each person has within him or herself the resources for self-understanding and for changing his/her self-concept, attitudes, and behaviors. However, these resources can only be tapped if there is basic acceptance and support of that person. This means suspending our urge to judge others based on what they say or do. This suspending of instinctual judgment will allow us to get to know the person more deeply, even as the person taps into those inner resources to change/grow toward a higher ground.

Harness Inchoate Emotions as Forces for Change

Walk into any meeting, and the people you are meeting already come in with emotions of all sorts. Some of these emotions may be hard to read if they come from a cultural context different from ours. If they grimace, for example, you may not be able to tell, absent additional data, whether they are reacting negatively to what you've just said or if they just have acid reflux from lunch.

But other emotions across many cultures and contexts are much more easily discernible and can become powerful allies to move toward +outcomes despite cultural barriers. The most prominent ones are — in our experience — fear, status, hope, and pride.

We have all experienced fear, and it is alive and well in us when we want to move away from what we don't want. Once the threat is removed, there is little to no renewable energy to move us forward and upward, so we stop. Fear also is known to stifle innovation and stop people from going the extra step beyond what is perceived to be the threshold requirements. Therefore, it is not a great resource for +influence.

Status is a universal need for standing because we are all social animals, so when we don't have status symbols — like rank, wealth, and material possessions — we invent other devices to assert greater status, if not dominance, over others. Thus, in any social group, there is almost always a pecking order[151] — who is on first, who gets first dibs, and who has the final say, especially when the rest can't agree. Chickens do it, monkeys do it, and we humans do it, too.

It behooves anyone who wishes to +influence to understand the power flow and dynamics in the social organization you are dealing with. In some organizations, such as family businesses, the formal structure and titles mean far less than the informal, real power hierarchy or pecking order. Observe its workings and, if possible, talk to members of the social organization to understand its evolution and reality. Then acknowledge to the power hierarchy that you know enough to respect the power and privileges of the most influential members. For most of the +influence envisaged in this book, this should go enough distance to engage them in +outcomes.

Changing the pecking order will typically take far too much time, effort, and patience to wait for a natural evolution (*e.g.*, a member joining or leaving) or a coup d'état from within. A special case can be made for a formal power transition such as the retirement of a CEO. At such junctures, the expectation that the pecking order may change in due course encourages members to contemplate several what-if scenarios and how that might affect their power, status, and opportunity to make a bigger difference. The stakes are naturally high, so LinHart is sometimes sought by controlling owners and boards to shepherd the transition to the new chief, but also help in guiding the smooth transition of the entire power hierarchy. A hallmark of LinHart's value-add is having the board/owners focus on a complete set of +outcomes, including how the new power flow will serve future business success. This is opposed to a narrower search for determining the next CEO, leaving it entirely to the new CEO to sort out the rest of the musical chairs of who is sitting in what roles. The power hierarchy should be examined with some guidelines for the newly appointed CEO to revert to, with a complete discussion of the likely power dynamics — not just structure and "reporting relationships."

That leaves hope and pride. Both can be sources of positive energy to tap into and harness for +outcomes. Of the two, pride is the more reliable source of energy to move a person, people, or organizations to +outcomes. Hope trumps fear in bolstering courage and confidence. Hope for a better future motivates people to voluntarily choose to go for achievement. So, hope motivates powerfully, but to a point — then it risks an implosion of energy if those hopes, especially with unbridled optimism, are dashed.

Lest we veer off into the negative zone of taking arrogance as pride, we define +pride here as "reasonable self-esteem, confidence, and satisfaction" derived from being associated with noble purpose, excellence, and meaningful accomplishments. Thus defined, the positive sources of pride are a strong ally in +influence. People who take appropriate pride in their work will, all things equal, consider others' viewpoints on what constitutes excellence and what accomplishments are meaningfully good. In doing so, they can be more open to consider perhaps a higher purpose and related +outcomes that would benefit others. Far less volatile than hope, the risk of pride becoming arrogance can be monitored by the +influencer, who can take timely steps to mitigate risks of growing arrogance while harnessing the constructive force of +pride.[152]

+Influence Personal Story:
Respecting Others' Pride and Needs

In China, business leaders, as Huijin learned, are also well versed in using pride as a powerful force. In a globally renowned company undergoing transformation, she ran across intense emotions bubbling just beneath the surface of many daily interactions. Mostly well contained, the emotions are, however, played out in political intrigue and cunning influence which scuppered otherwise good initiatives for change.

A high-potential senior executive was sinking into a quagmire of "noises" for being rough with people even though he always over-delivered on performance. He was ambitious to transform the organization and justly proud to be chosen to lead many of the critical changes. He had little patience for underperforming colleagues, especially if they were also engaged in power politics. His trajectory was marred by the undertow of resistance from such colleagues. Huijin counseled him to see that others' hopes and sources of pride were different, and that he needed to accept others as they were before attempting to influence them. Above all, he had to stop interpreting their behaviors and intentions as fundamental flaws in character. By encouraging him to explore his colleagues' sources of pride, Huijin helped him connect their pride in the company's past pioneering achievements to the pride in a transformed better future for all.

She stayed connected to his being throughout, acknowledging emotions while getting him to work toward a shared pride in the future company. His colleagues sensed a change: He became noticeably calmer and could stop his usual emotional hijacks as he learned to engage more with others' views.

Pursue with Passion and Value-Add Toward +Outcomes

——————————— ✝ ———————————

+Influence Personal Story:
Rallying People to Perform Again

When Tsun-yan arrived at the St. Marguerite auto assembly plant, the plant manager and the production superintendent were predictably skeptical. "What could this young, foreign chap tell us about auto assembly that we don't already know?" The truth was, other than being a generic good problem solver,

Tsun-yan had no domain knowledge of auto assembly to draw on. But his intense caring about the plant's survival and the livelihood of the 2,600 workers got their attention. They connected with his true regret over the Ontario plant story (recounted earlier in this chapter and in Chapter 14). They were moved by the sincere emotion Tsun-yan felt when he shared the story and his intent — to avoid another plant shutdown.

It showed them he understood what was at stake for them, their families, and indeed the entire town. He confronted their fears of losing everything and challenged them to regain their pride — by observing that they used to produce cars at half the current defect rates, and their current performance was highly variable, where on a good shift they could get within shouting distance of their competitor's performance. "You can do it because you've done it before! Just aim first at returning to your historical level of ('decent but not great') quality."

He also gave them hope that perhaps there was a way forward if he had a grasp of the proportion of the workforce who was unable and unwilling to improve. Highly unusual at that time, Tsun-yan got the plant manager to let him approach the local union leaders with his idea to research anonymously the workforce's will and skill to change. "I will let you do it if they (the union) agree," said the plant manager. Tsun-yan listened hard to the union leaders and shared the same Ontario plant story to explain why he was there. He also assured the union leaders he needed concrete evidence that the number of workers who were not willing or able to change was small enough so they could be given generous consideration while saving the jobs of the rest.

With the union on his side, he persuaded plant management to deploy the research, which indeed found that less than 2% of workers were either bad apples demotivating others or really preferred to have a career switch and move elsewhere. This allowed a good implementation plan to be made for transitioning those workers out, treating them fairly and well. The plant also introduced research insights into the work arrangement and the culture changes required to improve the plant's performance. Within six months, the plant halved the defect rate and went the rest of the way in another three months, moving to the upper half of the most successful assembly plants continent wide.

Intense caring about +outcomes is also essential in the boardroom. Guiding CEO succession is one of the mainstays of LinHart's work. In many cases, the board, owners and other stakeholders already have strong preferences for certain candidates. They form and socialize these opinions without necessarily having considered all the candidates' merits nor the best fit for the future demands of the job, let alone the impact of the selection on the leadership dynamics. While the path of least resistance is to go with the flow (*i.e.*, the preferred candidate) and just go through the motions in terms of process, Tsun-yan and Huijin do not accept a succession mandate on this basis. Instead, they painstakingly bring to bear all the relevant facts so that all candidates are presented in a fulsome, objective fashion and facilitate the decision makers to vigorously debate about the choice and the many consequences of their selection.

In a recent high-stakes CEO succession mandate, LinHart deployed 11 sources of input; roughly two-thirds were custom designed or proprietary, including a couple that provided insights on the candidates' humanity. The board was not just impressed with the comprehensive rigor and objectivity of the assessment but also engaged in reconciling revealing pieces of new evidence against prevalent opinions. Passion and a caring human connection bolstered by technical value-add helped this iconic institution make the best possible choice and won the respect of the most important stakeholders.

Value-add must therefore accompany passion and human connection for +outcomes to emerge. This can take many forms, as illustrated in the preceding CEO succession case. More generally, the value-add that is called for depends on the context of the situation and the +influencer's own being and resources. In LinHart's case, it is usually a unique situation-specific blend of the aforesaid leadership analytics, the ability to connect with stakeholders and +influence with a sharp focus on +outcomes, and the always-present humanity of LinHart counselors. In certain cases, we brought industry or functional skills from prior experiences, third-party experts or something learned over multiple episodes.

For example, in the case of automotive assembly, Tsun-yan started without domain knowledge, and after intense involvement in performance improvement in more than half a dozen situations, he had built a track record and became sought after for visits with assembly operations as far as the UK, continental Europe, and East Asia, where he could walk a plant front to back, review data, talk to supervisors on the shop floor, and then sit down with plant management for a compelling review of the top five rank-ordered changes that would improve plant performance — all this in three days. This domain knowledge was hard earned, and not every domain offers enough diet to develop the know-how, but the other capabilities outlined will connect, engage, and motivate the right people to make the right changes for +outcomes.

$+$

+Influence Personal Story:
Relating to Client's Unique Challenge

An industry leader in India was contemplating going global. It was 2008 and there was no precedent in their industry.

Theirs was an aggressive culture that challenged everyone and everything; unsurprisingly, they were not inclined to put in the time to prepare for the arduous process including likely government interventions in the target's home country. During a three-day workshop, the top 40 officers rolled up their sleeves in a compressed but highly realistic reenactment of a recent transnational merger involving a Chinese firm with a company in the same target country. With each two-hour slot devoted to every step in the approval process, these senior people were confronted with the reality of dealing with cross-cultural, cross-jurisdictional issues they thought could be handled by "lawyers and consultants." Much to their surprise, they (and the deal) met resistance almost every step of the way. New to India and to the industry, Huijin was resourceful and creative in getting the top Chinese executive who drove their successful transaction through to integration to share insights enlivened with war stories, while veteran politicians — regulators from the target country — were flown in to play their respective parts of the hearings and approval process. The top team emerged having thoroughly enjoyed the immersive experience and committed to doing their part in learning the necessary, including cultural preparation.

LinHart has also used its franchise with top management or the board to help the shop floor. Oftentimes, the two are disconnected due to a large cultural divide. Top management/board directors think they know what's happening on the shop floor and can prescribe what needs to be done. But the reality on the shop floor is very different, so there is a big gap in the prescription. In a recent situation involving a listed industrial company, the board had certain biases based on an occluded information flow emphasizing mostly good news. After a big performance glitch shocked everyone and tanked the stock price, the upward data flow was rejigged to be timelier and more balanced with good and bad news. A whole new sociology was developed, involving board challenges and the support of senior management to identify and provide the tangible help needed on the shop floor.

All roads lead to Rome. Other people who have effectively +influenced across boardrooms and shop floors and have crossed many cultural divides apply a variety of value-add. More importantly, across the most inspiring episodes we have seen or experienced, the common denominator is invariably a personal blend that fuses the +influencers' technical value-add with their unique beings, allowing them to be seen as genuine, deeply caring, and fully proficient in creating +outcomes for others — not just for themselves. If we suspend our urge to judge others immediately by what they say or do, we might discern another vital quality of inspiring +influencers: that they have faith in our shared humanity, that there are beautiful human qualities inside all of us, that we can all work to bring out the best from each other. We will examine this blend of capacities in the next chapter as a great opportunity for each of us in our life ahead.

16

Conduct, Craft, and Character

When people raise objections to an ambitious idea I have, I am not upset but instead positively energized by it. It motivates me to want to prove them wrong.

— *Susan Chong, entrepreneur*[153]

It was July 2006. Cambridge, England, was unusually sweltering hot. Huijin and several hundred new engagement managers (EMs) were at a plenary session of McKinsey's first-ever EM college. Equal parts celebration, boondoggle, and training, she and her peers were all furiously fanning, to add to the ginormous fans trying to cool down the hall where Tsun-yan was giving a mesmerizing plenary speech on "the Art of Seeing." He talked about the importance of seeing, and brought it alive with the help of Michael Weber, a guest speaker who, among other things, trained US federal agents to see more and better.

Huijin remembered thinking, this Tsun-yan guy is different from the usual senior partners. This sensation increased tenfold after she attended a small group training Tsun-yan offered on leadership being the starting point of strategy, based on unconventional work he did for his Asian clients. For Huijin, who had seen leadership be a footnote to most strategy projects, this really got her attention: how did he see the world so differently, and thus see so much more of the world and the people in it?

After 2008, when Huijin and Tsun-yan started working together actively, she began to see the character, craft, and conduct ("3Cs" for short) that undergird this extraordinary seeing of Tsun-yan's. The same 3Cs undergird his +influence and, indeed, all pursuit of truth and light, bringing out the better aspects of our human nature.

While each of us is unique, we all share an inexorable desire to seek higher ground — be it more impact on the world, a better life, or a higher station. This desire is irrepressible — sooner or later, it will be activated and even when suppressed by others or circumstances, will still try to find a way to emerge. It awaits inspiration from within ourselves and others. As we shall see, the development of the 3Cs is fueled by this desire, and in turn, such development will both direct and channel the energy to stay the course to reach higher ground.

Conduct

We start with conduct, the most observable and tangible of the 3Cs.

Conduct is the behavioral pattern of a person persisting over time, consistent across a wide range of interactive situations, and guided by a set of self-selected principles and corresponding norms. The norms set the standards by which the principles apply. Because these norms are self-selected by the person's own volition, they are adhered to much more sustainably than if they were imposed by others.

Two examples from everyday life illustrate what is meant by principles and norms governing conduct: The speed limit on the major road nearest Tsun-yan's home is 50 km per hour. Are drivers supposed to not exceed it at any time? Or just some of the time — when traffic is light, can we exercise discretion and go faster? The rules are clearly the former, but the socialized norms of frequent drivers seem to be the latter. The maximum speed sign displayed prominently thus appears to Tsun-yan to be a *de facto* suggestion to drivers.

More constructively, Tsun-yan chooses to not use disposable coffee cups on the rare occasions when he buys coffee outside, at least until all of them are recyclable in the cities he frequents. This self-selected norm inconveniences no one but him, and he adheres to it because of the principle he chose — to do his part for the environment. This is conduct, and not just a behavior of his, because the same principle and norm also apply to bottled water.

Such conduct is far less likely to depart from the norm, even when it is less convenient or if the circumstances make it convenient to do so. For example, someone whose conduct includes keeping public areas free of litter would refrain from throwing a used tissue on the ground, even when no one is observing or the nearest trashcan is inconveniently far — instead, keeping it in a pocket or bag until a trashcan is sighted en route to the next destination.

So, last October, when Tsun-yan was out on his morning walk in a new neighborhood, he paid $34 plus a tip for a 12 oz cafe latte, when the normal price with a single-use cup would have been $4 plus tax. Faced with the self-imposed choice of paying for a reusable mug to fill with the coffee versus skipping the coffee, he decided to pay for the reusable mug. Almost always there is an afterthought of, "I'm glad I did this/did it this way because I believe I'm better off and the world is (at least a bit) better off as a result of it." Never mind the actual carbon footprint of the options — what mattered to him was that the afterthought justified the extra costs, upheld the norm, and reaffirmed the principles. And, so, the conduct continues.

--- ✝ ---

+Influence Personal Story: What Else Could be True?

Tsun-yan's seeing ability can be traced back to Ron Oberlander, a demanding client and eventually a friend and mentor. About 15 years older than Tsun-yan, Ron would give Tsun-yan a hard time whenever he showed up with a tightly prepared PowerPoint presentation. As Tsun-yan would lead his project team through the presentation on what Ron and his company should do, Ron would interrupt and challenge him to put aside the team's presentation and think outside the box. "What you conclude is plausible. Other explanations could also be plausible." At first, Tsun-yan was flustered, even annoyed that Ron did not fully appreciate the rigor of the analysis and logic he and his team had worked hard to come up with. But Tsun-yan couldn't deny that the "other" (*e.g.*, people) factors and considerations Ron brought up were relevant and important to the positive outcomes being sought. This challenge made Tsun-yan reflect on whether his own thinking and seeing, though lauded by others, was too narrow and myopic sometimes. The thirst for truth won over pride.

Ron was able to make effective judgment and +influence in countless projects, bankruptcies, mergers, and international joint ventures across more than 15 years, in large part because of a set of principles that consistently guided his behavior. Some of these key principles that Tsun-yan has internalized into his own conduct will be illustrated in this chapter: "a conversation of possibility," "staying loose in the saddle," "parallel (or more complete) truths" ("If this is true, what else may also be true?"), and a "non-sequential thought process" (as opposed to a sequential argument to persuade others of a fixed preconceived position).

In every observable situation, big or small, high stakes or ordinary/low stakes, Ron practiced these principles and related behaviors because he believed they were essential to see the plethora of variables in a complex situation. In decision making, it can never be assumed that "we know what we don't know." Too often, though "we don't know what we don't know", we make the mental leap to: assume they do not exist or don't matter.[154] To Ron, that over-simplification is dangerous; instead one must always proceed with an open mind in an uncertain, changing environment. "Staying loose in the saddle," Ron says, "will keep you from being thrown off the horse!" This underlying belief makes his conduct consistent and sustainable.

Now that we have clarified the relationship between principles, norms, and the pattern of consistent behaviors called conduct, we should acknowledge the challenges of adopting principles and norms when social norms vary enough to cause consternation and possible friction with people around you. This is already the case in many developed countries, or at least certain regions within them. But the challenges need not be associated with any government or political regime; they abound in any corporate and community setting. Conventional understanding of conduct in these social settings is that behaviors are expected to comply with commonly accepted social norms.

The trouble is, as societies and corporate and community settings become increasingly heterogenous and social expectations become more ambiguous and shift unpredictably, a person's social norms are at a higher risk of differing from those of others. For example, what is the acceptance of varying degrees of public displays of affection? In the end, for those living in complex, heterogenous developed countries, they should be conscious of the range of social norms but self-select and self-impose norms. In other words, they are aware of the range of social norms, expectations, and conventional practices but recognize they have the autonomy to adopt a set that express their beliefs and values. It will help, however, to always be sensitive to other legitimate positions of others and to learn to live peaceably with those differences.

Not every norm behind conduct needs to be potentially difficult or conflictual. An example of one of Tsun-yan's, which is well-received everywhere, is to always bring a gift whenever he goes to someone's home for the first time. It is an act of social grace that he chose to adopt from his mother, while fully aware that it's not conventionally expected unless he has been invited there for a social function like a housewarming.

Ron practiced his behaviors even though it jarred the other people involved because he believed they were essential to see more of the reality and hopefully would yield +outcomes. One of Ron's frequent sayings was, "There is always more to see and more to learn." He'd not enter a discussion of an important matter by sitting still for a presentation of a tightly constructed, linear progression of a traditional persuasive argument that follows the rules of a situation description, a set of complications that have arisen, and thus a proposition for resolving the problems. He rejected completely the hidden assumption that the facts included in the situation and complications were all necessary and sufficient.

He'd insist on the jigsaw puzzle approach: take a piece of the jigsaw (or more likely a few pieces at the start), and have "a conversation of possibility," discussing what it might say about the situation or complications, but holding back on landing prematurely and with finality on a solution. He would say, "If this were true, what else could also be true?" Then, the next randomly drawn piece would be introduced and examined similarly. He would also ask, "How many pieces are enough to see the pattern of the jigsaw?" Well, that depends on the complexity of the jigsaw, the capability of the discussants, and the time available before the window closes for decision and action. Like any jigsaw, one does not need to have all the pieces to conclude what the final picture is. Rather, a running hypothesis will emerge from the picture when you have enough puzzle pieces. In real life and business, "Too many pieces, and you are wasting time; too few pieces, and you risk jumping to a wrong conclusion."

Conduct for +influence is not just about behaviors; the mindfulness with which the behavior is conducted is also essential. Consciously and purposefully. Because consciousness and purposefulness allow for the expression of the heart. It's a simple point easily seen in a common experience of all of us. Everyone is capable of understanding from the two simple words "I'm sorry" the sincerity with which they were said. When said while conscious of the wrongdoing and purposeful in expressing regret, remorse, and intent on correcting/compensating for the wrong, the tone is totally contrite compared with a perfunctory appeasement offer. When Tsun-yan interrupts others' well-practiced, singular argument, he shares with them why he is doing this, how Ron inspired him on the importance of seeing more and differently, and his wish to help others do the same.

Proficiency is also important for conduct. Proficiency comes from repeated, deliberate practice (see Chapter 9). Not all conduct requires superlative proficiency, but mindfulness is indispensable because it conveys the being so vital to + influence. "I'm sorry" really doesn't require proficiency, yet it is vital to be heartfelt and mindful of the feelings of the other person. Ditto when giving tough constructive feedback: how much the feedback giver cares about the feedback receiver will affect the receiver's openness to the feedback far more than the giver's articulateness.

Going from a jigsaw puzzle discussion of pieces to a piecing-it-together discussion *without cutting off further possibility* requires proficiency. Ron usually seized a juncture to have a higher-level discussion about the realm of the possible to generate interactively and iteratively the arc of the story that picks up every piece of pertinent information and weaves them into a coherent, internally consistent narrative (of the situation, problems, and likely solution). This is analogous to getting a trial balance in accounting, after assembling each pertinent piece of credit and debit entries that is material to the financial condition. After practicing his "realm of the possible" way of seeing consistently and constantly, Ron honed the skill to judge which pieces were significant to include/exclude, how to acknowledge the input of discussants, and how to remain open to other possibilities yet try for closing balance.

Consistency in conduct is not difficult to see. Don't take a person's declaration of principle easily; follow instead what the person does in different circumstances. Ask, does the person's behavior vary by circumstance? A person's character is that which guides him or her in making tough moral choices consistently, as we shall see next.

Character

Character is the habitual flow of moral biases unique to a person. Lest we think it is largely religious in origin, the biases are drawn from one's upbringing (*e.g.*, parenting, schooling, home environment), sources of inspiration (*e.g.*, philosophy, moral authority, religion, love) life-shaping experiences (*e.g.*, near-death illness), events (*e.g.*, being called upon to take up the leadership mantle in a crisis) and people (*e.g.*, a mentor). Because it is internalized and habitualized, it is, at best, subconscious when activated and expressed.

Holding it in place is a life narrative[155] that upholds all past incidents in which the exercise of one's character has helped endure sufferings, sustain stoicism, and produce good outcomes — if not eventual triumph over adversity. According to Dan McAdams, a psychologist and expert in life narratives, this story of a person's life evolves over time with life experiences and reinterpretation of past events and is internalized. Like all habits, it is reinforced with each use and weakened with every non-use when a situation avails itself for a moral decision. In a typical person's life, such moments occur many times every day, and some may even appear to be trivial.

For example, in a grocery store, you pick the best container of fresh strawberries. When no one is looking, do you open another container, pick some of the best-looking ones and add them to the container you chose to get more out of the $3 you'd pay for your container? You might say the difference doesn't add up to even $1. What if it had been $1 million? At what point does it become an act that beggars thy neighbor? More important than money, to us, the act informs and shapes one's character. A person who behaves only according to circumstances is a person without character — blowing with the wind, seemingly able to move with the direction of the wind but stalling/meandering in another direction when the wind changes.

Thus defined, character informs and undergirds conduct, and conduct builds character with every expression, particularly when tested in high-stakes challenges. Character drives +influence because it determines the +outcomes worth fighting for and delimits the moral boundaries within which the pathways are chosen. More precisely, character allows "dominion of an individual over his impulses and desires, so that he was in control of them, and not the other way around."[156] In short, character is the fuel for conduct; conduct in turn affirms and sustains character.

In Chapter 12, we talked about how Tsun-yan was inspired by Marvin Bower, the founder of McKinsey, whose conduct was always to challenge the CEO on what he might consider to be at the heart of the company's prolonged performance problems. Marvin was devoted to solving the client company's problem (good for the client company) — not maximizing the number of projects from the company (good for McKinsey). He knew that any leader of a company is bound to be a significant contributor and solution to the company's problems, but confronting the CEO is risky. The CEO may take offence, not give Marvin projects, or even truncate current projects. But that was a risk worth taking in service of the client's interest, and Marvin's consistent conduct in this regard was a manifestation of the principle of independence well embedded in his character. Inspired by Marvin, Tsun-yan and Huijin also engage the top leader of their prospective clients: "You should only retain LinHart if you give us permission to tell you where and when you are the problem. Sight unseen, you are likely to be at least 50% of the problem — and solution." Most clients respect this blunt truth.

To be sure, character is a product of judgment, discretion, and choice — born from intrinsic human agency. That is, we all have the capacity to make meaning of our environment through conscious reflection of what we see and the choiceful decisions and actions toward what to us is the higher ground. In terms of +influence, this autonomy is vital because our character gives us the autonomy to choose pathways according to our ingrained values and principles and use those cherished qualities that make us unique (*e.g.,* courage). Because of this, "alike the circumstances may be, no other being would do exactly what this character does, or says what it says. It is the seal of individuality which it sets on everything that comes out from it, which makes it a character."[157] Character ensures autonomy in our choices and informs our unique ways in +influence.

Another implication of character is that it takes a very long time, if ever, to evolve, let alone change. But during uncertain times and ambiguity, character can be the most powerful resource to cope with challenges and pressures because it channels those qualities reliably and readily in one's being to seek +influence pathways to resolve conflicts and move to better outcomes. Character, in other words, helps with the rapid access and harnessing of our being in +influence.

+Influence Personal Story: Acing a Big Bet with Savvy

Ron's lifelong practice of seeing the complexity of things and figuring out what really works paid off for him in the last innings of his leadership of a large industrial company in a sunset industry. He faced enormous internal opposition for merging his company with a larger competitor, yet stayed the course. Due to the decline of the industry across the board, he knew the company could not survive alone. Rather than fade into oblivion, he believed in a big wager for the future. Tsun-yan criticized him vehemently for foregoing the usual premium in selling the company and for not seemingly trying hard enough to negotiate choice roles for his top executive team members in the combined company. The only role Ron negotiated was that he become (non-executive) chairman of the board in the merged entity. When confronted by Tsun-yan, Ron's reply was cryptic but prescient: "I am not a schmuck. The cream will always rise to the top. Just wait and see." In a short span of two years after the merger, Ron consolidated power in the board and through its governance processes, and his influence and judgment enabled the "cream" among his former executive talent to rise and take over most of the key positions, including the group CEO role. Though the biggest wager of his business life, Ron brought to bear what he learned from all the earlier wagers; he was never one to sit around and let the river take him places, nor be bounded by his people's reluctance and fears.

Finally, Ralph Waldo Emerson, the famous American philosopher and essayist, shared in one of the most popular quotes on the subject that "character is this moral order seen through the medium of individual nature."[158] While the medium is clearly individual, character has always been about something higher and broader than the self because it commits the individual to a set of higher ideals and to do things and sacrifice, if need be, one's self-interest for the greater good of the community. Character, therefore, serves the pursuit of +outcomes that benefit others and the community at large. Ron asked his people to take a temporary step back in service for a stronger company: "The cream rises to the top." He challenged them to work hard, not give up, let their merit speak for themselves, and trust that he would have the political savvy and craft to ensure merit mattered in executive appointments that the board of directors would make in the ensuing years.

Craft

+Craft emerges when a suite of conduct covering work and life (and the overlap between them) is practiced as an expression of one's character in +influence. In its mature form, it is an internalized, tacit know-how combining creativity and emotionality of the being with the biases of one's unique character.

+Craft is distinguished from another general meaning of the word "craft" as in "crafty" — implying a certain deceit. Therefore, +craft supports +influence to yield +outcomes. The authors use the term "+craft" because it includes not only skills and knowledge involved in dexterity but also individually developed by one's character for unique and creative expression.

There are a lot of self-help literature, media, and training resources out there on communications, conversations, leadership, *etc.*, portraying techniques, tools, and methods to improve one's effectiveness in these areas. We applaud their value to the readers in general for providing timely uplift, but it is vital to point out that the ultimate payoff of LinHart's teachings is to build a sustainable craft unique to each person, expressing one's character in conduct productively and constructively for collective benefits.

To drive home this point, let us now examine two of the most outstanding self-help books on the subject of Influence.[159] First, take the landmark 1936 work of Dale Carnegie in *How to Win Friends and Influence People*. Perhaps the most impressive element of the book is that it never dwelled on the depressive setting of the massive economic downturn in the 1930s; instead, it is a sunny book on how people can make something better of their conditions. More importantly Dale shared some enduring, fundamental lessons on how to win friends — not just do well in public speaking, in which he was a master.[160] Some of the basic points, which included "smile," "remember names," "become genuinely interested in other people," "be a good listener," and "talk in terms of the other person's interests," were good advice for all seasons.

However, two major differences are important to note from LinHart's point of departure:

1. How to win people to your way of thinking: the starting point is the influencer's way of thinking as opposed to what the situation calls for and what the +outcomes are for all. The primary entity remains self and self-interest; whereas in LinHart's belief about the craft of +influence, it is "what's best for everyone" as a starting point to which the +influencer and +influencee are both contributing. Not just what the influencer wants, or what (s)he thinks is good for the influencee, but 'good outcomes for all', as a third entity which might encourage the +influencer to include outcomes (s)he hadn't thought of or even sacrifice some self-interests in favor of the greater good.
2. Six ways to make people like you: the tactics are all good, especially when one does them sincerely. Making people like you is also paramount perhaps in a depression-era economy and any other era when the buyers' market reigns. LinHart thinks, however, it will be better for today's environment to gain respect and acceptance of who you are and your character as a constructive resource to +influence others with joint interests as a third-party entity.

The seminal works by Roger Fisher and his collaborators on managing the differences between people have a much more similar starting point to LinHart's. He began his study of conflict with the question, "What advice could I give to both parties in a dispute that would be helpful and lead to better outcomes?" This work drove the thinking behind his draft guide *International Mediation: A Working Guide* (April 1978), and ultimately to the international bestseller, *Getting to Yes.*[161] We admire his sharp focus on negotiation and telescoping from any interpersonal negotiations to international conflicts and peacemaking. His later works focused more on dealing with relationship challenges, the principles of which could inform more broadly other influence situations.[162]

+Craft shares common characteristics with crafts across cultures, dating back to the Middle Ages and perhaps further back in time.[163] When we look at a variety of crafts, including those involved in decorative arts (*e.g.*, ceramics, metal), with their respective origins in functional or utilitarian products (*e.g.*, wine vessels, Samurai swords, and timepieces), the individual artisanship of these items is a paramount determinant of its value, mostly immune from the impact of mass production. Machine-made, alas, cannot replicate the beauty and rarity of handcrafted items. Each one is a unique expression of the craftsmanship; for example, the master craftsmanship involved in making authentic, individually certified Samurai swords made of hand-forged katana steel. The master's being is drawn upon in every instance and every stage in exercising his/her craft.

Speaking of Japanese swords, another source of inspiration and analog for LinHart is *shokunin*: the Japanese practice of artisanship or craftsmanship. It conveys not just superlative technical skills but also an attitude and social consciousness, including a social obligation to do one's best for the general welfare of the people, an obligation both material and spiritual.[164]

Ron's craft in consolidating power, seen through a purely non-executive chairman role, was essential to achieving the positive outcomes so quickly for the merger: stabilize the operations of the combined company, improve the economics of the combined business, and ensure the best people from either company rose to the top rather than the usual case of the acquiring company's leadership dominating all the key positions. He had to let go of his former executive power as a CEO and learn anew how to influence the new CEO from the acquirer and move the most important decisions through the CEO and his mastery of the board processes.

While many effective CEOs struggle in the transition to chairman, Ron was a natural in developing his +craft as a non-executive leader because of his lifelong practice of seeing complexity in situations and people and looking for ways to move everyone forward. He channeled his character and conduct in the boardroom and its well-honed processes on dollars, people, and strategy under the scrutiny of shareholders, acquirers, and other board members unfamiliar and therefore initially unaligned with him. This mastery of craft in turn inspired Tsun-yan in his journey to hone his own +craft, expressing it in every facet of his life and work, including as an influential board director and a leadership counselor in vastly different cultural, industrial, and institutional settings.

A Journey to Your Own Unique +Craft of +Influence

Putting it altogether, we, the authors, fervently hope each reader — regardless of age, seniority, or culture — will heed our call to go on a lifelong learning and apprenticing journey to develop a highly individual personal craft in +influence, thus enabling you to rise against challenges in life and work for the benefit of yourself, others, and the world.

We have seen how our character gives rise to individual autonomy in choosing how we respond in high-stakes situations; most, if not all, involve some form of moral choices. Its habitual expression through conduct makes our behaviors not just consistent over time but also across situations and stakeholders. Our character tells us why we ought to choose a certain way forward, and our conduct expresses how we actually blend our being with our skills and knowledge of the unfolding situation to move forward efficaciously. Integrated through daily use, we develop a personal craft of +influence that improves with experience in exercising each of the 3Cs and the reinforcement that, while unique in its blend, the craft is ours and works.

We can, again, look to historical crafts for inspiration of apprenticeship as another vital enabler in building our +craft. Apprenticeship, dating all the way back to the Middle Ages, is a system for bringing up a new generation of craftsmen and practitioners that typically involves more than just skill training. Studying under a master craftsman, apprentices gain knowledge not just of the science of what is involved in making the products but also the professional practices, the community of trade, and working with guilds (*i.e.*, community of craftsmen engaged in similar craft) and customers alike. The higher-order skills of mindset, discipline, and room for creative, individual expression are more likely to be brought out through apprenticeship rather than from rote training. Given the large number of variables, many of which are less/not visible, and the dynamic nature of influence situations, the mastery of +influence is more akin to learning how to make Samurai swords — apprenticing with a master craftsman — than cranking steel blades out from stamping machines.

That apprenticeship is not just an outdated way to employ (some might say exploit) cheap labor can be seen from the story of the master baker Wu Pao Chun. A world-champion in the Coupe du Monde de la Boulangerie (Olympics of Breadmaking), Pao Chun in 2010 had beaten 23 rivals from 16 countries to clinch the title of master baker in the bread category. His entry, now famous, was his special creation of a rose lychee bread made of millet wine, rose petals, and dried lychees — all ingredients from Taiwan, his native country. Pao Chun, now 53, was brought up in an impoverished single-parent family in Pingtung County, as the youngest of eight children. Living in poverty then, Wu started learning to bake bread right out of high school because he wanted a skill that would help him support himself and not be a burden to his mother. His inspiration came from the taste of a lychee macaron at the legendary Ladurée in Paris, his skills from his apprenticeship with traditional Taiwanese bakers making pork floss breads, spring onion buns, and traditional pineapple tarts. He even had an allergy to flour. To this day, his hands and face get a tinge of red when he kneads and bakes. How did the dots connect to produce this kind of mastery?

When interviewed by Michelin,[165] he spoke a basic truth of all crafts: "Every baker can bake from the same recipe and the results will be different from each." He learned this truth through his apprenticeship with multiple master bakers. For example, with master baker Chen Fu Guang of Donben Bakery in Taichung, he first learned the master's unique approach to European-style breads. Learning there to macerate fruits gave him the inspiration for his now signature longan red wine bread. His subsequent stint with Pasadena International Group in Kaohsiung gave him the insights of the high-end French and Italian dining culture and the clientele appreciation of top-quality pastries. His passion for the craft kept him going through his allergy and early-venture challenges when he elevated breads from "a staple to a work of art."

Anyone's struggle for a better life for their family, to contribute to something bigger than themselves, for self-expression, or to be recognized as a good and worthy person are, at any scale, no less dramatic than a fight to protect a country. Our fondest hope is that all of us will have the freedom — not to do as we please but to conduct ourselves as we ought, according to our unique character and our +craft.

Epilogue

Never underestimate the power of dreams and the influence of the human spirit. We are all the same in this notion: The potential for greatness lives within each of us.

— Wilma Rudolph

Do you believe after reading this book and trying some of the cases that you should and can be more effective in influencing, regardless of your starting proficiency? Have you discovered more of your inner being in applying the principles that have been shared, thus progressing to be a better leader and a better person? Are you inspired to persevere in a longitudinal effort to hone your personal craft in +influencing? If your answers to one or more of the foregoing questions are affirmative, then the purpose of this book has been accomplished.

+Influence is not a zero-sum game. You can benefit yourself and others as well in the same interaction. The authors discovered this truth much later in our lives than we'd have liked. But that made our wish to share it with you that much stronger. By learning from your mistakes and painful experiences, you may succeed sooner, scale greater heights, and all the while do more good. Why not?

I would encourage you to join the +influence Collective and/or try one of LinHart's programs to validate for yourself the truths in this book, discover your current state of influence, and learn how to be better at +influence in a very hands-on manner. If you are an alumnus of one of the programs, consider stepping up in our collective to share, encourage others and learn to master your +Craft. Our higher programs all came about because alums asked for them. So do help us know your needs and better still, sign up to pilot or facilitate a higher program. You will gain mastery faster by greater use of those +influence muscles.

From the thousands of students, executives, and business owners who have gained breakthroughs in influence skills and consciousness of their beings, LinHart has learned that two factors work in concert to bring the most uplift into reality. The first is tapping into your inner qualities that are otherwise submerged in negative self-talk and self-doubt. Your native inner qualities are what makes you a unique human being. That's why what works for you in +influence won't work as well for others. The second factor is that your conative that process cognitive and emotional signals are initially reflexive — most of us are hardly conscious of it, let alone try to direct it. We only know if we pay attention to our impulsive reflexes. That's why we all have the opportunity to hone consistency in conduct — longitudinally over years — by drawing more and more on our character. It is character that will enable ready, steady decisions in the moment to +influence in that unique way that is true to self. Like hybrid vehicles on the market, your batteries are charged even as you drive your car. So the same works for your character — it's strengthened every time you make a moral decision. Honing your personal Craft in +influencing, in a nutshell, is our ambition for you and the greatest gift you could give yourself if you keep at it.

I have persisted in improving my practice of +influence since 2003. It was painful, initially. Big gaps stood between my intent and effect on people. But then it became more and more joyful because the return on my efforts in psychic fulfillment far exceeded the discomfort of getting out of my comfort zone. The more I am conscious of the submerged inner qualities that can be put in service of better outcomes for all stakeholders, the more I'm energized to continue. The more I am attuned to the instantaneous energies flowing in the heat of an interaction, the more I feel alive to the opportunity to do good and well. It's truly inspiring that one can be indulgent in self-discovery and at the same time be magnanimous if not selfless in benefiting others. The journey has become self-sustaining! We fervently hope the same joy will attend your efforts in honing your personal craft in +influencing — along with bountiful benefits for yourself and others.

Tsun-yan Hsieh
Marco Island, Florida, USA

Mapping of +Influence Personal Stories

Chapter	Page Number	Story Title	Protagonist Name	Geographic Region Where Story Occurred
3	28	Going Beyond Cost Cutting	Tsun-yan Hsieh	North America
3	31	Taking the Road Less Traveled	Marie Cheong	Southeast Asia
3	34	Supporting Others to Grow	Mike Jackson	Southeast Asia
3	38	Developing Personal Formula for +Influence	Tsun-yan Hsieh	North America
5	67	From Reserved to Leader	Shaw Voon Hau	Southeast Asia
7	101	Connecting with the Person	Tsun-yan Hsieh	Europe
9	122	Overcoming Denial, Inspiring Self to Change	Tsun-yan Hsieh	North America
9	128	Uncovering Her Capacity to Care	Huijin Kong	China
9	143	From Doubt to Coaching Leader	Naithy Cyriac	Southeast Asia
10	157	Competing Fairly	Horst Kremer (disguised name)	North America
10	158	Embracing Her Emotions	Huijin Kong	China
10	166	Turning Down the Call to Become a CEO	Tsun-yan Hsieh	North America, Southeast Asia

(Continued)

(Continued)

Chapter	Page Number	Story Title	Protagonist Name	Geographic Region Where Story Occurred
10	167	From Too Many Choices to Clarity and Courage	Joseph Mocanu	Southeast Asia
12	195	Suspending Pride to Learn and Grow	Joydeep Sarkar	Southeast Asia
12	204	Telling Client he is the Problem	Marvin Bower	North America
13	216	Creating Opportunities for Mentee	Tsun-yan Hsieh, Aldo Bensadoun	North America
13	220	Learning from the World's Best	Tsun-yan Hsieh	North America
14	225	Interrupting a Powerful Person	Dominic Barton	North America
14	229	Courage to Ask for Debt Relief	European telecom CEO	Europe
15	237	Giving Up Too Easily	Tsun-yan Hsieh	North America
15	246	Sensing the Energy for Change	Tsun-yan Hsieh	India
15	256	Respecting Others' Pride and Needs	Huijin Kong	China
15	257	Rallying People to Perform Again	Tsun-yan Hsieh	North America
15	260	Relating to Client's Unique Challenge	Huijin Kong	India
16	266	What Else Could be True?	Ron Oberlander	North America
16	273	Acing a Big Bet with Savvy	Ron Oberlander	North America

Mapping of Cases

Seniority Level Legend

FOC = Founder, Owner, and CEO (16 cases)
EXE = Middle Management (11 cases)
YPL = Young Professional (7 cases)

	Case Name	Industry	Country	Seniority Level	Arena
2.1. A–B	New service launch	Facilities services	[not specified]	YPL/EXE	Management/ personal
5.1. C–E	New service launch	Facilities services	[not specified]	EXE/FOC	Management/ personal
7.2	Assigning a task to an uncooperative peer	Consulting	Europe	YPL/EXE	Management
7.3	Resetting investment expectations in start-up	Tech start-up	US	FOC	Management/ Boardroom
8.4	Rescuing a client relationship	IT services	US	EXE	Engaging customer

(Continued)

(*Continued*)

	Case Name	Industry	Country	Seniority Level	Arena
8.5	Convey news of a plant shutdown	Car assembly	Italy	EXE/FOC	Management/ Shop floor
8.6	Closing a deal with a stressed customer	Data analytics software	[unspecified]	EXE	Engaging customer
9.7	CEO dealing with under-performance of mentor	Oil and gas	Asia	FOC	Management
9.8	Last chance to retain a seasoned sales leader	Digital advertising	USA	FOC	Management
10.9	Failure to dissent makes everyone look bad	Consumer goods	Asia	YPL/EXE	Management
10.10	Overcoming past failures	[non-specified]	[non-specified]	EXE	Management
10.11	CEO persuading Chairman to improve governance	[non-specified]	[non-specified]	FOC	Boardroom
10.12	Leadership presence in a townhall	[non-specified]	[non-specified]	FOC	Management
11.13	Confirming starting a project	[non-specified]	[non-specified]	FOC	Engaging customer
11.1. F–G	New service launch	Facility services	[non-specified]	EXE/FOC	Management
11.14	Attracting talent via LinkedIn	Oil and gas	Global/Asia	YPL/FOC	Management
12.15	Colleagues making fun of you	Start-up	[non-specified]	YPL	Management

(Continued)

	Case Name	Industry	Country	Seniority Level	Arena
12.16	Inspiring staff to develop themselves	Accounting firm	[non-specified]	YPL/FOC	Management
13.17	Failing to grow together	Marketing	China	EXE	Personal
14.18	Leading a difficult transformation with low staff trust	Health care	USA	FOC	Boardroom/ Shop floor
14.19	CEO candidate with fixed preferences	Health care	USA	FOC	Boardroom
14.20	JV partners work out conflicting expectations	Education	Hong Kong	FOC (young)	Management/ personal
14.21	Misaligned views of the future	Finance (asset management)	Global	FOC	Boardroom
14.22	Family business leader with conative issues	Education	Asia (Singapore, India, China)	FOC	Boardroom/ personal
15.23	Turning around an automobile assembly plant	Car assembly	North America	YPL/EXE	Shop floor

Endnotes

1. See Tjan, T. (2017). *Good People*. Portfolio Publishing. Tony is one whose entry has made me continue on this commitment to bring the best out of everyone I work with.
2. LinHart Group (www.linhartgrp.com), founded by Tsun-yan with a singular mission to help people reach their best potential, selects CEOs, boards, owners, and senior executives to help them tackle their toughest business and people issues so that, in the process, they become better leaders and people.
3. MBA and Master of Technology. The course for MBA students at the National University of Singapore, Basic Managerial Communications, later renamed "Launch Your Transformation," was custom-built by LinHart Group on a build-operate-transfer basis.
4. Ian Davis was Tsun-yan's global managing director at McKinsey & Company between 2003 and 2009. He is, as of this writing, chairman of Rolls-Royce Holdings.
5. LinHart has created the netspace http://www.positiveinfluence.life/ for this purpose.
6. Growth versus fixed mindset is covered in depth in a book by Dweck, C. (2007). *Mindset: The New Psychology of Success* (updated ed.). Ballantine Books.
7. Intellectual Property (IP) of LinHart Group.
8. Parker, K., Horowitz, J.M., & Minkin, R. (2022, February 16). COVID-19 pandemic continues to reshape work in

America. *Pew Research Center.* Retrieved from https://www.pewresearch.org/social-trends/2022/02/16/covid-19-pandemic-continues-to-reshape-work-in-america/.

9. Most books on influence address persuasion or selling only. An all-time classic, *How to Win Friends & Influence People* by Dale Carnegie (1998), is an excellent example of the genre of effective communication, extended to lend advice on how to get others to see your side and how to make people like you. A more recent example is *Influence: The Psychology of Persuasion* by Robert B. Cialdini (2021).

10. See, for example: Turner, S. (2019). *Manipulation: Highly Effective Persuasion and Manipulation Techniques People of Power Use for Deception and Influence, Including 7 Laws of Human Behavior, NLP Tips, and Strategies of Dark Psychology.* Bravex Publications.

11. For an interesting scholarly study on the influence of social media, see: Romero, D.M., Galuba, W., Asur, S., & Huberman, B.A. (2010). Influence and passivity in social media. *SSRN.* Retrieved from http://dx.doi.org/10.2139/ssrn.1653135. The study pointed out that a lot of views does not translate into activity (*e.g.,* forwarding the information to others). For influence to take its course, it must overcome user passivity.

12. To avoid confusion with how others might see "indirect influence," in this book "direct" is defined as when the influencer is engaging the influencee directly and is not intermediated through another person. In *The Power of Indirect Influence* by Judith C. Tingley (2001), many of what Tingley considered to be "indirect" influences, such as the use of metaphors, acting in accord, and reframing, are very much "direct" in this book's definition.

13. www.positiveinfluence.life

14. The Myers & Briggs Type Indicator personality test is a psychometric assessment that proposes to determine personality types. In practice, it helps individuals understand their communication preference and how they prefer to interact with others.

15. Most often attributed to Maya Angelou, a poet, civil rights activist, and memoirist. See, for example: Smith, D. (2021). *100 Inspirational Quotes by Maya Angelou.* Self-published.

16. This is linked to the concept of generativity. According to McAdams, D. P., & Van De Water, D. A. (1989). Generativity and Erikson's "belief in the species". *Journal of Research in Personality*, 23(4), 435-449, generativity is the concern for guiding and promoting the next generation through such creative behavior as parenting, teaching, mentoring, leading, and generating products and outcomes that benefit others. Erikson (1963) has argued that in order to be generative in adulthood, people must have a fundamental "belief in the species" or a faith that human progress is possible and worth working toward.

17. Examples abound. Volkswagen's diesel emissions scandal first tipped off in 2014, ultimately resulting in a $14 billion settlement. See: Atiyeh, C. (2019, December 5). Everything you need to know about the VW diesel emissions scandal. *Car and Driver.* Retrieved from https://www.caranddriver.com/news/a15339250/everything-you-need-to-know-about-the-vw-diesel-emissions-scandal/.; Purdue Pharma in the opioid epidemic in the US; Wirecard found fraudulent financial reporting that led to insolvency; or simply someone taking undue credit for someone else's work.

18. See, for example: Goedhart, M., & Koller, T. (2020, June 16). The value of value creation. *McKinsey Quarterly.* Retrieved from https://www.mckinsey.com/capabilities/strategy-and-corporate-finance/our-insights/the-value-of-value-creation. The authors asserted that long-term value creation can and should consider the interest of all stakeholders.

19. This is consistent with the systems 1 and 2 explained in Kahneman, D. (2013). *Thinking, Fast and Slow.* Farrar, Straus and Giroux. System 1 is fast, intuitive, and emotional; System 2 is slower, more deliberative, and more logical, and must be consciously developed.

20. The original course was designed to run an entire semester in 2011. Two years later, the intensity was increased by running it continuously for an entire week. More than 85% of each cohort felt that they had been transformed beyond learning influence skills, in terms of becoming more confident and raising their readiness to accelerate their development.

21. Katzenbach, J.R., & Smith, D.K. (1992). *The Wisdom of Teams*. Harvard Business Review Press. See also: Katzenbach, J.R., & Smith, D.K. (1993, March/April). The discipline of teams. *Harvard Business Review*. Retrieved from https://hbr.org/1993/03/the-discipline-of-teams-2. The article discusses the distinctions between a working group and a team.

22. IP of LinHart Group. These elements and the team composition for a complete skill set form the heart of our interventions with top teams.

23. The issue map for subject-oriented analysis is only partially illustrated in the parable of apple picking. Full treatment of subject-oriented analysis and interventions has become the IP of LinHart Group.

24. The pilot course for Leadership Influence was taught over two semesters, then condensed to be delivered in one 7-day camp just prior to orientation week in the MBA program.

25. According to Oxford Languages via Google.

26. In the book *Thinking, Fast and Slow* by Daniel Kahneman (2011), the author talks about two aspects of our brain: System 1 is highly instinctive with many heuristics, best complemented by the effortful System 2, which is more systematic.

27. In *A Primer on Jungian Psychology* by Calvin Hall & Vernon Nordby (1999), personality is described as not being fixed but more like a range of traits and characteristics that are shaped by many factors, including how we make sense of, react to, and respond to the environment and challenges.

28. The prefrontal cortex's myriad of "executive" functions is described in Sapolsky, R. M. (2017). *Behave: The Biology of Humans at Our Best and Worst*. Penguin Press.

29. Unconditional positive regard (UPR), first developed by Stanley Standal and later popularized by Carl Rogers, is the basic acceptance and support of a person regardless of what the person says or does. He believed unequivocally that "Individuals within themselves have vast resources for self-understanding and for altering their self-concepts, basic attitudes, and self-directed behavior; these resources can be tapped if a definable climate of facilitative psychological attitudes can be provided." UPR requires empathy, warm and caring acceptance (as opposed to a selective evaluating attitude), and congruence. Attitude above all trumps any technique. Through UPR, counselors can provide the best possible conditions for personal growth, including taking responsibility for themselves.

30. Rogers, C. (1995). *On Becoming a Person: A Therapist's View of Psychotherapy* (2nd ed.). HarperOne.

31. Personality type 1 of the Enneagram Profile.

32. LIFE2, part of the series of LinHart's Leadership Influence for Executives, is for professionals or executives roughly 5–12 years post-graduation. LIFE3 is for mid-career executives contemplating a pivot to a different career, a new location, or taking a break. LIFE4 is for people post-45 who are contemplating a pivot to portfolio life or doubling down on their current career.

33. See, for example: Larson, E. (2022). *The Splendid and the Vile: Churchill, Family and Defiance During the Bombing of London.* HarperCollins. This is an account reconstructed from historical records and personal letters of the saga of Churchill during the Blitz, which was the first year of his prime ministerial role. Excerpts of his great speeches were well represented.

34. Braithwaite, S. (2022, February 26). Zelensky refuses US offer to evacuate, saying 'I need ammunition, not a ride.' *CNN.* Retrieved from https://edition.cnn.com/2022/02/26/europe/ukraine-zelensky-evacuation-intl/index.html.

35. Carrick, H. (2022, March 2). Volodymyr Zelensky speech: full transcript of Ukraine president's statement to European

Parliament. *National World*. Retrieved from https://www.nationalworld.com/news/world/volodymyr-zelensky-speech-today-full-transcript-of-ukraine-presidents-statement-to-european-parliament-3592244.

36. A Center of Excellence set up in the late 2000s based out of Singapore.

37. Cain, S. (2012). *Quiet: The Power of Introverts in a World That Can't Stop Talking*. Crown.

38. "Scuffle" may be more typical as not all high-stakes interactions end up in a confused scramble. That said, the authors in a real-life LinHart capacity have experienced more of this than the world would wish to see.

39. This is inspired by PDCA, Plan–Do–Check–Act, which according to Wikipedia is associated with W. Edwards Deming, who is considered by many to be the father of modern quality control; however, he used PDSA (Plan–Do–Study–Act) and referred to it as the "Shewhart cycle".

40. See our discussion of opaque areas and weak signals on our dedicated website: www.positiveinfluence.life.

41. If many of these contextual analyses need to be done (*e.g.*, private equity looking for investment opportunities), it may be useful to develop an order of magnitude assessment of financial flexibility. Tsun-yan uses "one torpedo company" versus "two torpedoes" to denote how many shocks a company could take before going belly up, as a simple measure of the company's resilience to financial shocks.

42. At LinHart, we have not found the values statement to be a useful guide; they typically represent some kind of ethos — something nice to have, desirable ethics we can all chin up to someday.

43. Examples of acknowledgement of emotional undercurrents: "This must be very difficult for you" or "How tough is it for you to shoulder this pain?" Avoid patronizing the person. It takes empathy, presence, and congruence; attitude is key.

44. See the Merriam-Webster dictionary definitions.

45. Dunbar, R.I.M. (2016). The Evolution of the Social Mind. Retrieved from https://www.rcpsych.ac.uk/docs/default-source/members/sigs/evolutionary-psychiatry-epsig/epsig-symposium-2-evolution-of-the-social-mind.pdf. A more extensive treatment of Social Mind can be seen in Dunbar, R.I.M. (2021). *Friends: Understanding the Power of our Most Important Relationships*. Little, Brown.

46. See 1) Lewis, P.A., Birch, A., Hall, A., & Dunbar, R.I.M. (2017). Higher order intentionality tasks are cognitively more demanding. *Social Cognitive and Affective Neuroscience*, 12(7), 1063–1071; 2) Kolb, B. & Wishaw, I.Q. (1996). *Fundamentals of Human Neuropsychology*. W.H. Freeman & Co; 3) Koziol, L.F., Budding, D.E., & Chidekel, D. (2012). From movement to thought: executive function, embodied cognition, and the cerebellum. *Cerebellum*, 11(2), 505–525.

47. Sapolsky, R.M. (2017). *Behave: The Biology of Humans at Our Best and Worst*. Penguin Press.

48. The faculty or power of using one's will.

49. Abridged from www.dictionary.com.

50. See definitions of key terms (pp. xvii–xxiii).

51. www.dictionary.com.

52. This is a real nugget when it comes to opaque areas and weak signals. Michael Weber, a former CIA member, taught Tsun-yan this.

53. The facts of the case are drawn from the book *Who Says Elephant Can't Dance?* by Louis Gerstner (2002), Chapter 4.

54. Europe, the Middle East, and Africa.

55. Kenichi Omae, a retired senior partner of McKinsey, wrote the notable book *The Mind of the Strategist: The Art of Japanese Business* (1991). McGraw Hill.

56. From 1945, the end of World War II, to late 1991, when the USSR was dissolved into component republics, historians regarded the Cold War to have been waged.

57. Augustus (63 BC to 14 AD) often chided his military commanders for rashness. To remind them constantly of

this often fatal error, he struck Roman coins then with the symbol of an anchor with a dolphin wrapped around it.

58. Being deliberate about achievability of +influence objectives in planning the +influence attempt is vital. The planning of multiple influence episodes that build toward a set of +outcomes is a more advanced skill, learned by our clients in actual LinHart counseling work and outside the scope of this book.

59. The phrase "moment of truth" is misused often to denote any juncture that is pivotal. A frequent usage in marketing, for example, is any opportunity for the (potential) customer to form an impression of a brand, product, or company and strive to seize these moments to create positive customer outcomes (*e.g.*, turning delight into purchase). Tsun-yan first came across the phrase as it was originally intended in Carlzon, J. (1989). *Moments of Truth* (revised ed.). HarperBusiness. In the book, Jan spoke of his turnaround experience at the airline where he became the CEO in 1981. He intended the phrase to indicate moments in which the airline and its staff members at the frontline (*e.g.*, at the check-in counter) are tested. They either failed or passed in the eyes of the customers at those moments and would impact the customers' relationship with the airline going forward.

60. As it was known at that time. More recently, McKinsey calls the highest tier of shareholders "senior partners."

61. Joe Keilty and Marshall Goldsmith were partners expounding a version of situational leadership, as Keilty, GoldSmith & Co., when Tsun-yan met Keilty. He credits Keilty's pithy advice at that dinner, *circa* 1985, to have planted the seeds to a lifelong journey, beginning in 1993, to be a better person, not just a better leader. Marshall Goldsmith went on to have a prominent career as a prolific author and leadership coach.

62. Michael (Mike) Murray is, among other things, the chairman of Aquilon Energy Services, Inc.

63. This four-stage learning model for skill building was initially developed by Gordon Training International by an employee, Noel Burch, in the 1970s.

64. Presence is the undivided attendance of the whole being in the moment. There is overlap with the notion of mindfulness, which is the basic human ability to be fully present, achieved mentally by focusing one's awareness on the present moment. Presence is less meditative and more physical; for instance, avoid distractions physically (*e.g.*, move to a quieter corner of the cafe) and emotionally (*e.g.*, remind yourself not to be overly excited). One can be present without meditation, for example. Presence is also experienced when the people surrounding you "are all there," focused, engaged, and attentive, besides being centered and grounded.

65. Huijin wrote about her childhood experiences in a book in Chinese.

66. "Helper" is a consistent towering strength on all of Tsun-yan's psychometric tests.

67. Enneagram is a personality test that maps a person's psyche against a model of nine personality types (*e.g.*, Reformer, Helper, Challenger). Origins of the Enneagram have been disputed, but it has been an instrument for spirituality and, more recently, business contexts for more than 50 years.

68. 77% of our alumni have confirmed that they have significantly expanded their influencing repertoire.

69. Gerstner, L. (2003). *Who Says Elephants Can't Dance? Leading a Great Enterprise Through Dramatic Change.* HarperBusiness. It is one of the business classics in turning around and transforming an iconic enterprise.

70. Oxford Languages via Google.

71. VUCA stands for volatility, uncertainty, complexity, and ambiguity. Originally coined by Warren Bennis and Burt Nanus (1985) in their book *Leaders: The Strategies for taking Charge.* Some military historians stated the world had entered a VUCA state in the early 1990s with the

collapse of the USSR and demise of the Eastern Bloc as the one enemy.

72. See for example: Cuddy, A. (2015). *Presence: Bringing Your Boldest Self to Your Biggest Challenges*. Little, Brown and Company. Professor Cuddy is a proponent of "power posing" as a self-improvement technique, essentially adopting certain physical postures to convey power.

73. Robert Cialdini terms it "law of reciprocity" even though he applied it first as a principle of persuasion, which states that humans are wired to return favors and pay back debts, treating others as they've treated us. While developed for selling purposes, this is likely to be true for many people.

74. There are many excellent resources on difficult conversations. They don't substitute for hands-on practice to see how you react when tensions rise, cope with pressure and continue to listen, ask questions, *etc.* For reading, see: Stone, D., Patton, B., & Heen, S. (2010). *Difficult Conversations: How to Discuss What Matters Most* (updated ed.). Penguin.

75. See footnote 54 on similarities and differences with mindfulness.

76. There are many breathing and visualization guides online. Mass General, for example, has specific step-by-step instructions for their patients. If the science of breathing is of interest, see: Nestor, J. (2020). *Breath: the New Science of a Lost Art*. Riverhead Books.

77. "FeedForward" is asking for two suggestions that could help you to achieve your goal (*e.g.*, behavioral change).

78. Howard Gardner's multiple intelligence framework describes eight different intelligences a human being can have: linguistic, logical/mathematical, spatial, bodily-kinesthetic, musical, interpersonal, intrapersonal, and naturalist. Gardner, H. (2011). *Frames of Mind: The Theory of Multiple Intelligences* (3rd ed.). Basic Books.

79. Anna Kiukas-Pedersen, Rohan Belliappa and Dany Bolduc, all long-time faculty at the +influence course at NUS Business School.

80. This is aligned with the stoic philosophy, as practiced by Marcus Aurelius, the Roman emperor, among others.

81. At LinHart, we define a habit of mind as a learned disposition toward thinking and behaving in a particular way when confronted with a problem to which there is no immediate answer. It is more of a mental pathway than any one specific algorithm and more generalized than a heuristic or a rule of thumb.

82. Steven Covey calls this being "response-able," part of Habit #1 of his book *The 7 Habits of Highly Effective People: Powerful Lessons in Personal Change* (revised ed., 2004). Free Press.

83. Dorian Lo is a practicing emergency room clinician even as he pursued a career in business. Among other appointments, he was EVP of pharmacy and health care of Shoppers Drug Mart and currently president of Express Scripts Canada.

84. Cain, S. (2012). *Quiet: the Power of Introverts in a World That Can't Stop Talking*. Crown. In this book, the author makes a compelling case that introverts can adopt highly extroverted behaviors in service of a worthy mission.

85. Hands-on practice.

86. He was promoted to Group CEO a few years later.

87. See: Larson, E. (2022). *The Splendid and the Vile: Churchill, Family and Defiance During the Bombing of London*. HarperCollins. It is a superb account assembled from archives and personal letters of that horrific first year as prime minister of a war-torn Britain.

88. Churchill told this to his cabinet on May 13, 1940, then repeated it in the House of Commons in the same day. See International Churchill Society, www.winstonchurchill.org.

89. Vaibhav is a male name in Sanskrit.

90. According to Wikipedia, "the complementary combination of the two concepts is an ancient concept." Nature is what people think of as prewiring and is influenced by genetic inheritance and other biological factors. Nurture is generally taken as the influence of external factors after conception (*i.e.*, the product of exposure, experience, and learning on an individual).

91. According to Simplypsychology.org, "Instead of defending extreme nativist or nurturist views, most psychological researchers are now interested in investigating how nature and nurture interact in a host of qualitatively different ways."

92. For a deeper look at deliberate practice and its role in producing excellence, see Ericsson, A., & Pool, R. (2017). *Peak.* HarperOne. And for a remarkable personal treatise on the inner journey to optimal performance, see Waitzkin, J. (2008). *The Art of Learning.* Free Press.

93. More on this in Chapter 6.

94. See Heifeitz, R., & Linsky, M. (2002). *Leadership on the Line: Staying Alive Through the Dangers of Leading.* Harvard Business Review Press.

95. *The Art of War.* Sun Tzu, ~500 BCE.

96. Though hotly debated, there is the concept of mirror neurons that lead us to pick up and unconsciously mirror the emotions and behaviors of others. This capacity is observed in primates and birds, in addition to human beings.

97. Stone, D., Patton, B., & Heen, S. (2010). *Difficult Conversations: How to Discuss What Matters Most* (updated ed.). Penguin.

98. This was created by the Ashland Institute, based in Ashland, Oregon.

99. The definitive treatise on EQ is by Daniel Goleman.

100. See: van der Kolk, B. (2015). *The Body Keeps the Score: Brain, Mind and Body in the Healing of Trauma.* Penguin.

101. Oxford Languages, via Google.

102. For this reason, we tend not to find it useful to separate the state of mind from the state of being. Rather, we find one informs the other.

103. Oxford Languages, via Google, defines conative as the tendency to act directly and ultimately in a certain direction.

104. Anderson, R. J., & Adams, W.A. (2015). *Mastering Leadership: An Integrated Framework for Breakthrough Performance and Extraordinary Business Results.* John Wiley & Sons.

105. Harris, B. (2016). *Becoming Whole: A Jungian Guide to Individuation.* Daphne Publications.

106. George, B. & Sims, P. (2007). *True North: Discover Your Authentic Leadership.* Jossey-Bass.

107. This is a proprietary LinHart methodology to get at the deep assumptions, beliefs, and instincts that drive a person's behaviors, thoughts, and feelings.

108. Minto, B. (1996). *The Minto Pyramid Principle: Logic in Writing, Thinking and Problem Solving* (expanded ed.). Minto Intl.

109. Strunk Jr., W. & White, E.B. (1999). *The Elements of Style* (4th ed.). Pearson.

110. Cadence is rhythmic sequence that is made up of frequency, format, and sequence.

111. LinHart has worked with thousands of business leaders on their leadership across four decades, 30 countries, and 30 industries, including CEOs, C-suite leaders, senior leaders, mid-level leaders, high potentials, younger professionals, and MBA and undergraduate students.

112. Excerpts from a Wikipedia entry on David (Michelangelo), https://en.wikipedia.org/wiki/David_(Michelangelo).

113. The finished statue weighs 12,000 pounds and is 17 feet tall.

114. Principals in those days were "junior partners."

115. Rooke, D. & Torbert, W.R. (2005). Seven transformations of leadership. *Harvard Business Review.* Retrieved from https://hbr.org/2005/04/seven-transformations-of-leadership.

116. Zhao, X., & Epley, N. (2022). Surprisingly happy to have helped: underestimating prosociality creates a misplaced barrier to asking for help. *Psychological Science, 33*(10), 1708–1731.

117. Brooks, A.W., Gino, F., & Schweitzer, M.E. (2015). Smart people ask for (my) advice: seeking advice boosts perceptions of competence. *Management Science, 61*(6), 1421–1435.

118. Schaffner, A.K. (2020, September 16). Perseverance in Psychology: Meaning, Importance and Activities. *Positive*

Psychology. Retrieved from https://positivepsychology.com/perseverance/.

119. Duckworth, A. (2016). *Grit: The Power of Passion and Perseverance*. Scribner. Professor Duckworth teaches psychology at the University of Pennsylvania.

120. For a full account of this innovator's remarkable inventions, see Dyson, J. (2021). *Invention: A Life*. Simon & Schuster.

121. See Chapter 10, case 10.10 for an example of a tough conversation.

122. LinHart doesn't believe a person will know everything about the inner being. It's a wonderful quality of being human — there's always more to discover and unleash.

123. See Carl Rogers's concept of unconditional positive regard: Rogers, C. (1995). *On Becoming a Person: A Therapist's View of Psychotherapy* (2nd ed.). HarperOne.

124. A term used by Robert Kegan, an authority on adult development, in: Kegan, R. (1982). *The Evolving Self: Problem and Process in Human Development* (reprint ed.). Harvard University Press.

125. The role of pride in corporate performance is well explored in: Katzenbach, J.R. (2003). *Why Pride Matters More Than Money: The Power of the World's Greatest Motivational Force*. Crown Business.

126. While in the army, Tsun-yan learned of the positive impact of a forced march: it is great for building *esprit de corps*, making it easier to cover longer distances, because of mutual encouragement, than one could normally accomplish alone. Rather than persuading, it can be an unusual +influence technique, appropriate in some circumstances when people are reluctant to try a new experience. It can also be figurative — not all forced marches are physical; it could be a mental exercise as well.

127. Lemov, D. (2010). *Teach Like a Champion: 49 Techniques that Put Students on the Path to College*. Jossey-Bass. "Too often teachers have not taken the time to teach their students, step

by step, what successful learning behaviour looks like ... the habits and processes of being a successful student and community member ... If they are not doing what you asked, the most likely explanation is that you haven't taught them ... to truly succeed you must be able to ... get them to do things regardless of consequence, and to inspire and engage them in positive work ... you care enough to know your students as individuals."

128. In the 1992/93 evaluation cycle, Tsun-yan was put in the "Issues" category, which meant he had one year to improve, or he had to leave.

129. By the 1993/94 cycle, Tsun-yan made this his personal mission and included it in the first line of his Activity Summary, a self-assessment cum business plan submission prior to the visit with the evaluator who would assess his contributions and direction. His evaluator thought it was far-fetched and advised him not to count the chickens before the eggs were laid.

130. Tsun-yan learned about this firsthand from his in-person visit to the West Point (US military) academy, where the teachers explained that their role was to observe how the cadets were doing, let them finish the exercise, and then step in to help the cadets debrief critical moments of decision and influence.

131. Co-author of *In Search of Excellence* (1982) with Tom Peters. It sold three million copies in the first four years. At that time, America was looking to Japan as the paragon of excellence in business. Their research went against this trend by studying what made the most successful American businesses successful. Forty years later, its legacy as one of the foremost business classics and influential books for leaders remains intact.

132. Ore-Ida is a well-known brand for frozen potato products such as fries. The name is a short-hand for Oregon-Idaho and was founded in Ontario, Oregon, in 1949. At the time of

the visit, Ore-Ida was owned by H.J. Heinz, later becoming Kraft Heinz.

133. In the practice of +influence, LinHart has found the concept of "presencing" to be compatible with our experiences. See, for example: Senge, P.M., Scharmer, C.O., Jaworski, J., & Flowers, B.S. (2004). *Presence: Human Purpose and the Field of the Future*. Society for Organizational Learning. A more conventional interpretation of presence as posture and facial and body expressions is espoused by such authors as Amy Cuddy in her book: Cuddy, A. (2015). *Presence: Bringing Your Boldest Self to Your Biggest Challenges*. Little, Brown and Company.

134. See, for example, https://toptrends.nowandnext.com/2018/01/24/how-to-spot-weak-signals/.

135. The ability to detect signals involves the field of psychophysics, which studies the relationship between intensity of stimuli and the person's sensitivity, *i.e.*, the (trained) ability to hear it. See, for example: Kingdom, F.A.A., & Prins, N. (2016). *Psychophysics: A Practical Introduction* (2nd ed.). Academic Press.

136. Gibson, E.J., & Pick, A.D. (2000). *An Ecological Approach to Perceptual Learning and Development*. Oxford University Press.

137. An easy-to-digest article on being judgmental is: Martin, P. (2019, July 8). How to recognize you're being a judgmental jerk (and what to do about it). *Fast Company*. Retrieved from https://www.fastcompany.com/90372138/how-to-recognize-youre-being-a-judgmental-jerk-and-what-to-do-about-it. For a more fulsome yet still accessible discussion of judgment, see: Plous, S. (1993). *The Psychology of Judgment and Decision Making*. McGraw-Hill.

138. The authors came across, in their engagements and travel in the business world, large differences in "social allegiances" within global MNCs and within regions in a country. Take one dimension, the significant visible divides on business due to culture or ethnicity: French and Anglo Canadians,

or the perceived prestige of French-speaking Belgian establishments in contrast with the Flemish-speaking business culture in Flanders, Belgium.

139. As explained elsewhere, human agency is an individual capacity to make unique meaning from the environment and, through conscious reflection and creative action, produce desired outcomes.

140. There is good general advice in books about working across cultures. It typically helps in deciphering culture and identifying "strategies" to better fit with certain cultural characteristics. Thus, it works within generalized assumptions about behaviors and not about the individuals in those contexts. See, for example: Hofstede, G., Hofstede, G.J., & Minkov, M. (2010). *Cultures and Organizations: Software of the Mind* (3rd ed.). McGraw Hill.

141. In some engineered material businesses, such as steelmaking or glassmaking, the manufacturer has the choice to scrap the defective end-product, melt it down, and start over to try and get it right on the second pass. In most family-owned/-controlled businesses, that's not an option. By the time the family has whittled the choices down to one or two candidates for succession, they have, at most, about 10 years — likely less if the current governing generation has failed to the reality that they are running out of time to provide the nurture and cultivation needed to grow tall timbers.

142. Including the expectations of the controlling family shareholders, which are often diverse and not aligned enough among influential family members.

143. Bharti Airtel, commonly known as Airtel, is a leading Indian telco MNC now operating in 18 countries, including South Asia and Africa. It had about 490 million subscribers in 2022, of which 326 million were from India.

144. In Collins Dictionary, "spiritual" means relating to people's thoughts and beliefs rather than to their physical beings and surroundings.

145. According to Merriam-Webster, "inchoate" means incipient, being only partly in existence or operation.

146. The name of the company town where the plant was situated has been disguised.

147. The LinHart leadership assessment is a proprietary approach that uses a combination of third-party and proprietary instruments on segmented business executives. Its CEO database has benchmarks that correlate empirically with executives that are, for example, "wobbly" and those who are "failing."

148. At that time, Tsun-yan did not get around to learn even the basic rules of popular games, like ice hockey and football, which would have made socializing with clients and colleagues alike much easier.

149. In the canning industry, the lid was applied manually to cans filled with processed food, largely by Chinese workers. In 1902, machines called "Iron Chinks" started to show up, initially in salmon-processing plants for butchering and canning fish, thus displacing the workers. The machine was invented by Edmund A. Smith, a Canadian from Ontario and patented in 1906 as the Iron Chink. For a fascinating account of the Iron Chink story, see Magnier, M. (2021, September 4). Chinese built the US salmon canning industry. 'Iron Chink' invention robbed them of their jobs — and insulted their ethnicity to boot. *South China Morning Post*. Retrieved from https://www.scmp.com/magazines/post-magazine/long-reads/article/3147341/chinese-built-us-salmon-canning-industry-iron.

150. See Rogers, C. (1961). *On Becoming a Person*. Houghton Mifflin. Unconditional positive regard was first developed by Stanley Standal in his unpublished PhD thesis titled *The Need for Positive Regard: A Contribution to Client-Centred Theory* (University of Chicago, 1954).

151. There is a century of scientific research (~26,000 papers) available on the pecking order, a particular term coined by a Norwegian zoologist, Thorleif Schjelderup-Ebbe, in 1921

while studying dominance hierarchy among chickens. For a fascinating read on the subject, see Strauss, E.D., Curley, J.P., Shizuka, D., & Hobson, E.A. (2022). The centennial of the pecking order: current state and future prospects for the study of dominance hierarchies. *Philosophical Transactions of the Royal Society B*, 377(1845), 20200432.

152. For further examples of how pride can be a motivational force, see Katzenbach, J.R. (2003). *Why Pride Matters More Than Money: The Power of the World's Greatest Motivational Force*. Crown Business.

153. Susan Chong is a Singaporean entrepreneur who founded and grown Greenpac into Singapore's leading environmentally friendly packaging provider and became the first female entrepreneur recognized by the World Economic Forum for leadership in the circular economy.

154. Ron Oberlander seemed to have preceded Donald Rumsfeld in the now famous quote: "There are known knowns. These are things that we know that we know. There are known unknowns. That is to say, there are things that we know we don't know. But there are also unknown unknowns. These are things we don't know we don't know." Defence.gov. News Transcript: DoD News briefing by Secretary Rumsfeld and General Myers, US Department of Defense, February 12, 2002. The original idea was rooted in the Johari window, created by psychologists Joseph Luft and Harrington Ingram in 1955.

155. Life Narrative is a powerful technique developed principally by Dan McAdam, a professor in psychology at Northwestern University. See for example: McAdams, D.P. (1997). *The Stories We Live By: Personal Myths and the Making of the Self*. Guilford Press.

156. Hunter, J.D. (2001). *The Death of Character: Moral Education in an Age without Good or Evil*. Basic Books.

157. Holland, H.S. (1887). *Creed And Character: Sermons*. Rivingtons.

158. Ralph Waldo Emerson (1803–1882) was an American philosopher, essayist, and poet. This quote was taken from his *Essays, Second Series* published in 1844.

159. There are a few other books on influence. But they tend to be focused on it as a skill (*e.g.*, Daley, D., & Burton, L. (2010). *Developing Your Influencing Skills*. Universe of Learning Ltd.) and 'compliance' techniques to get to a 'yes' to your pitch (*e.g.*, Cialdini, R.B. (2008). *Influence: Science and Practice*. Ally & Bacon.). +Influence does not exclude these narrower attempts but aims, as more of the reality in work and in life dictates, to encompass a broader set of stakeholder interests employing inner being, skills and habits in service of the greater good.

160. Carnegie, D. (1936). *How to Win Friends and Influence People*. Simon & Schuster. For a glimpse of his thoughts and tips on public speaking, see Carnegie, D. (1915). *The Art of Public Speaking: The Original Tool for Improving Public Oration*. Self-published.

161. Fisher, R. & Ury, W. (1981). *Getting to Yes: Negotiating Agreement Without Giving In*. Houghton Mifflin.

162. Examples: Fisher, R. & Brown, S. (1989). *Getting Together: Building Relationships As We Negotiate*. Penguin Books; Fisher, R., Kopelman, E., & Schneider, A.K. (1996). *Beyond Machiavelli: Tools for Coping With Conflict*. Penguin Books.

163. For a historical perspective on the emergence of craft, see Langlands, A. (2018). *Craft: An Inquiry into the Origins and True Meaning of Traditional Crafts*. W.W. Norton. Langlands, an archaeologist and medieval historian, reaches far back to recover our lost sense of craft through deep history and rich storytelling.

164. Nagyszalanczy, S. (2000). *The Art of Fine Tools*. Taunton Press.

165. *Michelin Guide*. March 30, 2018.

Acknowledgements

This book is a compilation of key principles distilled from decades of professional and personal experience. It has been written with several usages in mind: as an inspirational guide for CEOs and senior executives to better channel their talents and their inner beings to positively impact their environment; as a textbook to help leaders of all seniority in our LinHart programs to build leadership +influence; and as a handbook for trainers, coaches, and other avid practitioners of +influence and leadership. Along our journey to this point, we have many people to thank.

The person that deserves recognition first is Ron Oberlander — a client, mentor, and loving friend to Tsun-yan — who inspired him to delve deeply into the human aspect of business. He encouraged Tsun-yan to always look for other non-logical explanations for people's puzzling behaviors and to "stay loose in the saddle" while persisting in worthy outcomes for all stakeholders. Ron's being and superior leadership remind us of what is possible if we persevere in the arena of positive influence. It is a timely and proper tribute that the writing of this book helped crystallize in the authors' mind the many facets of Ron's +craft that inspired us in our pursuit of higher ground.

Tsun-yan's mentors in his McKinsey years have also helped him along in his +craft, by providing him with the learning opportunities through challenging assignments and sharing their abundant wisdom. They include Marvin Bower, Bob Waterman, Jon Katzenbach, Ed Michaels, David Meen, Julian Philips, Kenichi Ohmae and Rajat Gupta.

The second group of people that we would like to thank is Bernie Young, Susanna Leong, and Jochen Wirtz — respectively the (past) Dean, (past) Vice Dean (Graduate Studies), and (current) Vice Dean (Graduate Studies) of the National University of Singapore (NUS) Business School in Singapore. Bernie and Susanna took a leap of faith in allowing the authors to design and run a full-year pilot of the Basic Management Communication (MC) course for MBAs at NUS Business School, starting in 2010 and still ongoing every year. Over the past decade since its inception, more than 2,000 students have been through the course, and that number is expected to increase to 300 per year. Its success has proven that +influence principles and a self-leadership attitude can be learned and internalized at scale with significant individual uplift. The course, renamed Launch Your Transformation (LYT) to better reflect its true nature and impact, is now a degree requirement. We sincerely applaud and thank them for their wisdom. We thank Jochen for coming to his own belief in the transformative power of the course and his initiative in its renaming and continuing strengthening as it was intended.

It takes a village to develop a person, and that triply applies to carrying out such scale programs every year – from university courses, to the various LinHart program variants including LIFE (Leadership Influence for Executives) series for open enrollment and Leadership modules for Small Medium Enterprises (SMEs). One of the most joyful aspects of the work we do is finding natural mentors and avid +influence practitioners to serve as program faculty and executive mentors. These business leaders, with an average of 25+ years of executive experience, are devoted to mentoring other leaders while continuing to improve their own +influence craft. 60+% of them are still fighting the good fight, as executives, board members, investors, and coaches.

- Program/Faculty leaders (in alphabetical order, by last name): Nalin Advani, Lillian Cheng, Anna Kiukas-Pedersen, Huijin Kong, Mike Jackson, Phillip Lim, Mathia Nalappan, Zhi Min Wu
- Other long-time executive mentors who worked across multiple programs and/or corporate clients: Rohan Belliappa, Avital Carmon, Uen-li Chia, Wendy Chua, Dennis Khoo, Punita Lal, Robert Tan, Elvin Too
- Other executive mentors who have taught in one or more of our programs: Alp Altun, Dany Bolduc, Jean-Yves Broussy, Karen Caldwell, Andy Clay, Hak Peng Chg, Ian Faggotter, Adheet Gogate, Gracelyn Ho, Lucas Jiang, Geri Kan, Imran Khalid, Henrik Kofod-Hansen, Linus Koh, Jonathan Kwan, Davy Lau, Han Kiat Lee, Wai Hoong Leung, Jeremy Lim, Valerie Lim, Stacy McCarthy, Adeline Ng, Mark Powell, Andrew Quake, Raj Rawana, Nawal Roy, Kirpal Singh, Sze Meng Soon, Joktin Tan, Leong How Wee
- Assisting facilitators (eight or more per year) for MC/LYT programs: each faculty member was assisted by an alumnus of the program. There are just too many to name, but their passion for and commitment to helping others who enrolled in the program after them are truly outstanding.

For the writing of this book, we would like to thank the following:

- Our "editorial circle" who gave us comments and suggestions on the manuscript: Naithy Cyriac, Jasmine Cheng, Geri Kan, Marie Cheong, Joseph Mocanu, Jenny Xu, Faith Perh, and Lei Chen. In particular, we thank Joseph for asking us the difference between influence and manipulation, and Geri for encouraging us to talk about influence across cultures. Jasmine deserves special commendation for going through the book in great detail and creating the index for this book.
- Our publisher's team: Shaun Tan, Lee Hooi Yean, Yee-Hong Khoo, and Yubing Zhai
- Our editor: Janna Christie
- Tony Tjan — venture capitalist and Tsun-yan's co-author for the *New York Times* Bestseller *Heart, Smarts, Guts and Luck* — for his encouragement and suggestions for book marketing
- Hilario Bango (and the whole Martian Arts team) and Yixin Keller for their creativity in designing the book cover

Siauyih, Tsun-yan's wife, has been a strong pillar of support throughout his career and unstinting in rendering loving help to both authors in the writing process. Linhowe, Tsun-yan's son, taught Tsun-yan back in 1992 that he could change his parenting behavior and become a better person, and thanks to him, the latter pursuit is still ongoing.

Finally, we would like to give thanks to all the CEOs, senior leaders and professionals LinHart has worked with. You have continued to aspire to have more positive impact — on your work teams, your organizations and your families — and inspire yourselves to persist through challenges and setbacks. We are very privileged to be let in, not just to some of the most important business issues you are dealing with, but also your trust in us to help bring out the best in you. Even though most of your identities are disguised for obvious reasons, we want you to know we are indebted to your confidence that the anonymized insights shared in this book will benefit many more people in business and life.

And we hope you will inspire others to follow in your footsteps, by sharing this book with them and practicing with and mentoring them.

> *It is not the critic who counts; not the man who points out how the strong man stumbles, or where the doer of deeds could have done them better. The credit belongs to the man who is actually in the arena, whose face is marred by dust and sweat and blood; who strives valiantly; who errs, who comes short again and again, because there is no effort without error and shortcoming; but who does actually strive to do the deeds; who knows great enthusiasms, the great devotions; who spends himself in a worthy cause; who at the best knows in the end the triumph of high achievement, and who at the worst, if he fails, at least fails while daring greatly, so that his place shall never be with those cold and timid souls who neither know victory nor defeat.*
>
> — "Citizenship in a Republic" by Theodore Roosevelt, 1910

About the Authors

Across 48 years of working with 100+ CEOs and +500 senior leaders across 30+ industries and countries, Professor **Tsun-yan Hsieh** has always connected with them as human beings first, influencing them with his heart, fueled by an intense desire to help each and every one of them reach their potential and better cope with expectations and pressures. The same character and craft pervade his mentorship of hundreds of younger partners in McKinsey and younger leaders who are lucky enough to be part of his MBA course or scale-up CEO leadership courses. Unique at McKinsey, he was as fearless in boardrooms as he was in unionized shop floors. Harnessing human energies is his unifying passion; moving people toward shared outcomes is his special gift. He takes great joy in learning how his mentees have progressed, capturing their thank you/update notes in a Mont Blanc book.[1] Because his own influence and leadership skills were hard won, he is devoted to help all comers improve theirs. People may call

---

[1] The story of Tsun-yan's Mont Blanc entries, as a self-inspiring device, was retold by Tony Tjan, one of his mentees, in Tjan, T. (2017). *Good People: The Only Leadership Decision that Really Matters.* Penguin.

him a leadership guru, spiritual leader, but to himself, Tsun-yan is foremost a learner: "There is always more to see and learn."

To set a new standard in injecting humanity into business leadership, in 2010 he founded LinHart Group, a leadership services firm specialized in helping founders, owners, boards and CEOs address their most difficult leadership issues including transitioning leadership and uplifting top talent.

He is/has been an Independent Director of Singapore Airlines, Manulife Financial, Dyson, Bharti Airtel and Sony. For social interests, he serves on the board of SingHealth and Singapore Institute of Management. He has taught subjects related to leadership influence at the National University of Singapore Business School, the Lee Kuan Yew School of Public Policy and Nanyang Technology University, Singapore. He co-authored the New York Times bestselling book *Heart, Smarts, Guts and Luck.*

With nicknames such as Compass and Energizer bunny, **Huijin Kong**'s strong sense of direction, courage to call out the elephants in the room and relentless energy have enabled her to counsel CEOs, owners, and founders from 30s to 60s. She has pioneered LinHart Group's group leadership programs that have made deep learning and leadership development scalable, as evidenced by LinHart's program for a few hundred MBAs. She has also had to work hard to better influence leaders in USA, China, India, and Southeast Asia, digging deeply into herself to connect with them as human beings and gain the necessary insights to challenge and support them. Being able to overcome her handicap in compassion, empathy and emotional awareness gives her the conviction that everyone can get better in influence and leadership. Her passion for inspiring Chinese business leaders also propelled her to lead the expansion of LinHart's leadership program to China and Hong Kong. She holds an M.B.A. with Highest Distinction (Baker Scholar) from Harvard Business School, and a B.Sc. in Economics, summa cum laude from the Wharton School of Business, University of Pennsylvania, USA.

Index